The Connoisseur's Guide to Oriental Carpets

E. Gans-Ruedin

The Connoisseur's Guide to Oriental Carpets

Charles E. Tuttle Company: Publishers
Rutland, Vermont and Tokyo, Japan

Translated from the French by Valerie Howard

Published by the Charles E. Tuttle Company, Inc.,
of Rutland, Vermont and Tokyo, Japan

Library of Congress Catalog Card Number 70-157255
International Standard Book Number 0–8048–0988–7

© Copyright 1971 by Office du Livre S. A.,
Fribourg, Switzerland

Printed in Switzerland

Contents

PREFACE 7

HISTORY 9

CHARACTERISTICS OF CARPETS 13
Materials – Dyeing – Designs – Dating carpets – Weaving and knotting – The Ghiordes or Turkish knot – The Senneh or Persian knot – The Kilim or Karamani rug – The Soumak rug – The Verneh rug – Washing and glossing

BUYING AND CARING FOR CARPETS 27
The carpet trade – The choice and purchase of a carpet – Conservation and restoration of carpets

CLASSIFICATION OF CARPETS 31

TURKEY 32
Avanos – Bergama – Cal – Dazkiri – Dosemealti – Ezine – Hereke – Karakechi – Kayseri – Kirsehir – Konya – Kurd – Maden – Megri – Milas – Ortakoy – Saph – Sivas – Taspinar – Yahyali – Yuruk – Karamani – Kilim – Sileh (or Verneh)

THE CAUCASUS 83
Shirvan – Derbent – Gendja – Kazak – Karabagh – Kilim – Sileh – Soumak – Verneh

IRAN – AZERBAIJAN 112
Tabriz – Heriz – Ahar – Ahmedabad – Bakhshayesh – Bilverdi – Chekh Rajab – Karaja – Kolvanaq – Kurdlar – Meina – Sharabiyan – Mehriban – Merkit – Lanbaran – Ardebil – Mishkin – Sarab – Jin-Jin

KALAR DASHT 162
Kalar Dashti

VÁRAMIN 165
Varamin

ARAK, SERABAND AND LILIHAN 167
Mahal – Mir – Sarouk – Seraband – Lilihan

KIRMAN, YAZD AND AFSHAR RUGS 185
Kirman – Yazd – Afshar – Kirman-Afshar – Afshar

HAMADAN 213
Assadabad – Burjalu – Josan – Hosseinabad – Injilas – Khamseh – Malayer – Mehriban – Nobaran – Tuisserkan – Zanjan

KURDISTAN 237
Bijar – Senneh (Sanandaj) – Senneh Kilim – Songur – Koliayeh

ISFAHAN, NAIN AND THE CARPETS OF CHAHAR MAHAL: BAKHTIARI AND JOSHAGAN
Isfahan – Nain – Bakhtiari – Chalchotor Bakhtiari – Saman Bakhtiari – Joshagan – Luristan 254

SHIRAZ AND THE CARPETS OF FARS 275
Shiraz – A Horse blanket – Kashgai – Baharlu – Abadeh – Yalameh – Niriz – Gabbeh

KASHAN AND QUM   300
    Kashan – Qum

THE RUGS OF MASHAD, KHORASAN AND OF THE
TURKOMAN TRIBES   314
    Mashad – Mud – Baluchi – Kurd – Kachli-
    Turkoman

TURKESTAN   331
    Beshir – Bukhara – Bukhara Chuval – Buk-
    hara Jollar – Kachli-Bukhara – Kerki – Pen-
    deh Chuval – Yomud Chuval – Yomud

AFGHANISTAN   351
    Afghan – Beshir Chuval – Zaher-Chahi

PAKISTAN   364
    Pakistani Bukhara

INDIA   367
    Agra – Kashmir – Embroidered Rug – Kilim

TIBETAN RUGS   377
    Tibetan

CHINA   386
    Chinese – Khotan – Mongol – Ning-Hsia –
    Chinese – Peking – Pao-t'ou – Kilim

NORTH AFRICA   409
    El Djem – Gabès – Kairwan – High Atlas –
    Kilim – Hand-woven Rug

RUGS OF THE BALKAN COUNTRIES   422
    Balkan Rug – Kilim

BIBLIOGRAPHY   426

INDEX   427

Preface

Many works on the history of Oriental carpets show examples preserved in museums or in great private collections; and from these, the keen collector can learn a great deal. This volume, intended for the general public, takes another approach. After an historical account and several general chapters devoted to the technical or symbolic characteristics of carpets, the author deals with the essential and strictly original part of his study; he establishes a detailed classification by country and in the case of Iran by regions: each example is illustrated by one or several annotated reproductions. The lesser known products of countries such as Pakistan, India, Tibet, China, North Africa and the Balkan countries also figure in this vast panorama, so that nothing is omitted from the very wide choice currently on the market. The collector will be able to form a precise opinion on the rugs which he will have the opportunity to see, owing to the wealth of information provided on the origin, technique, style of patterns, colouring and finally the quality of each example.

This information, the result of lengthy experience, has all been verified on the spot by the author, during frequent journeys in producing countries. Indeed, the description of the motifs is as complete as possible, but it is often extremely difficult to obtain even from the rug-makers themselves the explanation of their designs; they use such and such a motif in accordance with tradition, but they are no longer aware of its original meaning. Another difficulty in getting information first hand lies in the inaccessibility of many villages. It can happen that in a town which deals daily with one type of carpet, nobody can tell you where the producing villages are, even though they might be less than 40 miles away. This is because the dealers have never been there, the villagers themselves arranging to bring their products into town. If you insist on making for one of these villages, nobody can understand your interest: why should you wish to undertake an uncomfortable journey, at all costs, since the local output is on sale in the market of the town?

Nevertheless, there are many people who have helped the author by their technical or linguistic knowledge, thanks to which he has been able to obtain the information he required. Their collaboration has been invaluable to him and he expresses here his deep gratitude.

E.G.-R.

History

In the last one hundred years the Westerner has come to see the Oriental carpet as a true work of art. For him its beauty evokes the luminous East, a land which has been the cradle of humanity and religion, where the most varied civilizations have flourished and decayed.

In general, when we refer to Oriental rugs we are thinking of carpets with a knotted pile, not simply woven carpets. In essence the process of making a knotted carpet consists of stretching warp threads on a loom, knotting the pile to these threads and, when a row of knots is complete, inserting a weft thread. The slow and painstaking task of knotting a carpet is in general the work of several people, now often women and children, seated at the one loom, and working to a traditional pattern. When the whole carpet has been knotted then the pile must be shorn. The precision of the design will depend largely on how tightly a carpet has been knotted and how short the pile has been cut – the number of knots per square unit of rug is a useful guide to the fineness of its texture and to its likely durability. There are, of course, Oriental carpets which do not have a knotted pile; reference will be made later to the tapestry-woven Kilims and Soumaks.

The precise origins of the knotted carpet are obscure. There are frequent enough references in the literature of Greece and Rome to carpets but there is no evidence that the references are to knotted carpets. In 1949, an expedition to Gorny Altai in southern Siberia discovered a carpet (the Pazyryk carpet) frozen and preserved in a tumulus. This carpet, used as a saddle-cover for a horse interred in the burial mound, dates from the fourth or fifth century BC and is by far the earliest surviving example of a knotted carpet. Even the frequent references to carpets by Arab and Persian writers between the eighth and the fourteenth centuries cannot with any certainty be taken as applying to knotted carpets. After the Pazyryk carpet the oldest surviving knotted rugs are fragments from eastern Turkestan dating from the third to the sixth centuries AD.

It may well be that the technique of knotting carpets was developed by the nomadic tribes of Central Asia. They produced rugs of modest dimensions decorated with summary geometric motifs inspired by plant and animal forms. That rug-knotting should have developed among nomadic people is in many ways remarkable, for the rug-maker is obliged to dismantle his loom each time that natural elements or the enemy menace his security, forcing him to move. Assembling and dismantling a loom are very delicate operations; the hundreds of warp threads must be kept from ravelling. In carpets of nomad manufacture one finds irregularities in the weave, differences between the selvedges, displacements in the lines and faults in the design, all of which indicate interruptions in the work but prove, too, the authenticity.

That the knotted carpet was the craft of nomads was an important factor in the dispersion of the technique. But one must also take into consideration the complex political upheavals, often involving large movements of population. Anatolia early on established a strong carpet-making tradition. According to Marco Polo, who visited Anatolia in 1271, the realm of the Seljuks of Roum produced the most beautiful carpets in the world. These splendid rugs were decorated with animal figures and geometric designs.

Following the Ottoman conquest of Asia Minor – Constantinople fell to them in 1453 – there developed a tradition of handsome geometrically-patterned carpets known to us now as Holbein carpets as a consequence of their frequent representation in paintings by Holbein the younger. From the evidence remaining, the golden age of carpet-making in Persia was from the sixteenth to the first half of the eighteenth century. The carpets of this period, quite a number of which fortunately are still preserved, are true jewels, incomparable in the harmony of their colours and in the originality of their designs. The Safavid dynasty ruled Persia during this time, which in the richness of its literature and art was comparable with the European Renaissance. The Afghan invasion brought to an end this great period of Persian history and carpet-making was among the arts and crafts which suffered.

The manufacture of knotted carpets spread from the Middle East to other centres. By the late fifteenth century carpets of distinctive colouring and design were being produced in Cairo. The Arabs introduced the art of knotting to Spain. The great mosques of Cordoba, Granada and Toledo, for example, were decorated with fine rugs of Spanish manufacture. In fact, Spanish carpets gained such a reputation for their beauty and quality that they were exported to Damascus, Egypt and Persia. In the fifteenth century carpets were manufactured in several centres in Andalucia on the commission of members of the nobility. They are decorated with armorial bearings and generally are of very elongated shape; as on the faience of Valencia there are vigorous border decorations of arabesques imitating Cufic script.

The decoration is dominated by stars of different dimensions and the colours are very vivid. In technique Spanish carpets are distinctive in having the knot tied to only one warp thread.

Two regions peripheral to the Middle East where carpet-making also developed are India and China. Despite the unsuitability of the climate for the preservation of fabrics the knotted rug spread throughout the sub-continent under the Timurids. The first carpets, dating from the sixteenth century, betray Persian influences. In the seventeenth century the fashion developed for rugs with figures and animals. With great boldness the designers transformed the cloth into a living painting, in the manner of the miniaturists.

It is only comparatively recently, at the end of the fifteenth century, that the Chinese learned the art of rug-knotting from the nomadic Turkomans of Turkestan. The Chinese gave to the carpet a unique character in complete harmony with the style of their decorative art.

Though the present interest in Oriental rugs dates only from the second half of the nineteenth century these rugs have long been known to the West.

It was largely through Italian merchants and travellers that the attractions of the Oriental carpet were revealed to Europe. Venice early established a privileged position as a trader with the East and became an important consumer as well as distributor of Oriental products. In this city the ownership of carpets was not reserved for the aristocracy. The Venetian school in general, and the paintings of Carpaccio in particular, reveal the use the Venetians made of Oriental rugs on the occasion of religious, civil or carnival festivities; they spread them along the narrow streets, hung them from the windows and decorated their gondolas with them. The northern painters, too, frequently depicted Oriental carpets in their works.

By the early sixteenth century, the great courts of Europe had important collections of Oriental rugs. The inventories of Charles V, Catherine de Medici, Mazarin, Cardinal Wolsey and Henry VIII, among others, show how valued these articles had become. Shahs, caliphs and sultans presented precious examples to the reigning houses of Europe. Many were sent to the doges of Venice, of which some can still be admired in the treasury of the Basilica of Saint Mark. There are, for example, rugs sent to Doge Marino Grimani by Shah Abbas the Great in 1603 and 1621.

The invasion of Hungary and Austria by the Turks contributed to the spread of the rug in Europe, until 1683, the date of the victory of Sobieski over the Mohammedans at Vienna. The imported rugs were for the most part of small size, prayer rugs, which are today to be found in large numbers in museums and churches in Hungary and Transylvania (now part of Romania). Some came from the army of the Mohammedan conqueror but many were imported on order by the Hungarians and Poles who, enchanted by the beauty of the colours and designs so close to their own taste, used them to decorate their houses and churches.

From the sixteenth to the eighteenth centuries the Western world, with the exception of a few connoisseurs of the exotic, ceased to be interested in Oriental rugs. It was only after the great exhibition in Vienna in 1891 that Europeans, and subsequently Americans, became fired with enthusiasm for Oriental carpets. Merchants set off for the Middle East, collected carpets at the towns and villages where they were manufactured and dispatched them to Europe and America. A phenomenon not unlike that which affected the production of Chinese porcelain in the eighteenth century took place: European importers encouraged the manufacturers to modify dimensions and occasionally also colours and designs to suit Western taste.

But perhaps the Oriental carpet is seen to best advantage in its own environment: in the nomad's tent, serving as floor covering, wall-hanging, curtain and saddle-bag, its utilitarian and decorative functions perfectly balanced; in the *talar* (reception room) of a Persian house where the most sumptuous carpets of the household are displayed; and most brilliantly of all, in the mosques of Islam where they decorate floors, walls and even tombs.

It must be admitted that very few of the rugs produced during the last forty years show the same artistry and craftsmanship as those of former times. Nevertheless, for the discriminating connoisseur there are still the wonderful early examples preserved in museums and private and public collections, which are fortunately richer than one might expect. One has only to leaf through the enormous publications by Sarre, Bode and many others to realize what treasures are contained in the old Imperial collections of Vienna, at Istanbul, in the East and West Berlin Museums, in the Textile Museum in Washington D.C., and finally in the museums of Paris, Lyons, Budapest, Florence, Milan and in private collections in both Europe and the United States.

Characteristics of Carpets

MATERIALS

The glossy, fine and supple wool of the sheep of the East has always been, and will always remain, the basic material used in the weaving of carpets. It is provided by the numerous flocks which, under the care of often nomadic shepherds, graze in vast arid and undeveloped regions.

In Anatolia, there is a breed of sheep which even in antiquity was famous for the fineness of its wool. At the time of the classical Greek civilization Miletus was the principal centre of the industry of raw and spun wool, which was exported in great quantity to Egypt and Greece. Today, the many wandering flocks which graze in the upper valley of the Tigris following the traditional tracks give a supple wool which is very white and has long fibres. An interesting type of sheep with a fat tail lives in Persia and Turkestan. When the pastures are plentiful, the fat of the animal is concentrated in the rump and tail. The fat accumulated constitutes a precious reserve of energy for when the grazing is poor.

Goat's hair is also frequently used, notably for the warp of the Baluchistan, Afghan and Bukhara rugs. The wool from northern Persia is fairly crude and thick, that from Khorasan and Kirman fine and velvety, and that from the Caucasus and Central Asia is lustrous and very strong. Lamb's wool has sometimes been used for certain very fine rugs as it gives a springy surface.

Camel-hair has been used, alone or mixed with sheep's wool, by the nomads of Turkestan for the pile or for the warp and the weft; but now it is used less and less as it is not hardwearing. At one time in Persia, silk was sometimes used for rugs destined for the court or wealthy patrons. On occasions the warp and the weft were both executed in silk, which gave the rug a sumptuousness amounting almost to ostentation, then the weft was brocaded with threads of gold and silver which were not covered over by knotting. A third type combined silk for the warp, with wool for the pile, in order to obtain a tighter knot.

In the Caucasus, silk was never used, but in Turkestan, it was employed to enhance certain designs on Bukharas, while the remainder of the carpet was carried out in wool. Today Persia and Asia Minor produce examples entirely in silk; but in those from Turkey the silk is generally of mediocre quality.

The material selected for the warp and the weft varies with the regions: in Turkey, especially in mechanized production, the warp and weft are of cotton, though in some prayer rugs they are of wool. In Persia – with the exception of the regions of Shiraz, Turkestan, Baluchistan and Luristan – cotton is usually employed for both warp and weft. In the Caucasus, although formerly only wool was used, in the modern rugs the warp and weft are of cotton.

The wool of the pile is usually of two-ply, that is to say of two threads twisted together. The weft and warp threads are, according to the region, of very variable thickness, but they always have several strands, numbering from two to sixteen.

In weaving with single warp, the warp threads are on the same level, while in the double warp method, the warp threads are brought down alternately, those at the top being seldom visible. This latter method has the advantage of giving the carpet a more compact structure.

Among nomadic peoples, shearing usually takes place towards the end of spring. Before being shorn, the animal is washed by the side of a river or lake or near a well. After the clipping, the wool undergoes a second washing in the river or in large basins; finally it is thoroughly trampled underfoot and dried in the open air. The spinning is carried out according to a method which is completely primitive: having first placed a certain quantity of wool under his arm, the spinner begins to twist the thread which, as it becomes longer, is wrapped around a rod. The wool is then ready to pass into the dye.

At the beginning of the century, Persia exported about 10,000 tons of raw wool each year, the produce from Khorasan being bought by Russia and France, and that from the regions of Faristan, Luristan, Azerbaijan and Kurdistan being particularly sought after by England and India.

DYEING

One of the attractions of Oriental rugs is the beauty of the dyes and the harmony of their colour schemes. There are, in the East, traditions of dyeing which produce not only the warm and luminous deep shades which give such a lively play of colours, but which also allow for the chromatic alterations colours will undergo during the life of a carpet.

Traditionally the mordant used is alum not bichromate. All shades can be obtained, from the golden yellow of the Kirmans to the dark tones of the Baluchistans, the iridescent colour of Tabriz to the wonderful pure tones of the flowers of the Shirvans and the Kazaks, in which the varied colours compensate for the geometrical austerity of the design.

The richness of the colour scale allows for magnificent decorative effects, through the contrast or the harmony of the colours. The recipes of the dyes, both vegetable and animal, have been handed down from century to century. The most important vegetable colouring agent is extracted from madder, the root of which supplies all shades of pink and red. A very common plant in Persia, the madder has been known in the Near East for a very long time and grows wild almost everywhere, notably in the provinces of Kirman, Zyd and Mazanderan. In some regions it is cultivated. Imported cochineal is another raw material of red. Reddish yellow is extracted from wild saffron, while cultivated saffron renders pure yellow; a light yellow is distilled from the root of turmeric. Blue is obtained through the soaking and fermentation of indigo, which grows in abundance in China and India, and which was already used by the ancient Egyptians. Although cochineal and indigo are not Persian products, they have been employed throughout the centuries to dye the wool of Persian rugs. The colour black, rarely used, is an extract of iron oxide: this is the only dye of mineral origin.

With these few dyes, skilfully thinned and wisely mixed, the Oriental people obtain all shades, not counting the natural white of the wool, or the browns, if camel-hair is being used. It sometimes happens that the necessary quantity of dyed wools is not calculated exactly before commencing a rug, particularly among the nomadic tribes, who take a certain pleasure in the unexpected. When the wool of one colour is finished, they are obliged to dye some more to complete the work. It is only rarely that the colour of the newly dyed wool corresponds exactly with the first dyeing. The rug-maker hardly cares about this, on the contrary he makes use of it to obtain decorative effects. This is why the early rugs which are called 'striped' or 'striated' retain all their beauty and value, in spite of this anomaly. To the eyes of the collector, the shading has a singular charm, provided it is not too marked.

The yarn is not dyed in the skein. Each long strand is plunged into the dye, then gathered together and dried in the open air, and finally exposed to the sun and to the dust. This system has the advantage of imparting to the shades of different strands an endless number of gradations, from the darkest to the lightest. We can verify this by closely examining the background colour of a good rug: each shade distinguishes the knot, the cloth comes to life, becomes a living thing, vibrant with infinite reflections. We are far from the sombre chromatic uniformity of wool dyed with synthetic colours.

This method of dyeing goes back to the distant origins of carpet-making. Until about 1870, it was to be found in almost all the Persian, Caucasian, Turkoman and Asia Minor centres. From 1870, synthetic dyes arrived first at the coastal regions, then at the large inland centres, and finally reached the nomadic peoples. It might seem surprising that the villagers abandoned their ancient methods so easily, but the aniline principally used to obtain the different shades of red was cheap-

er. But for browns and yellows they continued to use their own dyes (oak bark, pomegranate, vine-leaves) for these were even more economical than aniline.

The victory of Western chemistry over primitive empiricism was facilitated by the unending range of colours of aniline. Its ease of transport, its low price and the simplicity of its use allowed the craftsman to economize on time and labour. Aesthetically, however, the result was not a happy one, as was realized a little too late. At the end of the last century, Nasir-ud-din and his successor, Muzaffar-ud-din, attempted to restrain the invasion of chemical colours, by ordering the destruction of all stocks of aniline and the confiscation of rugs made from artificially-dyed thread. But smuggling hindered the strict application of these measures. Eventually, the law on chemical colourings was modified: instead of confiscating the rugs, they were penalized by a duty of three per cent on export. This tax was to cover the costs of research on the dyeing process; unfortunately, the Minister of Finance discovered a source of revenue in this decree and raised this tax successively to nine and twelve per cent, but the researches were forgotten.

The method of dyeing in general use in Iran is as follows: the thread is first scoured in hot water for about half an hour; if it is very greasy, three per cent of sodium carbonate is added with a little soap. Then, it is steeped for about twelve hours in a first bath of alum, then in a second, this second operation sometimes being replaced by cooking the yarn for one hour in the bath of alum.

The dyeing proper begins with the preparation of the colourant which is diluted in a vat, the amount of water varying according to the desired shade. The scoured wool is placed in this bath of dye, which is brought to boiling-point. After cooking for about one and a half hours, the wool is allowed to cool down in the dye for twelve hours. It is then rinsed, preferably in a river.

Some inhabitants of the region of Hamadan begin by exposing the wool to the sun for three days in a bath of whey of alum, then they rinse it before placing it in the dyeing vat. Once the colourant is absorbed by the wool, the latter is removed so that water and cow's urine can be added to the vat. The wool is replaced in the vat for fifteen minutes, before being dried out in the sun.

Between 1913 and 1914, according to more or less accurate statistics of Persian exports, 58 per cent of rugs exported contained chemical colourants, and 38 per cent were totally free of them. It must be noted that in the first percentage, chemical dyes were only partially used for a good number of the rugs. There is no exact information for the post-war years, but we can assume that the proportion of chemical colouring matters has increased, taking into account the increased use made of them. Greatly perfected, they now offer every guarantee of quality.

Western influence has also made itself felt in the field of production: in fact, as the use of the Oriental rug became popularized in the West, there were those who had the idea of increasing the output by creating large factories for mass production. This kind of production occurs today in certain regions of Turkey, Iran, the Balkan countries, Pakistan, India and China. One can talk of controlled production, that is to say production whereby manufacture takes place in accordance with the wishes of the client. From a commercial standpoint, this method undeniably presents huge advantages: the rugs are manufactured according to the size and design specified, which allows a better price to be obtained, while giving satisfaction to the customer. Unfortunately, the client is sometimes lacking in taste; the Persians have produced carpets to order which though technically sound have nothing to offer the connoisseur.

In 1892, a perspicacious observer, Doctor Feuvrier *(Trois ans à la cour de Perse),* described the scene in which the modern carpet industry developed. Speaking of the town of Sultanabad, he declared that this town would have possessed nothing worthy of interest, if it had not been one of the most important centres of rug manufacture. It resembled all other Persian towns, with narrow streets, for the most part dirty, bordered with grey walls, and with bazaars which extended from one end of the town to the other. But a loom was to be found in each house; the women who worked there earned on average three francs per week, a sum judged to be reasonable, the cost of living being low. As a result of this rug trade, Sultanabad grew rapidly and its population passed from four or five hundred to forty thousand inhabitants in fifty years.

DESIGNS

Oriental imaginativeness is expressed freely in the infinite variety of carpet designs. There are those which enable us to date examples and to determine the different production centres: in fact, each region develops its own designs and jealously maintains its tradition.

Each motif has a particular meaning, handed down from generation to generation and a tell-tale sign of the origin of each family of carpet.

With a little practice, it is fairly easy to differentiate between the six main areas from which carpets come: Asia Minor, Persia, the Caucasus, Afghanistan, India and China. The more difficult task of identifying the exact centre of production requires a more profound knowledge of styles.

These considerations hold good only for the early rugs, that is to say those prior to 1911. Carpets from after the First World War are less soft in colour and in design are no longer typical of the regions from which they come. If, in our time, manufacturing organizations also reproduce types which are foreign to the producing region, the blame must go to Western taste, which corrupted the tradition of the designs. A good number of these innovations have today become classic.

Among the orthodox Mohammedan people, the influence of religion on the decoration of the rug has been considerable. No follower of Allah and his Prophet can forget the commandment of the Koran: 'Take care not to depict the Lord or the created being; depict only the trees, the flowers, inanimate objects, because on the Day of Judgment, the beings who have been represented will come to reclaim their souls from the artist, who, powerless to satisfy them, will suffer the torment of the eternal fire.' The predominance of geometric design may seem to us to be an expression of primitive art; in fact, it shows remarkable inventive faculties. Iconographic restriction has never prevented or retarded the free development of a rich stylized art.

Having embraced the Islamic Shiite religion, Persia never submitted to it in the matter of this iconographic prohibition. Carpets from Persia are covered with lively animal and human figures set in fabulous dream-like surroundings. In this the Persian rug differs completely from the carpets of other regions, where representation plays a much less prominent role.

In Asia Minor, there are very varied types: the preference is for designs with broken lines, stylized, almost geometric figures which one tends to confuse, for this reason, with the motifs of the Caucasian production. The decoration is often floral, with motifs of Persian inspiration. The rugs with geometrical designs from Bergama, the Yuruks and Damascus are influenced by the contribution of the traditional art of the Turkoman tribes of Central Asia, who settled in Anatolia at the beginning of the fourteenth century.

In Caucasian rugs, there is a remarkable tendency towards stylization with a preference for geometric designs, human, animal and floral motifs being scattered on a ground dense with small lozenges, pointed stars, squares, triangles and other motifs arranged without symmetry. The only exceptions are some rugs with fairly large patterns and broad lines.

The carpets of Central Asia and Turkestan, in which geometric design predominates, show a predilection for symmetry and regularity, both in shape and in arrangement.

Chinese influences, which penetrated Iran following the Mongol invasion, were integrated into the Persian rug with remarkable skill. The harmony and vigour in the design of these carpets match that of the refined and splendid miniatures: there are interlacing branches, a rich profusion of flowers, and among them human figures, real and fabulous birds and wild animals. Particular importance is given to the borders, arranged in such a way as to surround the central motif in the most sumptuous manner possible. The many different motifs of Persian rugs are usually of small format and painstakingly executed down to the finest details. Some of them recall very ancient beliefs and superstitions; other motifs betray the influence of India or China.

In early Persian rugs, the dragon and the phoenix appear under various forms, but usually in combat position. The swastika and the cloud-band undoubtedly originated in China, like the *T'shi*, the sacred sponge, the symbol of immortality. This last motif is to be found from the sixteenth century, in different forms, in the famous carpets of the Persian court and also in numerous Caucasian rugs.

The lotus flower, held sacred in antiquity, is a highly-esteemed motif in Persia, as is the palmette, originally from India, which is reproduced in a thousand ways, whole or segmented, arranged in rosettes or in shield-shapes, in horizontal or vertical manner. This is perhaps the most commonly used motif in old and modern carpets, not only in Persia, but also in Anatolia, the Caucasus and in Central Asia.

The ancient running-dog frieze enlivens the borders of Caucasian rugs even today, notably of those made by Soumak craftsmen.

The austere Greek key motif often figures in the rugs from Samarkand on which it decorates borders and corner-pieces, while the narrow bands of the border are decorated with geometric or floral motifs of infinite variation. One of the most common is the pomegranate, with its fruit either complete or split open as a symbol of fertility or again the tree of life with symmetrically arranged branches topped with a flower.

A characteristic motif of Turkoman rugs, and particularly those from Bukhara, is that called 'flight of eagles'; we can recognize this heraldic symbol in the diagonally positioned lozenges which appear in two opposite corners, in white on a red ground, and which reveal, on examination, an eagle with outstretched wings. The Turkomans and ancient tribes of Asia Minor are very fond of the motif 'the roses of the Salors', a favourite of the tribe of the same name, the most civilized and numerous of Central Asia.

The eight-pointed cross, called the Maltese cross, must not be interpreted as homage to the Knights of Saint John, but merely as a decorative geometrical combination, comparable with the six-pointed star formed by the superimposition of two equilateral triangles, which reproduces Solomon's seal, recalling the influence of Jewish elements upon the formation of the Koran. Some equilateral polygons remind one of architectural plans.

Prayer rugs, known under the more general name of Turkish rugs, are made almost exclusively in Asia Minor and are characterized by a rich and minutely detailed decoration; there are some very fine examples, architectural in design and eclectic in style. The Turks, who originally came from the steppes of Central Asia, had no specific art at the time when they settled in Asia Minor. They learnt the Mohammedan art with Islamism, while borrowing from the Persian, Moorish and Arabic arts. Featured on the Turkish prayer rug is the Moorish arch, supported by fragile columns, which corresponds in Islamic symbolism to the niche of the *mihrab* of the mosque. This can appear as a broken arch or with several lobes, and can comprise an architrave decorated with delicate arabesques or sententious verses from the Koran. The mystical niche is often reproduced several times on the rug, thus forming a combination of two or three identical blind arcades. The borders are usually wide, containing plant designs with arabesques which are sometimes flowing and sometimes of broken lines. Usually, the colours are vivid. The ground of the prayer rug, which represents the niche, ought in theory to be devoid of all ornamentation, although this is not always the case, so that the attention of the faithful during prayer is not distracted.

DATING CARPETS

It happens fairly frequently that a rug bears a short inscription, contained within a light-coloured rectangle which stands out from the background and which is almost always situated close to the border: these are verses from the Koran, the name of the artist or of the place of manufacture and the date when the carpet was made. Having deciphered the Islamic date, in order to discover the corresponding date of the Christian era, one must reduce it by three per cent, and then add 622 to this (this is the date of Hegira, that is to say the year which marks the beginning of the Mohammedan calendar, with the flight of Mohammed from Mecca to Medina). For example, the carpet from the mosque at Ardebil, preserved in the Victoria and Albert Museum in London, is dated with the year 946 A H, which corresponds to the year 1539 of the Christian era. Imitations bear the early date of the model of which they are copies. Contemporary products are no longer dated.

Several criteria allow one to recognize the period of manufacture of a rug: the pattern, the process of weaving, the colours and the materials. Specialized study and long practice are essential to acquire sufficient knowledge to date carpets. Unfortunately, no early writings, from the East or the West, exist to help us; all that we know is the fruit of recent study, based on stylistic analysis. Perhaps only the painters of the Renaissance, by faithfully reproducing the designs and colours of the rugs from Asia Minor in the fifteenth and sixteenth centuries, can give us some precise references.

Carpets bearing a date also carry verses from the Koran and sometimes even, on the superb Persian examples of the sixteenth century, lyrical inscriptions in praise of the rug, often brocaded with gold and silver and enclosed within cartouches along the floral borders. The Poldi Pezzoli Museum in Milan, the Museum of Decorative Arts in Paris and the Hermitage in Leningrad possess important examples of this type. One of these, reproduced in the work by Sarre and Trenkwald would have been suitable for a standard of war of an Ottoman *condottiere*. It is completely covered with an interminable legend, in brown standing out on a golden yellow ground, the text of which seems to have been dictated by one of those zealous propagandists, who, by the word and by the sword, imposed the teaching of the

Prophet upon the whole of the East: 'Allah. There is no other God than He, living and eternal. He neither slumbers, nor does He sleep. All that exists in the heavens and on the earth is His. Without His permission, no one can intercede with Him. He knows the present and the future, and men can only know of this the little which He allows. His rule embraces heaven and earth, and without effort, He preserves them. He is great and sublime.'

A typical laudatory quotation is that on the carpet from the mosque at Ardebil, preserved in the Victoria and Albert Museum in London, of which the author declares with pride: 'Outside your Threshold, there is no refuge for me in this world, outside this door, there is no place for me where I can lay my head in complete safety. Made by the slave of the Threshold Maqsud Kashani in 946.'

WEAVING AND KNOTTING

There are four types of loom: the horizontal loom, used especially in Turkestan and by the wandering tribes of Shiraz, and the three different forms of the vertical loom: these are the village loom, the Tabriz loom and the loom with rollers. Of the three, the village loom is, as one might expect, the most simple: an upper and a lower beam, both horizontal, are firmly fastened to two vertical posts. The warp threads, normally twisted into a cord, are rolled around the lower beam and their free ends are brought together in a dozen 'bundles' fixed to the upper beam. Two lateral ladders make it possible for a plank to be placed in front of the loom on which the weaver can be seated for his work. As the work progresses, the seat is lifted. When the plank has been raised to a height of about 4 or 5 feet, the artisan takes out the wedges which hold the warp threads and unties the bundles, the knotted portion of the rug is drawn downwards and fixed to the lower beam, then the warp threads are once again attached to the upper beam. The seat is placed on the first rung of the ladder and the task of the knotting recommences.

The name of the Tabriz loom derives from the town where it was introduced and where it is the only type used. Simple and cheap to operate, it has spread to almost all urban centres of the north-west of central Iran. Its advantage over the village loom lies in the elimination of the complicated fixing of the upper warp threads and of the part of the rug that is already knotted. In effect, the warp threads are stretched around the loom, so as to achieve two continuous surfaces of yarn, one facing the weaver and the other behind the loom. The shifting of the rug is carried out by pulling the part which is already knotted towards the back of the loom.

The loom with rollers is technically even more advanced. The warp threads are rolled around the top roller and the rug, as it progresses, winds on to the bottom. Consequently it is possible to make carpets of any length, whereas the Tabriz loom only allows the execution of pieces of a length equal to twice the height of the loom. Moreover, the loom with rollers, because of a more uniform tension of the warp threads, has the effect of increasing the regularity of the carpet.

At Kirman, this type of loom usually has metal rollers. In China, the looms have been improved by the use of tension screws in the uprights. In Nepal and Tunisia, they are nowadays entirely of metal.

Each loom, whether horizontal or vertical, possesses a very simple mechanism which permits the weaver to divide the warp threads into two sets, in order to be able to reverse the threads after each shoot of the weft.

The manufacture of a rug begins with the weaving of a selvedge. Several shoots of weft are made, to obtain a narrow band, like a rough linen, which is intended as a firm edge for the knotted area. There are different sorts of knots, the most common being the Ghiordes knot and the Senneh knot.

The Ghiordes or Turkish knot

The knotting begins by leaving free three or four lateral threads of the warp, which, with the to-and-fro movement of the weft threads, will form a very narrow but indispensable lateral selvedge.

The knot is tied around two adjacent threads of the warp, both being encircled by the strand of wool, with the ends reappearing between. The operation is begun again by leaving a loop of wool, about one inch long between each knot, up to the last warp threads of the row. The weft then passes through the whole width of the warp, including the side threads upon which no knot has been made. Two rods are used to separate the warp threads to form a shed through which the weft is passed in two shoots, one in each direction. After each row, each shoot of weft is compressed against the row of knots with a heavy metal comb. A new row is begun, following the same procedure, and so on in succession, until the work is completed. The loops of wool, when cut, provide the tufts which after trimming, form the pile of the carpet. However, some weavers are in the habit of cutting the strand of wool as soon as the knot is made, thus doing away with the loops.

The Senneh or Persian knot

This is also made on two adjacent threads of the warp, after leaving the first threads free for the selvedges; but

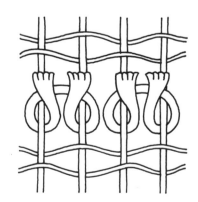

Turkish knot

Persian knot

unlike the Turkish knot, only one of the warp threads is encircled by the strand of wool, the other one merely being interlaced, so that the two ends of the strand reappear separately, the first between the two warp threads mentioned and the second between one of these and the following warp thread. Each knot is separated from its neighbour by a loop, which is cut after the shoot of the weft. The Senneh method of knotting can be carried out equally well from right to left as the other way round, which is why it is sometimes called the 'two-handed knot'. When several craftsmen are working at the same carpet, one begins the knotting from the right, and the other from the left.

The knotting can be carried out on three warp threads, by holding two threads together and one by itself, or on four threads, by separating them into two pairs. This procedure is becoming more and more widespread in the East: thereby the work gains speed, but to the detriment of the strength of the rug. A highly skilled Oriental worker can execute on average from eight to ten thousand knots per day. This laborious and monotonous task requires unremitting attention and dexterity. Various attempts made by European manufacturers to produce hand-knotted carpets have not proved successful: the rugs obtained were coarse both in workmanship and in materials, and could be distinguished immediately from their Persian models.

The Kilim or Karamani rug

The Kilim could be thought of as a stage on the road which led to the discovery of the knotted rug. It is made according to a technique which reminds one of embroidery. Having stretched the threads which form the warp onto the loom, which has been placed in a vertical position, the craftsman weaves under and over these threads with a strand of wool threaded through a needle. These threads serve as the weft and at the same time form the fabric, which is thus devoid of pile. Each shoot of weft reverses the course of the previous one, passing over instead of under a given warp thread. Wool of each colour used is taken as far across the loom as the pattern allows. On changing the colour, the warp threads are not fastened together, so that a small opening like a lengthwise slit can be perceived in the warp at this spot. When the work is complete, the Kilim presents two identical faces. The perfection of the weave depends upon the fineness of the threads of the warp and weft.

The Kilim seems to have originated in the Caucasus, whence it would have been brought by the nomadic tribes who settled in this mountainous region at some indefinite period. It is produced also in southern Anatolia, more precisely in the region of Karaman, (hence the name Karamani), Iran, the USSR, China, Tunisia, Yugoslavia, Egypt, Romania and, in a slightly different manner, in India.

The very primitive designs consist of broken lines, arranged in zigzag fashion lengthwise, so as to form superimposed rectangles and lozenges; the colours, light and dark blue, red, yellow, white, green, are fairly bright, and the material is strong.

The Kilim can be formed of a single piece, measuring up to about 8 feet 3 inches to 12 feet or of two pieces

*A loom operated out of doors
(Kalar Dasht)*

joined by a seam: in the latter case, it is very rare for the designs to coincide perfectly, because there is usually a difference in length between the two pieces. This is not a shortcoming, but a characteristic of the Kilim, the beauty of which rests rightly in the decorative character of its pattern. The two-piece Kilim is also used as a door curtain, whereas an example made from a single piece serves to cover furniture and to decorate the walls.

Rugs similar to Kilims are made in the province of Senneh, in Persia, and these have been christened Senneh-Kilim for this reason. Their very fine workmanship, the geometric elegance of their patterns, minute and precise down to the smallest details, and the sobriety of the colours make these very pleasing rugs. They are always of a single piece and their dimensions vary from approximately 5 foot by 3 foot 3 inches to 6 foot 6 inches by 5 foot 3 inches.

The Soumak rug

This differs from the Kilim in that, at the point of the changing of the colour, the weft thread is passed under the warp and cut on the reverse side about an inch away from the material; the right side of the carpet might be smooth, but the reverse presents a tangle of hanging threads.

The Soumak, always woven in wool, originates from the Caucasus, more precisely from Derbent on the Caspian Sea where manufacture continues still today. The geometric designs are very varied, with fairly large central motifs in the shape of lozenges or stars, at times asymmetrical, but in consistently discerning taste. Here and there we find small flowers, stylized human and animal shapes of fine decorative effect. The borders are richly decorated, the very wide central band echoing the motifs of the field, the outer and sometimes the inner band being decorated with the ancient running-dog motif. As far as colours are concerned, two shades dominate the ground: blue and russet. In some examples, the figures are in ivory white.

Because of its smooth and compact surface and ease with which it can be cared for, the Soumak lends itself to diverse uses: it serves as a floor rug, but also as a covering for divans and tables or as a wall decoration. Its dimensions range from 3 foot 3 inches by 5 foot 3 inches to 13 feet by 16 feet.

The Verneh rug

This rug is executed according to the same technique as the Kilim, but is more delicately made and embroidered. Its relief designs are almost always of small size. It is made at Susca and in the southern Caucasus, Anatolia and Iran. At Shiraz and in Baluchistan, it is partly knotted.

Another rug also woven in the southern Caucasus is the Sileh which belongs to the same family; it is strictly speaking more compact and consequently harder wearing. It is easily recognizable owing to its design which consists of large embroidered S-forms of whitish colour, scattered without symmetry on a ground of rather sombre hue. It is composed of two joined pieces and its current dimensions are approximately 6 feet 6 inches by 12 feet.

Turkoman horizontal loom

WASHING AND GLOSSING

Most of the carpets of the European and American markets have undergone a chemical washing aimed to give them a sheen or patina they would otherwise have lacked. Indeed, the carpet leaving the loom is nearly always lustreless and often has very bright colouring, too garish for Western taste. It is at this point that the expert in the technique of washing intervenes; he knows how to give the pile its gloss and the colours their mellowed appearance. Although this last operation can impart an antique finish to new pieces, owing to an almost total fading, it does harm the quality of the wool and therefore the strength of the rug. On the other hand, a simple washing intended to make the pile glossy does not cause much damage to a rug thus treated.

Buying and Caring for Carpets

THE CARPET TRADE

Although the principal production centres are situated in Asia Minor, Iran, the Caucasus, Central Asia, India and China, the centres of the carpet trade, where the most important transactions take place, are, besides Tehran and Istanbul, London, Leningrad, Hamburg and Zürich.

In Asian Turkey, Izmir, the former Smyrna, constitutes the principal outlet for the products of Anatolia, which, apart from prayer rugs, provides also low-priced pieces. At the present time, Turkey has lost her importance as supplier of carpets on the world market: Istanbul, which was a great centre before 1914, has ceded her primacy to London first, then to Tehran. The capital of Iran takes in a large part of the Persian output, and distributes it in Europe and America.

Of recent years, the production of Oriental carpets has been organized industrially. In some regions of Iran, it is placed under the control of the Iranian Carpet Company, whose headquarters are in Tehran and in whose workshops the old methods of dyeing with a base of natural colours, that is to say vegetable, have been resumed. One also finds large private factories at Kirman, Nain, Isfahan and Tabriz, as well as in the region of Arak. However, most of the output comes from families who work at home following traditional methods.

Recently Greece, Yugoslavia, Bulgaria, Romania and Albania have produced rugs of fine and glossy wool, with fairly deep pile, generally known under the name of 'Spartan' or 'Macedonian'. Iranian and Turkish weavers supervised the installation of the looms.

At Hereke, in Asia Minor, there exists an old industry, created in 1845 by Sultan Abdul Mecid, who wished to emulate the early rugs produced under the reign of the shahs of Persia; they were copied with remarkable fidelity. Among these high quality pieces (with up to 650 knots per square inch) are some examples in silk which are highly coveted today.

Russia was one of the first countries in Europe to appreciate the carpet. The imperial and princely palaces and governors' residences were decked out with magnificent and rare examples. At Leningrad and Moscow, the collections of Caucasian and Persian carpets had been built up from the spoils of war collected by the tsars during their struggles against Mohammedan states. The old cathedrals and convents also possessed beautiful rugs received as gifts from soldiers and diplomats taking part in the movement of Russian expansion in the East.

Before the First World War, Russia exported Caucasian and Turkoman carpets in great quantity, for example approximately three hundred tons in the year 1913; a temporary interruption followed the events of 1917, but already in 1930 export was flourishing more than ever before. In 1928, according to the information of the Bureau Sakgostorg (USSR), Caucasian rugs to the value of ten million roubles had been exported, while the export of rugs from Russian Turkestan had increased by 30 per cent in one year.

In Nepal, the carpet industry took root only a few years ago, brought by the Tibetan refugees to that country in 1961. Swiss technical aid has allowed this industry to develop. It has also helped to spread a production hitherto practically unknown, different technically in that the knots, of Persian type, are made upon an iron rod and cut only when the latter is full (see diagram). The wool for these carpets comes from Tibet which has preserved, in spite of the situation, normal commercial relations with Nepal.

Tunisia has also been endeavouring to manufacture quality rugs for some years. The National Craft Office, a state organization, has installed in all regions of the country model workshops, perfectly organized, which respect the ancient traditions of the classic craft. Here the old patterns of Kairwan are reproduced in examples, sometimes of silk, containing 250,000 to 500,000 knots.

Formerly the European carpet trade took place almost exclusively on the Italian markets, notably at Palermo, Pisa, Genoa, Florence and especially Venice, where the merchandise of the Orient abounded. In the fifteenth century, the Queen of the Adriatic controlled the monopoly of carpet imports, which she redistributed in Europe. Already in the fourth century, the Venetians had established this trade at Pavia. It is certain that the rugs which so much delighted Holbein came to Germany from Turkish or Venetian shops.

THE CHOICE AND PURCHASE OF A CARPET

In buying a carpet one should take the same care as one does when buying a jewel: the purchaser should go to a reliable specialist house, where prices will correspond with the quality of the goods. The expert is also a man of taste, capable of guiding the choice of the client according to the use to which the carpet is going to be put.

In general, the Oriental carpet blends easily with the interior of Western homes; its colours are restful to the eyes, and are so harmonious that they are incapable of detracting from the beauty of either tapestries or furniture. It is preferable to choose a compact rug of good wool. Some rugs have a slacker texture: the dealer will indicate to the collector for what use the rug is intended. A carpet must always be examined on the reverse, where one will find again the pattern of the right side, more or less distinctly. It goes without saying that the more compact, fine and careful the knotting, the better the example.

CONSERVATION AND RESTORATION OF CARPETS

The Oriental carpet is made to last a long time; a good example can be used for several generations, according to the use to which it is put: if it covers the floor of a drawing-room, it will naturally stand up better to wear than if it is laid in an office. With regard to rugs hung on walls, these can last for centuries, as is borne out by the wonderful examples in the museums of Florence, Milan, London, Berlin, Vienna, Paris and those in American museums and in private collections throughout the world. Some of these, almost undamaged, date from the end of the fifteenth century or the beginning of the sixteenth century. In the East, and especially in Persia, it is the practice to remove the shoes before treading on a carpet, to prevent wear. The correct conservation of a rug poses hardly any special problem; it is sufficient to take some very simple precautions against dust and moths, the most insidious enemies. A carpet should be beaten only very rarely. Vacuum cleaners now on the market ensure sufficient cleaning and dispense with this laborious and often inadvisable task: in fact the warp and weft threads suffer from beating a carpet which has been slung over a rail. It is preferable to spread it out on the grass or on the snow, and beat it on the reverse side. Not only will it be cleaned this way, but also it will help restore the colour. Before a carpet is spread on snow it should first be allowed to cool down otherwise it will become wet.

Early rugs and those made of silk need special consideration: they must not be beaten but simply run over lightly with a vacuum cleaner. During the summer months, if a person leaves his home for any length of time, he runs the risk of having his rugs attacked by moths. To prevent this commercial insecticides should be used. As soon as the carpet shows the slightest tear, or when the pile has been eaten and the warp and weft become uncovered, one must call in the services of a specialist restorer who will fill in the empty spaces by remaking the missing knots. Frequently, particularly with carpets of recent manufacture, some of the weft threads adjacent to the fringe become loose, so that they leave the row of knots unbound; these latter gradually become undone and risk destroying the carpet little by little. When this happens it should be seen to promptly.

Classification of Carpets

The name 'Oriental carpet' is given in general to all hand-knotted carpets; this denomination is not inexact in view of their common Asiatic origin. However, the immensity of the producing areas, and the variety of techniques, styles and materials used necessitate a detailed classification. As a rule, Oriental carpets are divided into four groups: Turkish or Anatolian rugs, rugs from Persia or Iran, rugs from the Caucasus, and finally rugs from Central Asia or Turkestan, to which one must add those from Afghanistan, Pakistan, India, Nepal and China. Even in these distant regions, exclusively commercial criteria direct the manufacture, so that the art of rug-making has become truly industrialized. In China and India, the early production drew to a close in the eighteenth century. Today attempts are being made in India and Pakistan to re-establish the old methods of carpet-making. Once again one finds rugs with classical designs with a delicacy worthy of the best traditions.

In the second half of this century an important production of the knotted rugs has developed in Europe and North Africa; although they cannot be classed with Oriental carpets, they merit no less of our attention, because, woven according to the same procedure, they attain today a worthwhile quality.

Turkey

Turkey, that massive Asiatic peninsula bounded by the Black Sea, the Sea of Marmara, the Straits of the Bosphorus and the Dardanelles, the Aegean Sea and the Eastern Mediterranean, is a very active producing country.

The name 'Anatolia', which signifies 'land of the rising sun', dates from the conquest of the Turkomans, who came from Turkestan in the fourteenth century, led by Osman. The Anti-Taurus chain of mountains separates Anatolia from the Asiatic continent. She embraces approximately ten million inhabitants, distributed throughout an area of 200,000 square miles. This vast territory saw a succession of the most varied civilizations. Succeeding races – Greek, Roman, Byzantine, Persian and Turkoman – have left a complex mixture of religions, languages, cultures and customs. The final decline of Anatolia began with the Turkoman conquest; towns were destroyed and only ruins remained, even the earth, formerly fertile, became arid; with cultivation abandoned, vast regions were transformed into deserts.

Lately, under European influence, Anatolia is awakening from her long sleep: the organization of the ports and the creation of roads has revived local trade, and Anatolia's role as a distribution centre – especially since the construction of the railway linking the Bosphorus to Baghdad and the Persian Gulf – steadily increases in importance.

The carpet trade has for long been one of the most prosperous in Anatolia for the region has so many natural advantages. Few countries are as well suited to breeding sheep which give a strong high-quality wool, and the country has, by virtue of its geographical position, easy communication with the West. Finally, the poverty of the indigenous population has enabled it to adapt easily to the patient labour of rug-knotting.

Anatolian rugs, generally designated 'from Smyrna' or 'from Anatolia', are erroneously believed to be of inferior quality. There are Turkish carpets which equal or surpass many rugs of illustrious origin, both in the fineness of the work and in the harmony of the colour schemes. The most noteworthy are the famous Ghiordes prayer rugs, the Ushaks which charmed the painters of former days, the Siebenbürgers, and many others made throughout the past centuries. It is true that present-day output tends to bow to purely commercial criteria, particularly in creating rugs of deep pile, with a central medallion on a light ground. But the ancient traditions have not been completely stifled and continue today in several centres. The now settled nomads specialize in small carpets among which the prayer rug is the most sought after by Western admirers, because of its decorative character. Formerly, the weaving of these was limited to certain regions, since it was reserved exclusively to the Mohammedan cult.

Five times daily, the Mohammedan, punctilious in respecting the Koran, spreads out his rug on the ground and kneels down to recite his *salat,* the prayer which he must make with his face turned towards Mecca. He calls fervently to Allah in his ritual invocations, opening his arms from time to time, folding his hands on his breast and lowering his head until he touches his rug with his forehead.

The design of these carpets is well known: a niche,

the arch of which can be broken, or of ogival or trilobe shape, occupies the field, usually of a plain colour, so as not to distract the worshipper during his prayers: however this rule is not absolute, and some prayer rugs are decorated with verses from the Koran above the niche or even with a lamp or a vase of flowers, common Islamic symbolic motifs, suspended at the top of the niche. The rugs which bear two or several niches are intended for communal prayer. Usually, the warp and weft are of wool, especially in the early rugs; but many modern rugs have the warp and weft in cotton.

All carpets from Asia Minor have the Turkish knot. The best known are: Avanos, Bergama, Bursa, Cal, Canakkale, Dazkiri, Demirci, Ezine, Ghiordes, Hereke, Incesu, Isparta, Karakechi, Karamani, Kayseri, Kirsehir, Konya, Kula, Ladik, Maden, Milas, Megri, Malatya, Mujur, Nodge, Ortakoy, Ushak, Siirt, Sivas, Yahyali, Yuruk.

AVANOS

Origin: Turkey
Dimensions: 63×42 inches (161×107 cm)
Turkish knot: 40 per sq.inch (62,500 per sq.metre)
Warp of two strands of natural wool
Single weft in mauve wool
Pile of two strands of wool of medium thickness, chemically washed
8 colours: 2 reds, 1 blue, 2 greens, 1 yellow, 1 white, 1 brown

Avanos is a small village of Cappadocia, which produces rugs with loose knotting and deep pile.

The example reproduced, a prayer rug, has a *mihrab* of red ground, upon which the weaver has inscribed his name: Fadimea. It is surrounded with a beige band, ranged with small octagons. The blue ground of the main border is decorated with large flowers; this precedes a green outer band of stars.

BERGAMA

Origin: Turkey
Dimensions: 45 × 43 inches (115 × 108 cm)
Turkish knot: 67 per sq. inch (104,000 per sq. metre)
Warp of two strands of natural white wool
Double weft of red wool
Pile of two strands of wool of medium thickness
12 colours: 3 reds, 3 blues, 1 orange, 1 white, 1 green, 1 black,
1 yellow, 1 violet

Bergama, the ancient Pergamum, a town of about 22,000 inhabitants, situated at the foot of the ancient acropolis at an altitude of 203 feet, was the capital of the ancient kingdom of the same name, which had known glorious days. It rivalled Alexandria and the great Antioch. The sovereign Attalus III had the curious idea of bequeathing his kingdom to Rome, who created it the capital of the province of Asia.

In the sixteenth century, Bergama was an important religious centre where Dervish scholars preached. Pergamum was one of the main centres of the Hellenistic civilization and today attracts numerous tourists.

Bergama is also very well known for the rustic, but charming, carpets made in the region.

In the example reproduced, a large dark-blue hexagon surrounded by latch-hooks fills the field; it encloses a diamond shape formed of flowers. In the centre is a lozenge crossed by bars, the two lengthwise ones terminating in stylized trees. The other motifs scattered in an irregular fashion within the hexagon, include miscellaneous stars, flowers, and even a motif in the shape of a cooking-pot; the corners are decorated with large flowers, probably sunflowers. The main border is most characteristic of the Bergama: all manner of stars and flowers are placed freely between slantwise stepped lines. A band of embroidered Kilim weaving completes this gay and imaginative rug.

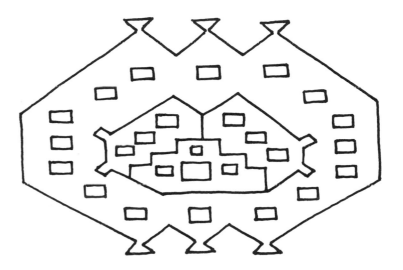

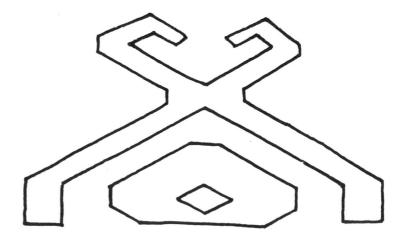

37

CAL

Origin: Turkey, Anatolia
Dimensions: 70 × 46 inches (178 × 118 cm)
Turkish knot: 64 per sq. inch (99,200 per sq. metre)
Warp of two strands of wool
Double weft of grey wool
Pile of two strands of wool of medium thickness, slightly washed
8 colours: faded in parts by the light

Cal is a village which has only a small carpet production. It is situated at a distance of 62 miles from Ushak, towards Denizli.

The field of the example shown is occupied largely by a hexagon of red ground, bordered inside by a half serrated and half stepped line, and on the outside by a band of small repeated motifs; at the top and bottom, a row of latch-hooks are terminated by a variant of the diamond-shaped motif called *mahi-tu-huse* standing out against the yellow ground, which is edged with six multicoloured stepped lines. The central serrated motif encloses another lozenge of elongated shape crossed by two lateral bars. A large motif made up of stylized leaves decorates the grey ground of each of the corners.

Around the field is a pretty band of stylized carnations, found again outside the main border which is decorated with pairs of leaves with latch-hooks, and accentuated by two small serrated bands.

The dominant yellow colour gives this carpet a rather unusual appearance.

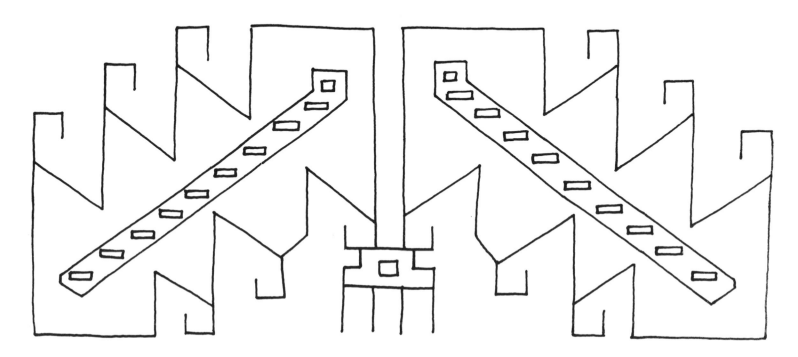

DAZKIRI

Origin: Turkey, Anatolia
Dimensions: 67 × 53 inches (170 × 135 cm)
Turkish knot: 52 per sq. inch (81,200 per sq. metre)
Warp of two strands of undyed wool
Double weft of red wool
Pile of two strands of wool of medium fineness, chemically washed
10 colours: 3 reds, 2 blues, 2 greens, 1 white, 1 brown, 1 beige

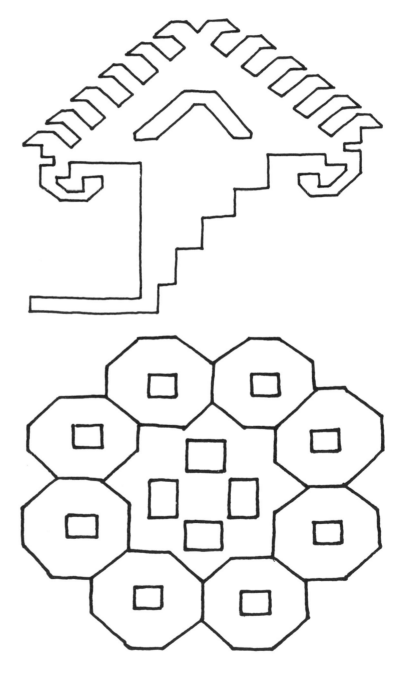

The style and colours of Dazkiri rugs resemble those from the village of Ortakoy.

A large hexagon, the frame of which is partially stepped on four sides, covers the major part of the field of this carpet. Carnations of various colours stand out against the green ground. These alternate with roses which border a lozenge of red ground in which is inscribed a star with latch-hooks.

Ewers, flowers and leaves are arranged on the ground of the corners, also of red. The ground of the principal border takes up the green shade with a decoration of large flowers. There are little flowers on the narrow band alongside the field and flowers and branches on the outer edge. A band of Kilim weaving precedes the border at both ends of the rug.

DOSEMEALTI

Origin: Turkey
Dimensions: 63 × 45 inches (160 × 115 cm)
Turkish knot: 39 per sq. inch (60,000 per sq. metre)
Warp of two strands of natural beige wool
Double weft of natural brown wool
Pile of two strands of wool of medium thickness, with natural sheen
8 colours: 2 reds, 2 blues, 2 greens, 1 brown, 1 white

Dosemealti, a small place approximately five miles from Antalya, does not produce a large quantity of carpets but the quality is fairly good. The one reproduced is of the prayer-rug type, but there seems to be only a half *mihrab,* of red ground: below are three motifs terminating in points, from which spring large tulips on a green ground similar to those on Ladik rugs.

A wide border of white ground is decorated with large motifs, more slender at the sides than at the ends. A second fairly wide border of stars is separated from the first by a small band through which runs a zigzag line.

This is an original carpet, of good quality wool, with a thick but lustrous pile.

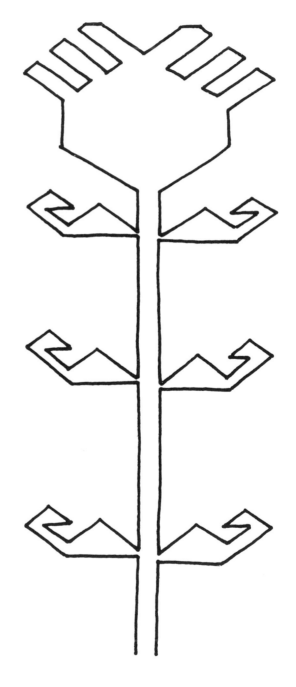

EZINE

Origin: Turkey
Dimensions: 87 × 56 inches (220 × 142 cm)
Turkish knot: 31 per sq. inch (48,300 per sq. metre)
Warp of two strands of natural white wool
Double weft of red wool
Pile of two strands of rather thick wool
7 colours: 1 red, 1 blue, 1 green, 1 beige, 1 white, 1 black,
1 yellow

The rugs of Ezine, a small locality situated in the Bergama region, have, characteristically, a long tuft of wool in the centre when they come off the loom. This tuft is often cut later on, as in the example shown.

The geometric decoration is similar to that of many Caucasian carpets. Two large motifs are placed on both sides of the central medallion, the rooflike part of which they repeat in larger form: here one can see the chevron, a rare motif in Oriental rugs. Octagons decorated with latch-hook motifs ornament the corners and run along the border. The remainder of the decoration is floral, with rosettes of varying sizes. The border, of Caucasian type, is preceded by a band of Kilim weaving.

HEREKE

Origin: Turkey
Dimensions: 69 × 49 inches (174 × 125 cm)
Turkish knot: 379 per sq. inch (588,000 per sq. metre)
Warp of two strands of natural silk
Double weft of beige cotton
Pile of two strands of natural silk
14 colours

The ancient Ancyrona, where Constantine the Great died in 337, was situated on the site of Hereke, set inside a bay of the Gulf of Izmit, 42 miles from Istanbul.

In the past, the Hereke production was famous for the beauty of its carpets. The sultans had copies made here of early models, often in silk.

In this example, which dates from the end of the nineteenth century, the whole field is covered with lozenge shapes decorated with flowers. Arranged in the very wide principal border, flanked by two sets of three small bands, are some extremely beautiful vases of flowers. The photograph is unable to reproduce exactly the delicacy of the design, particularly the silky reflections of the pile, which vary with the light. The overall impression is light and elegant, proof of the perfection reached by the Hereke rugs.

KARAKECHI

Origin: Turkey, Anatolia
Dimensions: 73 × 59 inches (185 × 149 cm)
Turkish knot: 50 per sq. inch (78,000 per sq. metre)
Warp of two strands of natural wool
Double weft of natural dark-brown wool
Pile of two strands of wool of medium thickness
9 colours: 1 red, 2 blues, 1 white, 1 black, 1 brown, 1 mauve, 1 green, 1 yellow

The decoration of the field of this early example consists of bands of latch-hooks arranged in such a way as to form two large lozenges, which are accentuated by a frame of lighter colour. The whole field is thus filled, except for two narrow strips ornamented with stars which form a frame across the width. The principal border, separated from the field by a narrow floral band, repeats the motifs. The corners show an interruption in the sequence of the bands, a characteristic of carpets knotted from memory. The design of this rug is rather curious and not widespread in Anatolia.

KAYSERI

Origin: Turkey
Dimensions: 79 × 55 inches (200 × 140 cm)
Turkish knot: 142 per sq. inch (220,000 per sq. metre)
Warp of five strands of undyed cotton
Double weft of three strands of pink cotton
Pile of one strand of wool
12 colours: 3 reds, 2 blues, 2 beiges, 1 black, 1 brown, 1 grey, 1 olive, 1 white

Kayseri, a large and fine town of approximately 100,000 inhabitants, situated at an altitude of 3,471 feet in the foothills of the ancient Mount Argaeus, is quite close to the site of the antique Caesarea, which in the first century of our era was the capital of Cappadocia. The town had to suffer numerous invasions, notably by the Arabs. At the time of their march to the Holy Places, the crusaders took possession of it, but they could not keep it and had to cede it to the Seljuks. It finally became part of the Ottoman empire in 1515.

The rugs of Kayseri, often called Caesarea, have no unique motifs. Between the two world wars, imitations were made of seventeenth- and eighteenth-century carpets from other regions of Anatolia.

The example reproduced here is of 'medallion' type, which is found rather rarely in Anatolia. It appears that the weaver worked without a cartoon, for the lozenge-shaped motifs of the corners of the main border and of the two bands which surround it are not exactly in place. The weaver must have improvised from a model of different dimensions from those of his own piece of work. There is a striking contrast between the strict geometry of the border, of Anatolian or Caucasian style,

and the rest of the carpet with its luxuriant floral pattern of Persian inspiration. The azure blue corners with their stylized flowers are reminiscent of a Kirman rug. The field, of red ground with bracket-shaped fretwork, and the blue medallion are in simpler style, that of northern Iran. The number of colours indicates that the weaver wanted to make a particularly beautiful piece.

50

KIRSEHIR

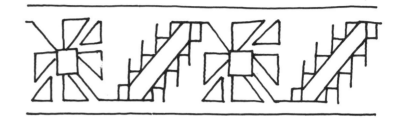

Origin: Turkey, Anatolia
Dimensions: 67 × 37 inches (170 × 95 cm)
Turkish knot: 79 per sq. inch (122,400 per sq. metre)
Warp of four strands of wool
Double weft in red wool
Pile of a single strand of wool of medium fineness
12 colours

The town of Kirsehir, with a population of 20,000, lies 118 miles from Ankara in the direction of Kayseri. In the fourteenth and fifteenth centuries it was the spiritual centre of the powerful sect of the Ahis, certain of whose members occupied important positions, such as that of governor of the province.

Even today it is rare for the pious Moslem to pray upon a rug with a *mihrab*. The production of prayer rugs is especially intended for the Western clientele.

In this example, the *mihrab*, in a fine red, has an upper part in steps, crowned with a motif of double latch-hooks; the whole circumference of the field is bordered by a row of small stylized carnations. The arch stands out against a blue ground scattered with little touches of red; the flowerbeds set above and below are identical.

In the principal border, tulips and stylized cypresses are arranged in regular fashion. On either side, a narrow band precedes a small border with floral patterns on a white ground.

KONYA

Origin: Turkey
Dimensions: 70 × 43 inches (179 × 110 cm)
Turkish knot: 69 per sq. inch (106,400 per sq. metre)
Warp of two strands of wool
Single weft of two strands of red wool
Pile of two strands of wool of medium thickness
8 colours

Konya, a town in Anatolia of about 125,000 inhabitants, is also the chief town of the province of the same name. It is situated at an altitude of 3,366 feet on the edge of a vast plain which occupies the centre of the Anatolian plateau. Its origins go back to the third millenium BC. Towards the eleventh century, Konya became the capital of the Seljukid sultanate of Roum. It remains one of the principal towns of present-day Turkey.

Already in the twelfth century rugs from Konya were held in high repute, since Marco Polo declares that he had seen in this town the most beautiful carpets in the world.

The example shown here is a prayer rug. The main border, of Georgian (Caucasus) type, is surrounded by two bands decorated with classical *shekeri* motifs (broken lines and rosettes) of Iranian origin. On the two narrow bands which complete the border the same variation of the double 'T' border is repeated, on a yellow ground for the outer strip, and on a white ground for the inner one. The major part of the field is occupied by the *mihrab* of strong red ground, devoid of decorative details, the outline of which is emphasized by a yellow notched band. The triangular top of the *mihrab,* cut out in steps, is crowned by a tree of life flanked by two large

motifs which vaguely recall the carnations of the eighteenth century. At the foot and above the prayer arch, two flowerbeds of rather smaller scale and very simple style repeat the motif of the steps. A two-coloured Kilim weave frames the rug at both ends.

KURD

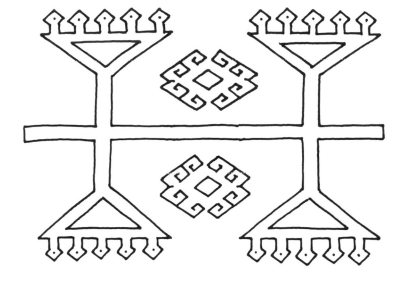

Origin: Turkey
Dimensions: 59 × 43 inches (150 × 109 cm)
Turkish knot: 87 per sq. inch (134,400 per sq. metre)
Warp of two strands of natural beige wool
Single weft of natural black wool
Pile of two strands of wool of medium fineness, chemically washed
8 colours: 2 reds, 1 green, 1 brown, 1 orange, 1 white, 1 black, 1 greyish-blue

In this prayer rug the upper part of the *mihrab* is cut out in steps and terminates in a point decorated with latch-hooks; the ground is of a green colour, which is rather unusual. It is decorated with motifs which resemble cups surmounted with candles. The octagons and the lozenges arranged on the warm red field are all surrounded by latch-hooks. In the principal border of reddish-orange ground, are octagons and stars, outlined on every side by a fine triple band.

Because of its design and unusual colours, this is a warm and pleasing rug.

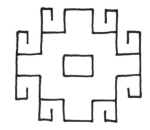

KURD

Origin: Turkey
Dimensions: 86 × 36 inches (218 × 92 cm)
Turkish knot: 43 per sq. inch (67,200 per sq. metre)
Warp of two strands of natural black goat's hair
Double weft of the same material
Pile of two strands of wool of medium thickness, chemically washed
9 colours: 1 red, 2 blues, 1 green, 2 browns, 1 orange, 1 white, 1 yellow

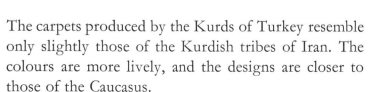

The carpets produced by the Kurds of Turkey resemble only slightly those of the Kurdish tribes of Iran. The colours are more lively, and the designs are closer to those of the Caucasus.

In the example reproduced, three large hexagons cover almost the whole of the red ground of the field. They are surrounded by a double line of latch-hooks, white on the outside and red on the inside. Double latch-hooks trim two sides of the rectangles contained within the hexagons, and also figure in the decoration of the field, as in that of the principal border of white ground, where they adorn the flowers.

The pile is thick and the colours strong. Note that the selvedges have knotted fringes.

MADEN

Origin: Turkey
Dimensions: 74 × 43 inches (187 × 109 cm)
Turkish knot: 48 per sq. inch (74,400 per sq. metre)
Warp of two strands of undyed wool
Double weft of beige cotton
Pile of two strands of wool of medium thickness
10 colours: 3 reds, 1 black, 1 white, 2 yellows, 1 violet, 1 blue, 1 grey

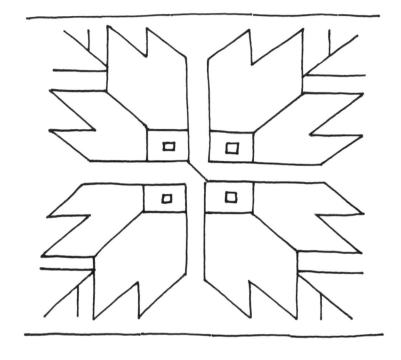

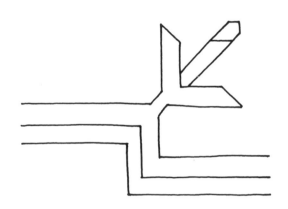

Maden is a small village situated in the neighbourhood of Yahyali, some 43 miles from Kayseri.

This rug has a fine *mihrab* of purplish red, the arch of which, rising up in steps, is emphasized by three lines, with a stylized flower at each step. The two flowerbeds above and below are identically decorated with thick notched lines, carnations and insects with eight legs, the centre one inset within a medallion. A border of large carnations frames the field; the outer band is decorated with daisies.

MEGRI

Origin: Turkey, Fethiye
Dimensions: 76 × 51 inches (185 × 129 cm)
Turkish knot: 34 per sq. inch (52,000 per sq. metre)
Warp of two strands of natural beige wool
Double weft of red wool
Pile of two strands of thick wool
12 colours: 3 reds, 1 black, 1 white, 1 grey, 2 yellows, 1 green,
2 blues, 1 chestnut-brown

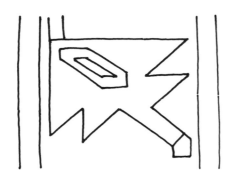

The Megri rug was fairly widely distributed at the end of the last century. It was also called 'rug from Rhodes', the island being exactly opposite Fethiye. Nowadays, it is rarely seen: the example reproduced is an early one. Two large elongated motifs almost cover the whole area of the field, one with a red ground decorated with large stylized carnations, the other with a blue ground, with long-stemmed carnations.

The same flowers ornament the first border, while the second, the outer one, is decorated with diamond shapes.

MILAS

Origin: Turkey
Dimensions: 71 × 49 inches (181 × 125 cm)
Turkish knot: 68 per sq. inch (105,000 per sq. metre)
Warp of two strands of light natural wool
Double weft of brown wool
Pile of two strands of wool of medium thickness
8 colours

Milas, a small place of approximately 12,000 inhabitants, is situated quite close to the Mediterranean, in a plain encircled by wooded mountains. The old name of the town, whose origins go back to furthest antiquity, was Mylasa. The art of rug-making has been known there for centuries, and the design and colours of Milas rugs have not undergone any important modifications for more than a hundred years.

The *mihrab,* with the upper part of its niche narrowed, is typical of Milas rugs; it always has a brick-red ground. The top of the arch is surmounted with a flowering tree of life, which is framed by four rose bushes in flower.

In addition to the form and colour of the *mihrab* with its floral pattern, the yellow colour of the main border of stylized carnations is also characteristic of Milas rugs; very broad in relation to the field, it is separated from the latter by a series of small diagonal multicoloured bands. On the outer edge, two serrated lines surround a band decorated with various octagonal motifs.

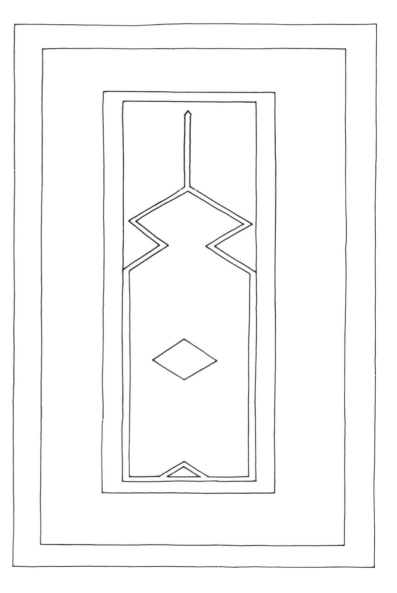

ORTAKOY

Origin: Turkey
Dimensions: 58 × 41 inches (148 × 105 cm)
Turkish knot: 44 per sq. inch (67,500 per sq. metre)
Warp of two strands of natural beige wool
Double weft of red and brown wool
Pile of two strands of wool of medium thickness
8 colours: 1 red, 1 blue, 1 beige, 1 white, 1 green, 1 mustard,
2 brown

The carpets of Ortakoy, a village 29 miles from Kayseri, are rustic and coarse, but show a completely original character.

On a mustard-coloured field are two large beige hexagons extended to both ends by an area of bright red, the design of which is accentuated by stepped lines on the field. The border is of only one band, very wide at the sides and narrower at the ends. The floral decoration is heavily stylized. This is an interesting, rather than beautiful, piece.

SAPH

Origin: Turkey, Kayseri
Dimensions: 94 × 33 inches (239 × 82 cm)
Turkish knot: 148 per sq. inch (229,600 per sq. metre)
Warp of seventeen strands of white cotton
Identical double weft
Pile of one strand of schappe silk
10 colours: 2 pinks, 3 browns, 2 greys, 1 white, 2 greens

The name of Saph is given to prayer rugs made at Kayseri. The early rugs, of which they are replicas, were of much larger format, which permitted each niche to receive one person at the time of prayer.

Here, the *mihrabs* are nine in number and their arches, supported by two double columns, are of various types: cuspidate, lanceolate, stepped. They are separated from each other and surrounded by a narrow flowered band, which is repeated as the outer frame of the main border with graceful arabesques; at both ends is an additional border, narrower at one side than at the other. The colours of this rug are very soft and pleasing.

SIVAS

Origin: Turkey, Anatolia
Dimensions: 79 × 58 inches (200 × 148 cm)
Turkish knot: 88 per sq. inch (136,000 per sq. metre)
Warp of three strands of natural beige wool
Double weft of natural brown wool
Pile of two strands of wool of medium thickness
12 colours

In the Roman period, Sivas, which was then called Sebastia, was an important commercial metropolis. As early as the second century, Christianity took root there, and in the fourth century, under Licinius, the Christian community of the town paid heavy tribute to the martyrology of the new faith. But after the Turkoman conquest in 1400, the town lost its importance. In modern times it has only begun to develop since the construction of the railway linking Ankara to Erzurum and Samsun. Today it is an industrial town of 94,000 inhabitants which has completely abandoned the tradition of fine carpets formerly held in high honour. Even trading in carpets has lapsed; at the very most one finds an occasional furniture salesman offering a meagre choice of coarsely knotted pieces. Formerly, Sivas rugs, whether the work of independent craftsmen or factory made, were renowned for their fineness and good workmanship.

The rug reproduced belongs to the coarsely knotted type. It is a most attractive piece, with a *mihrab* bordered with latch-hooks, enclosing a rather elaborate motif in the arch of the niche. The two flowerbeds have the same pattern of stylized pomegranates; flowers and little stars fill the corner above the niche. A similar little floral strip surrounds the flowerbeds, the field and the two borders, the inner one with carnations and the outer one with pomegranates.

70

TASPINAR

Origin: Turkey
Dimensions: 68 × 45 inches (174 × 114 cm)
Turkish knot: 96 per sq. inch (148,200 per sq. metre)
Warp of two strands of natural beige wool
Double weft in natural brown wool
Pile of two strands of wool of medium thickness, with natural sheen
8 colours: 2 reds, 1 blue, 2 beiges, 1 grey, 1 yellow, 1 brown

The small village of Taspinar, which produces rugs of the same name, is in distance about 152 miles from Ankara and 46½ miles from Bor.

In this example the major part of the field is occupied by a red hexagon decorated with flowers, of which the upper and lower edges are serrated. It encloses three superimposed medallions, the first beige, the second blue and the last red. Apart from the floral decoration, one can see combs and the motif of the guinea-fowl, the sign of protection. On the blue ground of the corners are stars and large flowers. At both ends of the field, a band half grey, half red, is decorated with rams' horns and flowers. A wide main border, flanked by two floral bands of blue ground, bears *boteh* and floral motifs on a beige ground. The whole effect is not lacking in originality.

YAHYALI

Origin: Turkey, Kayseri region
Dimensions: 78 × 46 inches (197 × 117 cm)
Turkish knot: 100 per sq. inch (15,800 per sq. metre)
Warp of two strands of wool
Double weft in red and brown wool
Pile of two strands of wool of medium thickness, chemically washed
12 colours

This is a prayer rug of a particular type, in which the *mihrab* fills only part of the field. Among other motifs are a mosque flanked by two slender columns terminating in a hand; exactly above, a lamp intended to give light to the believer; around the *mihrab*, elongated motifs each decorated with a stylized tree; and high up, two small pendentives bearing an inscription. The two 'flowerbeds' above and below the *mihrab* are decorated with large flowers (daisies?).

A small grey band trimmed with leaves runs all round the field and the flowerbeds. Another floral band precedes the principal border of rosettes alternating with double latch-hooks. Lastly, the outer band is decorated with the old Persian motif *medahil*.

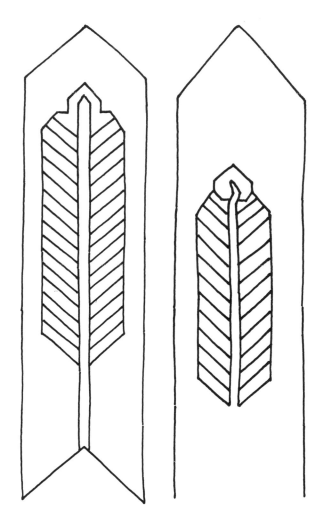

YURUK

KARAMANI

Origin: Turkey, Anatolia
Dimensions: 96 × 50 inches (245 × 125 cm)
Turkish knot: 44 per sq. inch (68,200 per sq. metre)
Warp of two strands of natural wool
Double weft in brown wool
Pile of two strands of wool of medium thickness, in bright colours
10 colours: 2 reds, 1 yellow, 2 blues, 2 greens, 1 mauve, 2 browns

Yuruk rugs, also called *tapis de montagnards,* are produced by the Kurdish tribes. The example reproduced is a typical nomad rug (Yuruk means 'nomad') with its very strong tones and simple geometric design.

Two large square motifs spread out over the field. The decoration which surrounds them is not the same in both halves of the rug: at one end, there are four small squares, while at the other are two, as well as a motif in the form of a fir-tree. Other motifs in the form of a stick with latch-hooks are sometimes furnished with a frame with hooks, sometimes surrounded with a simple linear frame. The main border is decorated with contiguous hexagons, with a central cross.

Both colours and pattern denote a whimsical imagination, with little regard for regularity. The general style is Caucasian.

Origin: Turkey
Dimensions: 167 × 39 inches (424 × 98 cm)
Technique: Kilim
Warp of three strands of natural brown wool
9 colours: 3 reds, 3 blues, 1 mauve, 1 brown, 1 white

The Turkish town of Karaman which has a population of 22,000, lies 64½ miles from Konya in the direction of Adana. The beautiful oasis which surrounds it has been made famous in several poems by Mevlâna Celal al Tin Rumi. From the thirteenth century and until 1467, Karaman was capital of a powerful emirate. It was then that numerous monuments, still to be seen today, were built.

Karamani rugs are Kilims usually of elongated, narrow shape, like the piece illustrated. This is one of a pair which could be used as curtains.

The geometric decoration is fairly plain, with rather soft colours, blue predominating.

KILIM

Origin: Turkey, Anatolia
Dimensions: 51 × 41 inches (157 × 103 cm)
Warp of two strands of natural goat's hair, black and white mixed
Thread of two strands of wool
12 colours: 2 reds, 1 blue, 1 mauve, 1 grey, 1 black, 1 orange, 1 white, 3 browns, 1 yellow

Constructed in the manner of the classical Kilim the Anatolian Kilim often shows threads on the reverse which are picked up later on in the course of the work, so that it can only be used on one side.

The piece reproduced, of this type, shows a clear difference in the colours of the right side, where they are mellowed, and the reverse, where they are stronger.

The red ground of the field is decorated in the centre with four hexagonal medallions each containing several triangular motifs with latch-hooks and serpents. Irregularly arranged at the sides of the field are hexagons, triangles and large combs. In the border of white ground are triangular motifs facing one another, which look like pendants worn by women.

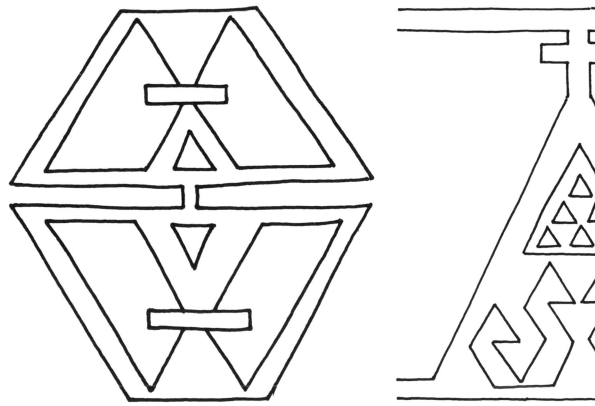

SILEH (VERNEH)

Origin: Turkey, Anatolia
Dimensions: 63 × 44 inches (160 × 112 cm)
Warp of two strands of natural wool
Thread of two strands of wool
10 colours: 2 reds, 2 blues, 1 black, 1 white, 1 orange, 1 mauve,
1 green, 1 grey

It is rather rare to encounter rugs employing the Sileh or Verneh technique (flat weaving with embroidery) with an Anatolian provenance; indeed, these pieces usually originate in the Caucasus.

The whole of the red ground of the field is here covered with embroidered squares, the white ones forming two large diamond shapes. The border is of double latch-hooks. The colours are fairly bright and warm: mauve, although little used here, is a common shade in Anatolian rugs.

This example could serve as a table cover or as a wall-hanging.

The Caucasus

The Caucasus, a harsh, wild and mountainous region, separates Asia from Europe. Situated between the Caspian, Azov and Black Seas, it constitutes the great overland communication route between the two continents.

Strabo mentions that more than three hundred clans of diverse race and religion speaking seventy different languages occupied the area. Precious Oriental merchandise crossed it before reaching the West. The Romans established colonies here, and later it was an area dominated by Byzantium. Subsequently the Genoese developed commercial traffic and built fortified castles whose ruins still remain. In time came Arab domination and then that of the Mongols, which brought with it decline. The Caucasus suffered besides under the yoke of the Turks and the Persians, and was only eventually subdued by Russia in the nineteenth century, after a bitter struggle.

The southern part of the Caucasus is considered to be the cradle of rug-making and of wool-dyeing. The early inhabitants, forced by the savage and inaccessible nature of their mountains to live in caves, from early on used the wool from their flocks to weave rugs. They were able to make these long-lasting and strong. For centuries, the particular style of these rugs remained free of all outside influences. Their designs follow an almost absolute geometric schema, with some lively stylized plant and animal motifs. The colours are usually bright, but one also finds examples where more sombre tones predominate.

The classic production is the work of nomads: therefore, these pieces are of small size. The pile is short-napped, with a fine natural gloss and thick and compact knotting, a guarantee of strength. Warp and weft threads are of wool, but in modern pieces, which are the work of sedentary workers employed in State workshops, the wool has been replaced by machine-spun cotton for the warp and weft threads, while the pile is executed in wool, also machine-spun. Mechanical spinning of the wool imparts a very even appearance, relating them more closely to entirely machine-made pieces.

At the present time, Caucasian rugs are made in four Soviet republics: in Azerbaijan, at Baku, Divichi, Jebrail, the Kazak region, Kariguin, Kalajikh, Kirowbad, Konakhkend, Kuba, Kusary, Tauz, Khizy, Shemakha, and Stepankert; in Armenia, at Aparan, Basargechar, Nor-Bayazet, Gori, Erivan, Ijevan, Kirovakan, Keninakan, Sisian, Stepanavan, Krasnoselsk, Karabakhliar, Nijneakhty, Noemberian, Shamshadi; in Georgia, at Borchalo and Signakhi; finally in Daghestan, at Arkit, Buniak, Kabyr, Kandyk, Kizliar, Kuchin, Mejgul, Mikrakh, Ortostal, Rukel.

The main rugs are the following: Shirvan, Derbent, Erivan, Gendja, Karabagh, Kazak, Kuba, Khila, Seichur, Chichi. Although most of these rugs differ little from each other, the Kazak is distinguished however by its large motifs, slightly less elaborate central field and a surface that is not so close-cropped. Some classical Kazaks knotted in Armenian villages can be recognized by their dark-blue weft. The USSR has latterly undertaken the production of rugs, which are known in the trade under the name of Kalinska and Piatigorkin. Soumak and Kilim rugs, described elsewhere, also come from the Caucasus, the Soumak more specifically from Daghestan, but it is also made in Azerbaijan.

SHIRVAN

Origin: USSR
Dimensions: 83 × 52 inches (211 × 132 cm)
Turkish knot: 101 per sq. inch (156,400 per sq. metre)
Warp of natural wool: 1 thread brown, 1 white
Double weft in undyed cotton
Pile of two strands of wool of medium thickness, with natural sheen
10 colours: 1 red, 1 straw, 2 blues, 1 orange, 1 black, 1 white, 2 browns, 1 grey

The centre of the rug is occupied by an elongated octagon of steel-blue ground, inside which are to be found several rows of hexagons, flowers and dogs, arranged in irregular fashion, some with legs and tail only. Around the centre, on a red ground, are stars, double latch-hooks, a comb at each end and more dogs. The light-blue corners are decorated with flowers. The field is framed by a running-dog border. In the geometric motifs of the principal border of white ground we again encounter the orange colour of the early Shirvans. This

shade, which is certainly of natural origin, has the dis-advantage of running when the carpet is dampened; on the other hand, neither sun nor light makes it fade.

This early example has very beautiful colours, bright but harmonious.

SHIRVAN

Origin: USSR, Azerbaijan
Dimensions: 60 × 40 inches (152 × 102 cm)
Turkish knot: 128 per sq. inch (197,600 per sq. metre)
Warp of three strands of natural beige wool
Double weft of three strands of grey wool
Pile of two strands of wool of medium thickness
12 colours

The decoration of this piece, which dates from the beginning of the century, is interesting. A large rectangular motif terminates at either end in an octagon. This encloses two smaller octagons, flanked by two small rectangles, themselves placed on either side of a central octagon, which is of the same colour as the field. Note four more triangles at the corners of the octagons. Thus there is a very well-balanced arrangement of geometric motifs. Another point worth mentioning is the remarkable use of double latch-hooks as a decorative element, in all details of the central motif, whether in the terminal octagons, in the white crosses which decorate the central octagon or in the four small motifs which surround each cross, separated by a double rectangle trimmed with a flower.

The principal border of the wine-glass type is enclosed on both sides by a zigzag band, and at the outer edge by a band of small multicoloured lozenges.

The harmony of the composition corresponds with that of the colours.

SHIRVAN

Origin: *USSR, the Caucasus, Republic of Azerbaijan*
Dimensions: 73 × 41 inches (186 × 104 cm)
Turkish knot: 75 per sq. inch (115,500 per sq. metre)
Warp of two strands of natural beige wool
Double weft of two strands of natural grey wool
Pile of two strands of wool, with naturally mellowed colours
12 colours: 2 reds, 2 blues, 1 brown, 1 white, 1 orange,
1 brownish-black, 3 greens, 1 grey

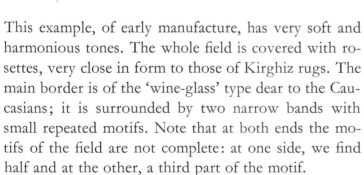

This example, of early manufacture, has very soft and harmonious tones. The whole field is covered with rosettes, very close in form to those of Kirghiz rugs. The main border is of the 'wine-glass' type dear to the Caucasians; it is surrounded by two narrow bands with small repeated motifs. Note that at both ends the motifs of the field are not complete: at one side, we find half and at the other, a third part of the motif.

This example owes its charm neither to the delicacy of its workmanship nor to its pattern, but to its simplicity and colour harmony.

DERBENT

Origin: The Caucasus, Republic of Daghestan
Dimensions: 90 × 53 inches (229 × 135 cm)
Persian knot: 88 per sq. inch (136,800 per sq. metre)
Warp of six strands of undyed cotton
Single weft of double cotton: one white, one grey
Pile of four strands of fine wool, chemically washed
10 colours: 2 reds, 2 browns, 2 blues, 1 yellow, 1 green, 1 black,
1 white

The running-dog motif, characteristic of early Caucasian rugs, decorates the principal border and two pairs of narrow bands with small repeated motifs form a frame for it.

The regions of Arkit, Buniak, Kabyr, Kandyk, Kizliar, Mejgul, Mikrakh, Ortostal, Rukel, and Kuchnin produce rugs of the Derbent type.

The example opposite reproduces an old design: the eight wide bands in parallelogram formation terminated by stylized sunflowers fill up a good part of the field, with floral decoration for the remainder.

GENDJA

Origin: The Caucasus, Kirowbad region (formerly Gendja)
Dimensions: 129 × 56 inches (327 × 145 cm)
Turkish knot: 42 per sq. inch (64,400 per sq. metre)
Warp of three strands of natural beige/brown wool
Double weft of two strands of red wool
Pile of two strands of wool of medium thickness, with natural sheen
8 colours

are simplified. In this piece, the four octagons of the medallions are decorated with motifs like stylized serpents, called in Germany *Wolkenband*. The main border, of the double latch-hook type, is surrounded by two narrow bands strewn with stars. The field has an irregular decoration of stars, double latch-hooks and stylized flowers. The very soft, warm colouring adds to the charm of this example.

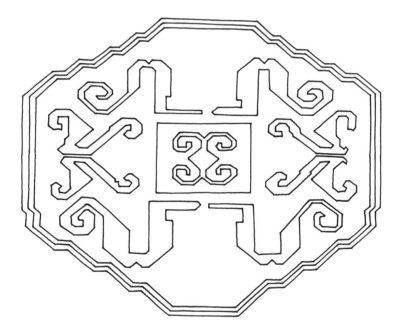

This rug of classical type of the early manufacture, which, alas, has disappeared gradually from the market, shows numerous irregularities in design which give it its charm and for which one can search in vain in present-day carpets. The same type of design can still be found but the treatment is strictly exact and the borders

KAZAK

Origin: The Caucasus, Kazak region
Dimensions: 98 × 58 inches (249 × 147 cm)
Turkish knot: 56 per sq. inch (86,400 per sq. inch)
Double warp of two strands of natural wool
Double weft of two strands of red wool
Pile of two strands of fine wool, with natural sheen
9 colours: 2 reds, 2 blues, 1 yellow, 1 black, 1 white, 1 green,
1 brown

This slightly worn early Kazak owes its beauty to its very warm tones, bright but harmonious, with red predominating. The pattern does not comply with a strict axial symmetry, but this clumsincss, if this is what it is to be called, adds to the charm of the piece. The rectangular medallion which occupies the centre is decorated with double latch-hooks and two large stylized fircones. On either side is a group of three large wineglass motifs each adorned with a ewer. On the red ground of the field are stylized animals and stars. The three bands of the border bear floral decoration: large identical motifs for the guard bands, and a more slender and elaborate pattern on a white ground for the principal band.

KAZAK

Origin: The Caucasus, Kazak region (Republic of Azerbaijan)
Dimensions: 61 × 41 inches (155 × 103 cm)
Turkish knot: 75 per sq. inch (115,600 per sq. metre)
Warp of twenty-four strands of undyed cotton
Double weft of twelve strands of blue cotton and twenty-four strands of undyed cotton
Pile of two strands of medium thickness, chemically washed
8 colours: 1 red, 4 blues, 1 brown, 1 grey, 1 white

The modern Kazak, in contrast to the early examples, has the warp threads in cotton, and no longer of wool. Collectors view with regret the loss of the originality and lack of constraint of weavers of former days: indeed, contemporary production, of which this piece is a good example, aims for an extreme regularity in design.

Three large diamond-shaped medallions with lateral extensions spread over the dark-blue field. These are interlinked and decorated with latch-hook motifs identical in shape; the centre medallion, however, differs from the other two in colouring. The ground of the field is decorated with eight rhomboid shapes called *mahi-ku-hos*. On the border two narrow guard bands encircle the central band of wine-glass type.

KAZAK

Origin: USSR, the Caucasus, Republic of Azerbaijan
Dimensions: 112 × 47 inches (285 × 120 cm)
Turkish knot: 45 per sq. inch (68,200 per sq. metre)
Warp of three strands of wool, partly beige, partly beige-brown
Double weft of pink wool
Pile of two strands of wool, with natural sheen
8 colours: 3 reds, 2 greens, 1 orange, 1 white, 1 black

This is a rug of the multiple medallion type: fourteen lozenges with latch-hooks are set out in two rows upon the field. Inside each medallion is an eight-pointed star motif formerly called 'jewel of Mohammed', in the centre of which is depicted the symbol of the divinity of the sun.

Outside the main border of wine-glass type, we find an old Oriental border in the form of sugar-loaves.

This rug has very soft colouring, with pastel reds predominating; two shades of green and one of orange combine to give an effect of great harmony.

KAZAK

Origin: The Caucasus, Republic of Azerbaijan
Dimensions: 85 × 57 inches (217 × 145 cm)
Turkish knot: 85 per sq. inch (131,200 per sq. metre)
Warp of two strands: one thread of undyed cotton twisted with
one thread of white goat's hair
Double weft of two strands of red goat's hair
Pile of two strands of wool
8 colours: 2 reds, 2 greens, 1 orange, 1 black, 1 grey, 1 white

This Kazak rug, with its three irregular diamond-shaped medallions upon a red ground, is a classic example of the early manufacture.

Inside the medallions are pomegranates, tulips and stylized carnations. Note that in two of the medallions one finds crosses, which are absent in the third.

The plain field which surrounds the medallions assumes a diamond-shaped indentation, accentuated by a partially stepped line which simultaneously determines the outlines of quarter and half diamond shapes along the border. These spaces are decorated with various motifs: stylized horses, little squares, flowers and symbols of the divinity of the sun.

The border is formed of three bands of equal width with a pattern of stylized carnations.

The pastel colours impart a rather soft appearance. The wool is without sheen.

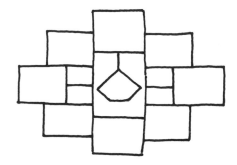

KARABAGH

Origin: USSR, Azerbaijan
Dimensions: 124 × 53 inches (315 × 134 cm)
Turkish knot: 61 per sq. inch (95,200 per sq. metre)
Warp of three strands of wool
Double weft of beige wool
Pile of two strands of wool
12 colours

Four bright red medallions, of jagged form decorated with large flowers, occupy a large part of the field. A series of symmetrically arranged motifs fills up the remainder. Apart from stylized flowers, one can particularly distinguish some four-legged animals which look more like cocks than dogs.

The principal border of double latch-hooks is surrounded by two bands called 'serpent borders'.

This example is of early manufacture, but the colours have remained strong. The wool has no sheen.

KILIM

Origin: USSR, Azerbaijan
Dimensions: 98 × 73 inches (250 × 185 cm)
Warp of two threads of natural beige and brown wool
Kilim weave of two strands of rather fine wool
8 colours: 1 red, 2 blues, 1 black, 1 white, 1 yellow, 1 violet,
1 green

This Kilim, called Palas in the Caucasus, has a very
simple design of repeated stripes; those which have a
zigzag line are decorated with small squares, while in
the adjacent row, little crosses ornament the centre of
each of the lozenges.

The tones are soft and the weaving is compact: this
is a fine example of early manufacture.

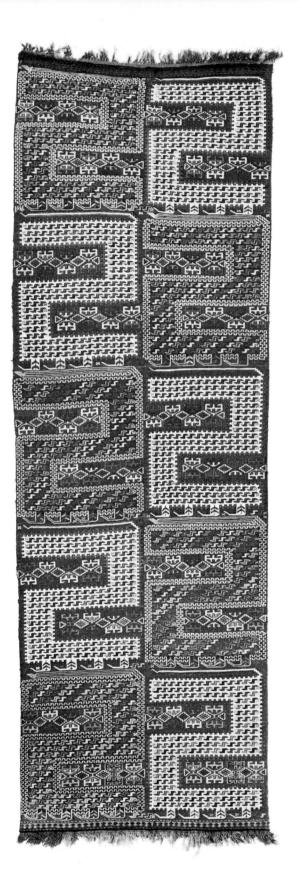

SILEH

Origin: USSR, Republic of Armenia
Dimensions: 142 × 47 inches (361 × 120 cm)
Warp of three strands of natural white wool
Weft of the same material
Two strands of wool and three strands of white cotton
12 colours: 3 reds, 2 blues, 3 greens, 1 white, 1 black, 1 beige, 1 brown

The Sileh, originating from the town of the same name, is connected by virtue of its technique with Soumak rugs.

The field is covered by two rows of large inverted S-forms, alternately light and dark. These are surrounded by a jagged line and completely filled with a multitude of little S-shaped motifs this time in normal position. Among other motifs are ram's horns and diamond shapes.

Rugs of this characteristic style are rather rarely seen in the trade.

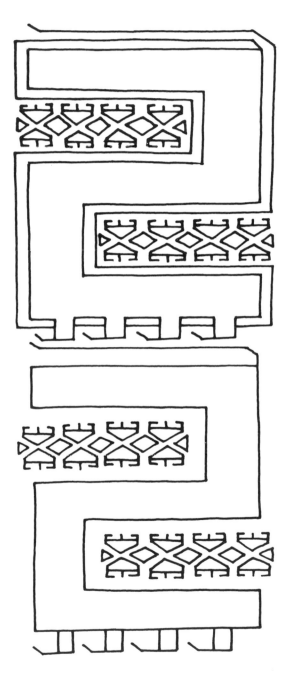

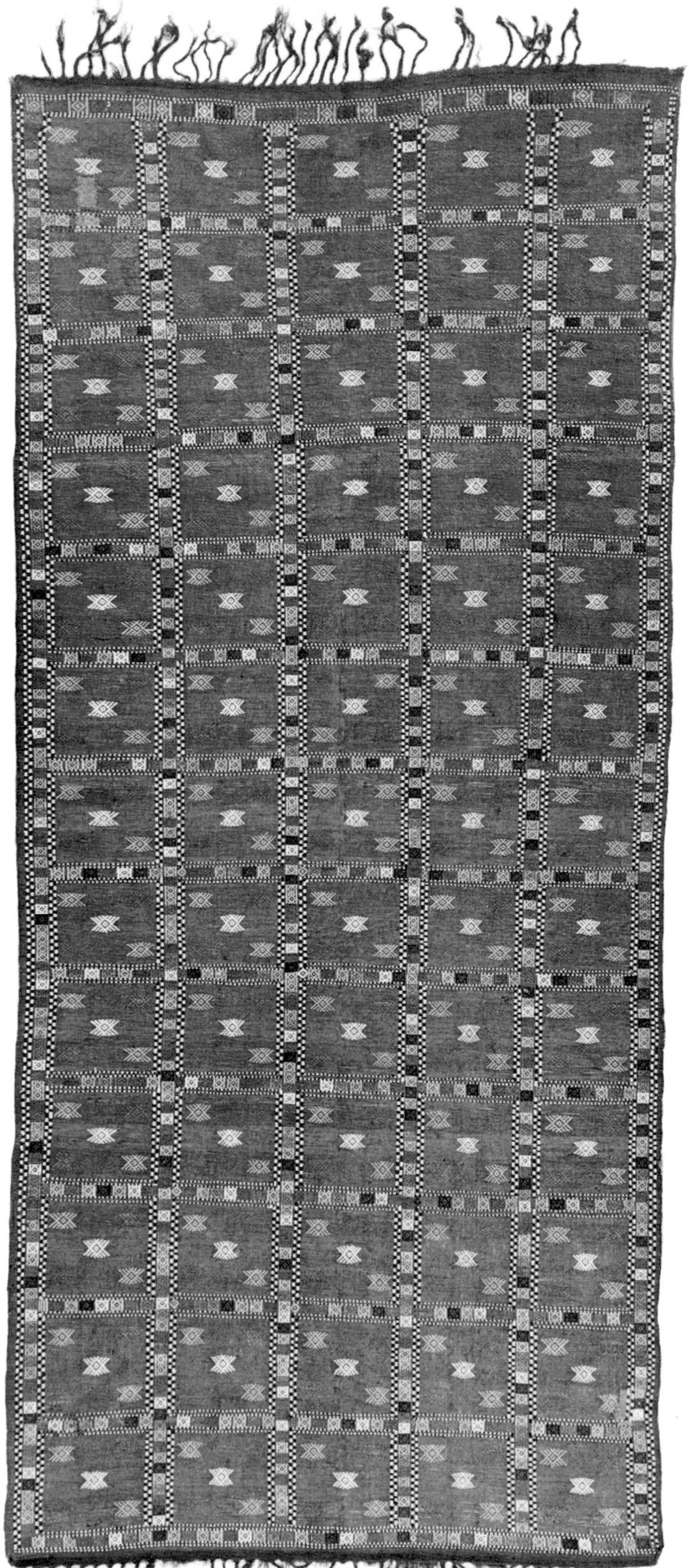

VERNEH

Origin: USSR, The Caucasus
Dimensions: 128 × 56 inches (326 × 142 cm)
Warp of two strands of red and blue wool, mounted in strips of approximately 2¾ inches (7 cm)
Tapestry weave of two strands of wool
8 colours: 2 reds, 1 blue, 1 yellow, 1 white, 1 black, 1 orange, 1 green

The design of this rug is embroidered on a flat ground, woven in the Kilim technique, with the warp in plain strips of 2¾ inches, blue and red alternately. Each stitch of the tapestry weave forming the squares of the design is carried out on three warp threads.

Unfortunately the Sileh is no longer produced in the USSR; the carefully chosen colours of its tapestry weave gave it a distinctive character which the Kilim cannot match.

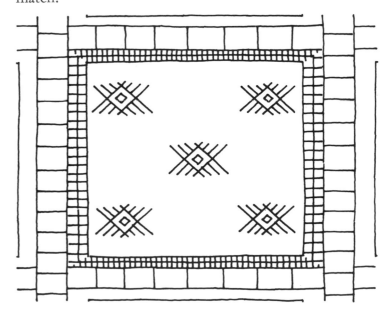

Iran-Azerbaijan

Azerbaijan, a very fertile province of northern Iran whose climate is suited perfectly to the breeding of sheep, is rightly renowned for the excellent quality of its wool. This guarantees the strength of rugs produced in this region, in particular those from Heriz.

The capital, Tabriz, is the third town of Persia and since the seventeeth century it has been one of the most important production centres of the country. Before the First World War, it used to control all Iranian trade between tsarist Russia and the West. It was at that time the richest town in Persia. Old accounts of journeys describe it as a city full of refinement. Today, it contains several factories which make the most beautiful Tabriz rugs. The weavers of Tabriz are the most skilled in all Iran and work very rapidly, using a special hook for making the knots.

Two other regions of Azerbaijan well known for their rugs are Heriz and Mehriban; these general classifications cover the products of numerous villages which can be distinguished by small differences in the design. They are as follows:

(a) rugs with a central medallion, known under the name of Heriz. The most beautiful examples are woven at Heriz itself, at Ahar, Sharabiyan and Kargha while the most everyday pieces come from the neighbouring villages of Ardalan, Asnak, Bakhshayesh, Bari, Bilverdi, Bissovan, Gorji, Gorevan, Jamalabad, Jangur, Karaja, Kirncjuvan, Kolvanaq, Kordh-Kandi, Kuva, Meina, Mianbasur, Ostelak, Rajul, Sehen-Sara, Taze-Kand, Turkan-Burg, Valhi, Zarma.

(b) rugs with an all-over design, without a central medallion; sold under the name Mehriban, they can also come from Arbatan, Chekh Rajab, Kaissareh, Merkit and Zarma.

Carpets commonly called Karaja have often originated in Ahmedabad, Bilverdi and Khursmalu.

Barjid, Lanbaran, Sahadabad and Hachterud have their own typical production, akin in character to the Karajas. One also occasionally finds them in the trade under this name.

One must mention two more weaving centres, the regions of Ardebil and Mishkinshahr, which make rugs of the Shirvan (Caucasian) type, without however equalling their quality and colour harmony.

Sarab, a village of the Ardebil region, has specialized in the weaving of long rugs with medallions standing out upon a beige-brown ground. The knotting is very thick on a double warp.

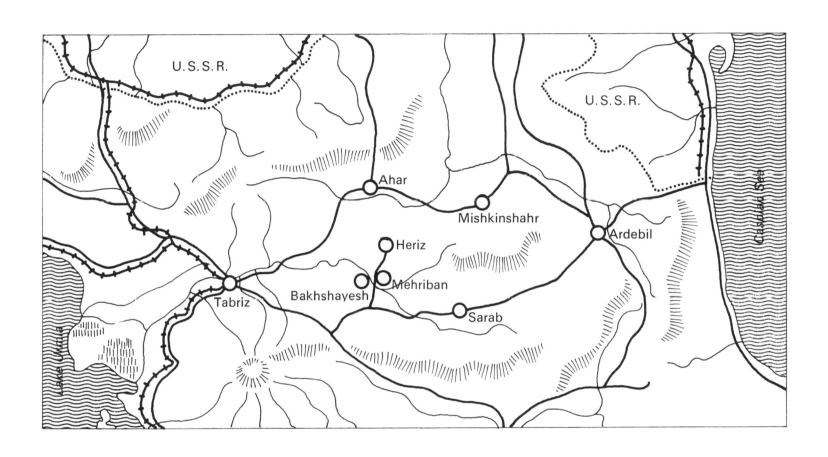

TABRIZ

Origin: Iran
Dimensions: 98 × 67 inches (250 × 170 cm)
Turkish knot: 111 per sq. inch (172,200 per sq. metre)
Warp of twelve strands of undyed cotton
Double weft: one thread of five strands of thick beige cotton,
one thread of three strands of fine blue cotton
Pile of two strands of wool of medium thickness, chemically
washed
12 colours: 2 reds, 2 yellows, 2 blues, 2 greens, 1 pink, 1 black,
1 white, 1 grey

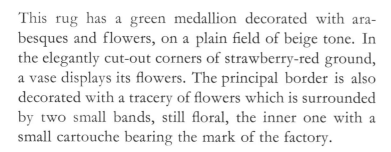

This rug has a green medallion decorated with arabesques and flowers, on a plain field of beige tone. In the elegantly cut-out corners of strawberry-red ground, a vase displays its flowers. The principal border is also decorated with a tracery of flowers which is surrounded by two small bands, still floral, the inner one with a small cartouche bearing the mark of the factory.

TABRIZ

Origin: Iran
Dimensions: 63 × 49 inches (160 × 125 cm)
Turkish knot: 382 per sq. inch (591,600 per sq. metre)
Warp of two strands of natural silk
Double weft of beige cotton
Pile of two strands of natural silk
12 colours

This type of carpet, of early manufacture, has unfortunately disappeared from the market. This is an example received, in thanks for his services, by a Dutch official, who had helped to organize the Iranian postal services at the end of the last century.

A large *mihrab* with broken arch supported by two narrow columns is adorned with a lamp. The 'flower-bed' underneath is embellished with arabesques and flowers, the upper one with little domes sheltering trees of life.

Two borders each of three bands encircle the principal border trimmed with roses.

The softness of the tones is heightened by the use of silk.

TABRIZ

Origin: Iran
Dimensions: 110 × 72 inches (280 × 184 cm)
Turkish knot: 145 per sq. inch (225,600 per sq. metre)
Warp of seven strands of undyed cotton
Double weft: one of four strands of thick grey cotton, one of twelve strands of thick grey cotton
Pile of two strands of wool of medium fineness, chemically washed
16 colours: 4 reds, 2 blues, 1 beige, 2 browns, 1 grey, 1 black, 2 yellows, 2 greens, 1 white

The pattern of this carpet, which comes from a Tabriz factory, represents a garden, such as one finds also in Kirman, Qum and Bakhtiari rugs. The decoration of the rectangles presents a great variety of motifs: diverse trees, animals, bouquets and vases of flowers between two columns or under a dome. The principal border includes no less than fourteen poems inscribed in cartouches, which are separated from each other by rosettes. The luxuriant effect is enhanced by the very great number of soft-toned colours.

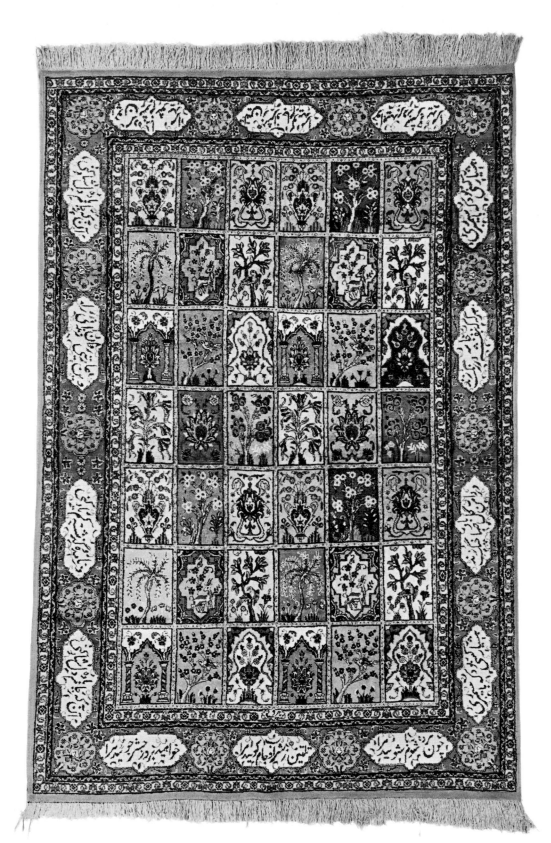

TABRIZ

Origin: Iran
Dimensions: 67 × 49 inches (171 × 125 cm)
Turkish knot: 188 per sq. inch (291,200 per sq. metre)
Warp of seven strands of undyed cotton
Double weft of cotton: one thread grey, one thread blue
Pile of two strands of wool of medium fineness, chemically washed
14 colours: 4 reds, 4 greens, 2 blues, 1 black, 1 white,
2 beiges

rather blurs the outlines of the small motifs. The main border is decorated with animals and flowers upon a bright brick-red ground.

The colours are soft and the whole effect is pleasing to the eye.

This is an example woven in a Tabriz factory from a cartoon which reproduces a hunting scene: this ancient Persian design has already been used in the rugs of the seventeenth century.

The hunters, animals, trees and flowers stand out well against the cream ground of the field, although the thickness of the pile, which reaches almost half an inch,

HERIZ

Origin: Iran, Azerbaijan
Dimensions: 130 × 141 inches (330 × 230 cm)
Turkish knot: 52 per sq. inch (81,200 per sq. metre)
Warp of thirteen strands of natural cotton
Double weft of blue cotton
Pile of two strands of rather thick wool, chemically washed
10 colours

Heriz, a large village of 25,000 inhabitants, can be reached during the fine season by a small secondary road leading off from the arterial route which links Tabriz to Ahar. Its rugs have been known for a long time, not for their delicacy or their beauty but for their robustness. They always have a large central motif, as in the piece reproduced, which is typical of this type. A hexagon of red ground with sides partially stepped covers the major part of the field. This encloses two superimposed star-shaped medallions the centre one decorated with eight large tulips, the other with cypresses alternating with bunches of stylized ears of grain. The whole is surrounded by a very varied pattern of flowers and leaves, with vases in the corners and plantlike interlacings in the main border surrounded by two narrow bands.

The rugs from the actual village of Heriz are in general of better quality than those of the same type from the neighbouring villages.

AHAR

Origin: Iran, Azerbaijan
Dimensions: 132 × 94 inches (336 × 239 cm)
Turkish knot: 39 per sq. inch (61,600 per sq. metre)
Warp of four strands of thick undyed cotton
Double weft of thick blue cotton
Pile of two strands of thick wool, chemically washed
10 colours: 3 reds, 3 blues, 2 beige-browns, 1 white, 1 black

Ahar, a town of approximately 20,000 inhabitants, situated at an altitude of 4,900 feet and 70 miles from Tabriz is already mentioned in the thirteenth century by the geographer Yaqut. The carpets bearing its name are made in the town itself and in the vicinity. In their manufacture and texture these carpets are much the same as those of Heriz, but their patterns have more rounded outlines, as can be seen in this piece on the central medallion and the corner motifs with large stylized flowers. The field is red, with a dark-blue medallion and corners of cream ground. The main border, decorated with large leaves and stylized flowers, is edged by narrow bands with stylized carnations upon a beige-brown ground.

This thick and robust rug stands up well to daily wear.

AHMEDABAD

Origin: Iran
Dimensions: 47 × 51 inches (120 × 129 cm)
Turkish knot: 38 per sq. inch (58,900 per sq. metre)
Warp of six strands of thick undyed cotton
Single weft of six strands of thick blue cotton
Pile of two strands of thick wool
9 colours in bright shades

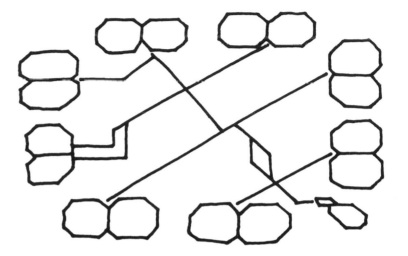

Ahmedabad is a village in the province of Azerbaijan, situated approximately 37 miles from the Tabriz-Ahar road. About 3 miles have to be travelled on a track, fording the saline Talkeh Rud, as there is no bridge. The inhabitants of Ahmedabad can thus transport their rugs on horseback as far as Tabriz during the fine season or in winter when the river is frozen; but there are periods when they are cut off from the road and cannot dispose of their products, unless they cross the mountains, which triples the distance, quite apart from the inconvenience of the route.

Ahmedabad specializes in pieces of small dimensions; the looms usually can take rugs with a maximum width of about five feet.

The example reproduced is of almost square shape. Its pattern is similar to that of a Karaja, with its characteristic repeated medallions, decorated with key motifs on a white ground, and its wide border of small leaves and stylized flowers which frames a field of warm red colour. The single weft gives an interesting appearance to the reverse of the rug.

BAKHSHAYESH

Origin: Iran, Azerbaijan
Dimensions: 196 × 133 inches (498 × 338 cm)
Turkish knot: 54 per sq. inch (84,000 per sq. metre)
Warp of seven strands of undyed cotton
Double weft of blue cotton
Pile of two strands of wool of medium thickness
14 colours: 3 reds, 3 blues, 2 greens, 1 yellow, 1 beige, 2 greys,
1 black, 1 white

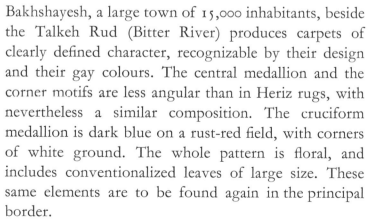

Bakhshayesh, a large town of 15,000 inhabitants, beside the Talkeh Rud (Bitter River) produces carpets of clearly defined character, recognizable by their design and their gay colours. The central medallion and the corner motifs are less angular than in Heriz rugs, with nevertheless a similar composition. The cruciform medallion is dark blue on a rust-red field, with corners of white ground. The whole pattern is floral, and includes conventionalized leaves of large size. These same elements are to be found again in the principal border.

The thick wool used does not permit a great number of knots to the square inch, but the rug is no less compact. The wool is of good quality and the fourteen colours are evidence of a search for harmonious beauty.

BILVERDI

Origin: Iran, Azerbaijan
Dimensions: 137 × 102 inches (347 × 259 cm)
Turkish knot: 60 per sq. inch (92,400 per sq. metre)
Warp of eleven strands of undyed cotton
Single weft of six strands of blue cotton
Pile of two strands of wool of medium thickness, of rather soft shades
10 colours: 2 reds, 2 blues, 2 greens, 1 black, 1 white, 1 beige, 1 yellow

The small village of Bilverdi, situated between Tabriz and Ahar, produces single-weft carpets, as does Karaja, which it is quite near. This technique gives the reverse of these pieces a different appearance from other types of Heriz rugs.

The field is covered with a very large hexagon framed by a stopped line which is decorated with an angular central motif of large dimensions forming a sort of star. The decoration is entirely of plant forms, both on the field and border of large flowers and leaves.

The ground colour is reddish-brown, with white corners. This example in rather soft colours has been mellowed in the open air, undoubtedly according to the usual procedure in Iran, which consists of exposing the rug to bright sunlight after having rubbed the pile with dampened earth.

CHEKH RAJAB

Origin: Iran, Azerbaijan
Dimensions: 135 × 103 inches (343 × 261 cm)
Turkish knot: 26 per sq. inch (40,000 per sq. metre)
Warp of thirteen strands of thick undyed cotton
Double weft of thick blue cotton
Pile of two strands of thick wool
10 colours: 3 reds, 2 greens, 1 blue, 1 beige, 1 white, 1 black,
1 greyish-black

The decoration of this example is very simple: three small medallions stand out against a red ground, ornamented with stylized flowers and leaves, and in the principal border are lozenges and hexagons encircled by latch-hooks. The weaving is not very compact, with a low number of knots.

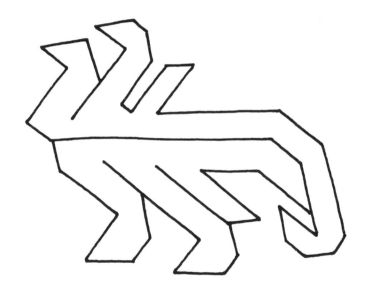

Chekh Rajab is to be found on the Talkeh Rud (Bitter River) not far from Bakhshayesh about 4 miles from Merkit. The carpets made there conform to the pattern of the classical Heriz and the Afshar type, an example of which is reproduced here. This group is less esteemed in the country than the Heriz with large central motif.

KARAJA

Origin: Iran, Azerbaijan
Dimensions: 77 × 55 inches (195 × 139 cm)
Turkish knot: 69 per sq. inch (106,400 per sq. metre)
Warp of seven strands of undyed cotton
Single weft of blue cotton
Pile of two strands of wool of medium thickness, chemically washed
12 colours

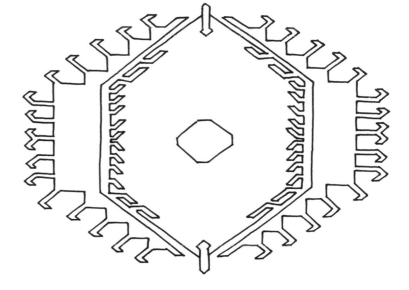

Karaja is a small mountain village near Shahsavar, which lies on the road between Tabriz and Ahar. It is difficult to reach as there is no access by road. Its rugs have a character all their own, different from those of other production centres of the region, which belong to the Heriz or Mehriban types; here the warp threads are single and the motifs smaller and more delicate.

The red ground of the field is patterned with stylized trees, leaves and flowers. Of the three medallions, two are square-shaped with four little bars. These also have floral decoration, and in each corner a stylized scorpion. The central medallion is a hexagon encircled by latch-hooks.

Three little strips surround the central floral border. The style is simple; good quality wool gives the carpets of this region great strength.

KARAJA

Origin: Iran
Dimensions: 133 × 93 inches (339 × 237 cm)
Turkish knot: 46 per sq. inch (71,300 per sq. metre)
Warp of nine strands of white cotton
Thick single weft of blue cotton
Pile of wool of medium thickness, chemically washed
8 colours: 3 reds, 2 blues, 1 green, 1 brown, 1 white

Karaja is a village in Azerbaijan, in the Heriz region, approximately 34 miles from Tabriz. Its rugs are distinguished from all others of the same type by a design of repeated medallions, partly encircled by white latch-hooks, which are reminiscent of those of the Yomud rugs of Turkestan. The Karaja is always made on a single warp, while almost all the villages of the region work upon a double warp.

The example reproduced opposite, the main colour of which is a warm red, contains eleven medallions with latch-hooks and ten other less conspicuous geometric motifs on the greenish-blue ground of the field. The main border of dark-blue ground is of the type with rosettes interlinked by fine lines, with stylized flowers and leaves. This border is framed by two narrow bands of white ground, the outer one bearing palmettes and the inner one with motifs of the wine-glass type.

The Karaja is a plain rustic rug, the major quality of which is its solidity, which results from the very strong wools produced in Azerbaijan.

KOLVANAQ

Origin: Iran, Azerbaijan
Dimensions: 146 × 106 inches (372 × 270 cm)
Turkish knot: 57 per sq. inch (88,800 per sq. metre)
Warp of twelve strands of undyed cotton
Double weft of thick blue cotton
Pile of two strands of wool of medium thickness, chemically washed
10 colours: 3 reds, 3 blues, 1 black, 1 white, 1 yellow, 1 green

Kolvanaq (also known as Kilvana) is a village 7 miles west of Mehriban and 7 miles from Bakhshayesh. Its rugs belong to the Heriz medallion type, however with a smaller and denser pattern. The large red hexagon which covers the major part of the field has sides which are cut out in steps, as is the central motif of blue ground, itself decorated with a sort of star in red. The corners, of a darker red than the hexagon, are separated from the latter by the white ground of the field. The principal border is dark blue and has a floral decoration, as does the rest of the carpet.

This is a hard-wearing carpet.

KURDLAR

Origin: Iran, Azerbaijan
Dimensions: 144 × 103 inches (367 × 262 cm)
Turkish knot: 41 per sq. inch (63,000 per sq. metre)
Warp of six strands of thick cotton
Double weft of blue cotton
Pile of two strands of thick wool
10 colours: 2 reds, 3 blues, 1 white, 1 black, 1 beige, 2 greens

Kurdlar, one of the numerous small villages of Azerbaijan, provides rugs of the Heriz type.

A large leaf enclosing a tree of life upon a royal-blue ground is to be found on either side of the large star-shaped medallion of geometric lines. The corner motifs stand out against a white ground. All of the decoration, including that of the border, is composed of large stylized leaves and flowers. The small striped red and white band on either side of the main border is characteristic of Kurdlar rugs.

This is a sturdy piece, with a compact hard-wearing weave. The thickness of the warp threads and of the wool used for the pile accounts for the low number of knots.

MEINA

Origin: Iran, Azerbaijan
Dimensions: 146 × 100 inches (355 × 254 cm)
Turkish knot: 54 per sq. inch (83,200 per sq. metre)
Warp of twelve strands of white cotton
Double weft of thick blue cotton
Pile of two strands of wool of medium thickness, in soft shades
10 colours: 3 reds, 2 blues, 1 green, 1 black, 1 white, 1 beige, 1 yellow

Meina, a small village of the Heriz region, produces rugs of the same style as those of other villages of the region, but which can be recognized by their characteristic colouring.

The three central motifs superimposed in the form of a star have a stylized floral pattern of geometric lines. A very large flower lengthens the medallion and adorns

the corners. The principal border comprises large rosettes separated by leaves.

This simple, but robust rug is the work of poor craftsmen, whose mode of life changes very little.

SHARABABIYAN

Origin: Iran, Azerbaijan
Dimensions: 137 × 100 inches (348 × 253 cm)
Turkish knot: 88 per sq. inch (136,800 per sq. metre)
Warp of nine strands of thick undyed cotton
Double weft of grey cotton
Pile of two strands of wool of medium thickness, chemically washed
12 colours: 2 reds, 3 blues, 1 green, 1 gold, 1 white, 1 black, 2 greys, 1 brown

Sharabiyan lies about 22 miles from Bostanabad; the road from here to Sarab goes through Kuzduzan from where a track leads to the village.

In general composition, the rugs are of the Heriz type, although the motifs are less angular; moreover, the weave of Sharabiyan rugs is heavier. Made of good quality wool, the Sharabiyan rug enjoys, like the Heriz, an excellent reputation.

As always with these carpets the field has a red ground; it is decorated with a fairly important central medallion, and with large leaves and flowers, which are to be found again on the white ground of the corners and on the blue ground of the principal border. The latter is completed by three narrow bands on the inside, and by two others on the outside. The colours are bright and warm.

MEHRIBAN

Origin: Iran, Azerbaijan
Dimensions: 77 × 54 inches (195 × 137 cm)
Turkish knot: 70 per sq. inch (108,800 per sq. metre)
Warp of eight strands of white cotton
Double weft of blue cotton
Pile of two strands of fairly thick wool, chemically washed
10 colours: 2 reds, 2 blues, 2 greens, 1 white, 1 orange, 1 black,
1 beige

The large village of Mehriban, 16 miles from Heriz, is well known for its carpets, which belong to the Heriz type, although devoid of the central medallion.

Flowers and leaves cover a field of red ground, or white as in this example. Two small borders of carnations frame the main border of arabesques of plant forms.

Like the Heriz, the Mehriban is a very robust carpet of rustic style; it is frequently found in European dining-rooms.

MERKIT

Origin: Iran, Azerbaijan
Dimensions: 111 × 75 inches (283 × 191 cm)
Turkish knot: 40 per sq. inch (62,000 per sq. metre)
Warp of four strands of thick undyed cotton
Double weft of thick blue cotton
Pile of two strands of fairly thick wool, chemically washed
10 colours: 3 reds, 2 greens, 1 blue, 1 beige, 1 white, 1 black, 1 greyish-black

Merkit is a village of approximately 2,000 inhabitants situated quite close to the Tabriz-Ahar road, beside the Talkeh Rud. It is some 31 miles from the first rug manufactory of the Heriz medallion type and of the design called 'Afshan' or Mehriban: in fact the name of Afshan defines the pattern, Mehriban being more exactly the name of a large village which produces rugs of this type.

The rug reproduced has a decoration typical of the Heriz group, with its large leaves and stylized flowers which completely cover the field. The main border is ornamented with large leaves with a flower in the middle, arranged regularly upon a dark-blue ground. Two narrow bands on the inside and one on the outside surround it. This is a rustic piece, with loose knotting because of the thickness of the wool used, but none the less sturdy enough to stand up to daily wear.

LANBARAN

Origin: Iran, Azerbaijan
Dimensions: 68 × 46 inches (173 × 118 cm)
Turkish knot: 53 per sq. inch (81,600 per sq. metre)
Warp of eight strands of white cotton
Double weft of grey cotton
Pile of two strands of wool of medium thickness
12 colours: 3 reds, 2 blues, 1 white, 1 orange, 1 black, 1 beige,
1 brown, 1 green, 1 yellow

The rugs from the village of Lanbaran are made in small sizes and in narrow strips (runners). The decoration is geometrical and shows some resemblance to that of the rugs from Russian Azerbaijan.

The major part of the field is occupied by three large medallions, with the outer ones of hexagonal form and surrounded by latch-hooks, while the central one has tulips and carnations for adornment, formalized in rather diagrammatic fashion.

Various flowers are strewn over the ground of the field, which is framed by a multicoloured serrated line.

The main border of light ground like the central medallion is decorated with flowers and trees and flanked by two narrow bands with floral motifs.

This rather simple and colourful rug is the product of a rustic workshop.

ARDEBIL

Origin: Iran, Azerbaijan
Dimensions: 111 × 43 inches (282 × 110 cm)
Turkish knot: 107 per sq. inch (165,600 per sq. metre)
Warp of five strands, four in cotton and one in goat's hair
Double weft of undyed cotton
Pile of wool of medium thickness, chemically treated to tone down the colours and to make them glossy
10 colours

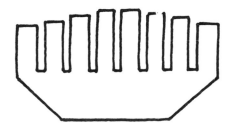

It is at Ardebil, an important town of 90,000 inhabitants situated at an altitude of 3,600 feet to the east of the ancient extinct volcano of Kuh-i-Savalan, that Zoroastra, according to tradition, would have written the Avesta. In the north-west of the town stands the mausoleum of the holy man Sheikh Safi al-Din Ishaq, who died in 1334. Nadir Shah was crowned at Ardebil in 1736.

The geometric decoration of this carpet is of the same style as that of Caucasian rugs; with many double latch-hooks, flowers, combs, dogs, and trees of life. The principal border, decorated with crosses and rosettes is encircled by two narrow bands.

The Ardebil rug is distinguished from the Caucasian rug by its knotting and less lustrous wool.

MISHKIN

Origin: Iran
Dimensions: 57 × 43 inches (146 × 110 cm)
Turkish knot: 78 per sq. inch (120,900 per sq. metre)
Warp of seven strands, six of undyed cotton and one of natural wool
Double weft of six strands of dyed black wool
Pile of two strands of wool of average thickness
8 colours: 2 reds, 2 blues, 1 beige, 1 green, 1 brown, 1 black

Mishkinshahr, formerly Khiov, 115 ½ miles from Tabriz and at an altitude of 6,000 feet is a small place at the foot the Kuh-i-Savalan. The rugs produced there, like Ardebil rugs, are very close in style to those of the Caucasus.

The example reproduced is characterisic of the current output; it has three octagonal medallions, two of beige ground and one of red ground, which remind one of Kazak rugs. The decoration conforms to a strict axial symmetry. The field is strewn with diverse motifs among which are stylized animals, the four cocks in the corners being especially memorable. The main border of red ground is a variant of the wine-glass border of the Caucasus; this is surrounded by two bands of S-forms upon a white ground.

The production of Mishkinshahr is of interest to the collector. These rugs, still little known, are worthy of attention.

MISHKIN

Origin: Iran, Azerbaijan, Mishkinshahr
Dimensions: 111 × 52 inches (283 × 132 cm)
Turkish knot: 65 per sq. inch (100,800 per sq. metre)
Warp of five strands of undyed cotton
Double weft of grey cotton
Pile of two strands of wool of average thickness
12 colours

form another diamond shape, with a jagged border furnished with eight small latch-hooks.

A little black denticulated line encircles the field. The frame includes four floral bands, separated from each other by a small dotted line.

This is a fine piece, rather restrained in design, but with numerous colours blended with confident taste.

The small settlement of Mishkinshahr, formerly Khiov, lies about 6,000 feet above sea-level at the foot of Kuh-i-Savalan. The decoration of its rugs, which enjoy high repute, remind one of Caucasian carpets.

Two floral zigzag bands are arranged upon the dark-red ground of the field forming five diamond shapes of large size, inside each of which four joined triangles

SARAB

Origin: Iran, Azerbaijan
Dimensions: 85 × 37 inches (215 × 94 cm)
Turkish knot: 49 per sq. inch (75,900 per sq. metre)
Warp of three strands of natural wool
Double weft of natural beige wool
Pile of two strands of rather thick wool
8 colours

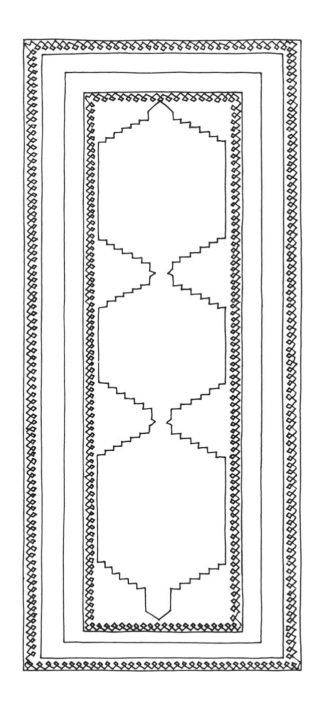

Sarab, a small place in the Ardebil region, is known for its rugs of elongated shape and heavy quality and of which the design varies little. Large medallions cover the field, which is usually of a beige ground, or less frequently of red, as is the case here.

The three hexagonal medallions enclose a second hexagon, ornamented with latch-hooks and flowers. At both ends are triangular motifs resembling pendants.

The border includes two bands, one decorated with stylized pomegranates, the other of white ground with large and small squares surrounded by latch-hooks. A row of sugar-loaves runs right round the outside and alongside the field.

JIN-JIN

Origin: Iran, Azerbaijan
Dimensions: 72 × 68 inches (184 × 173 cm)
Warp of two strands of grey cotton
6 colours: 1 red, 1 green, 1 white, 1 blue, 1 black, 1 yellow

The Jin-Jin rug employs the technique of the tapestry-woven Kilim and is made in bands approximately 12 inches (30 cm) in width, which are then sewn together. The example reproduced consists of six of these, closely woven. The colours are of warm tones, with blue predominating.

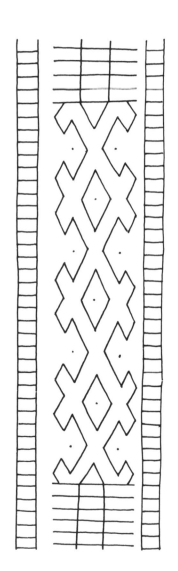 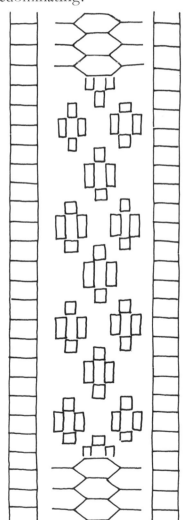

Kalar Dasht

The plain of Kalar (Kalar Dasht) owes its name to Mount Kalar. It dominates a verdant valley reached by Marzanabad, which is to be found on the Karaja-Chalus road. About ten miles of mountainous road separate Marzanabad from the entrance to the valley, situated at an altitude of about 6,550 feet. Rug manufacture is carried on in almost all villages of the valley, especially Kalino, Rudbar, Makulud, with the exception of Hassan Kif, the administrative centre.

For design the Kalar Dasht rug has mainly the *jangali* (of the jungle) and *majmei* types. Its production is not of long standing, since it goes back only fifty years.

Another curiosity of Kalar Dasht is that the weavers work in the open air. The vertical looms are in fact mounted against the façades of the houses, under the eaves. In bad weather they cover the top of the looms with a sheet of plastic, to prevent the rug and the warp threads from becoming wet.

KALAR DASHTI

Origin: Iran
Dimensions: 100 × 70 inches (254 × 178 cm)
Turkish knot: 49 per sq. inch (75,400 per sq. metre)
Warp of six strands of undyed cotton
Double weft of natural brown wool
Pile of two strands of wool of average thickness
9 colours

With its broad style and large hexagonal motif of red ground, decorated with two *sandugh* motifs, each containing a samovar, this example recalls the rugs of the Caucasus. The small diamond-shaped motif in the centre and at each end of the hexagon is called *pialeh* and the white zigzag line which borders the hexagon is called *karim khani*. The absence of axial symmetry is striking; the animals (goats and dogs) are all arranged in the same direction, whether on the field or in the principal border, which also includes *kadradomes* (stylized foxes). On either side of the latter are bands with floral motifs of different colours.

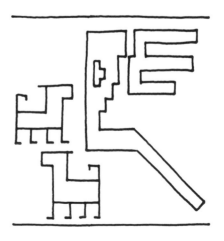

Varamin

Situated at a distance of 29 miles from Tehran on the railway line from Tehran to Mashad, Varamin is a small town dominated by a tower of the Mongol period. After the sack of Ray by the Mongols in 1220, it knew a certain prosperity. Today, Varamin preserves only one proof of its past importance: the Friday Mosque, completed in 1325.

The production of carpets is not large. The main pattern, and almost the only one, of Varamin rugs is of big daisies called *mina khani*, easily recognizable.

VARAMIN

Origin: Iran, Tehran region
Dimensions: 88 × 60 inches (225 × 153 cm)
Turkish knot: 218 per sq. inch (334,800 per sq. metre)
Warp of twelve strands of white cotton
Double weft of blue cotton: one fine one of four strands and one thick one of six strands
Pile of one strand, of rather fine wool, chemically washed
10 colours: 2 reds, 2 blues, 1 black, 1 white, 1 yellow, 2 greens, 1 brown

In the thirteenth and fourteenth centuries, Varamin was counted among the important towns of the Tehran region. It was then surrounded by fine gardens and orchards and its cultivated lands extended from the first foothills of the Alburz mountains to the north, and as far as the desert to the south.

The carpets of Varamin usually have a field of blue ground with a regular floral pattern, as in the example reproduced. This design is called *mina khani* (daisy). The principal border is adorned with arabesques, with large flowers of the same style as those on the field. The two bands which encircle it have also a floral pattern. The overall impression is of extreme regularity, some people will perhaps call it monotony.

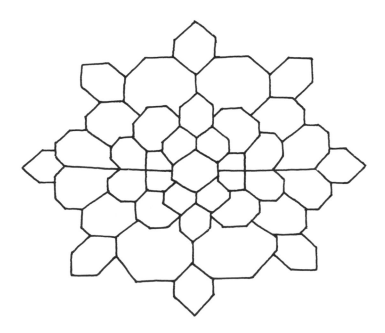

Arak, Seraband and Lilihan

Arak, formerly called Sultanabad, is situated at an altitude of 5,750 feet at a distance of 185 miles from Tehran on the railway line which links the capital to Khurramshahr. This town which has a population of 60,000 was founded by Fath 'Ali Shah at the beginning of the nineteenth century. It rarely attracts foreigners and many of the stalls of its huge bazaar are unoccupied, due to the fact that for some time much of the merchandise intended for export has been dispatched directly to Tehran without passing through Arak. However, Arak has been one of the most important production centres of Iran for more than a century. Indeed it was about 1875 when the merchants of Tabriz organized the export of their rugs. In 1883, an English firm of Swiss origin in Manchester, Ziegler & Co., established offices at Sultanabad and had rugs made to their own designs, to be sold under the name of Ziegler rugs. Other companies, European and American, installed themselves at Sultanabad, but they eventually disappeared one after the other; the last foreign offices closed in 1929.

Unlike other regions, Arak has no villages which produce a specific quality or design: the Sarouk, Mir, Mahal, Mushkabad and Vis types are made all over the region according to demand. For a very long time the weavers have been used to working from cartoons: the dealers can thus easily get work done to order.

The best carpets of the region are the Sarouks, originally from the village of the same name, 25 miles to the north of Arak. However, no rugs have ever been woven here in a size larger than 55 by 79 inches whereas one can find Sarouk rugs in the trade of all sizes and even exceeding 120 by 160 inches.

Mir carpets have the same construction as the Sarouks, but they are distinguished by their design, which makes use of the characteristic *boteh* motif.

The Vis rug is a fairly recent innovation, of which the first examples came from Gulpaigan. The Mushkabad and Mahal carpets, which were formerly very common on the market, are now only made in very small quantity since they have lost the favour of buyers. For the same reason, the Sultanabad and Ferahan rugs have almost completely disappeared.

The main villages of the Arak region are Dulakhor, Ferahan, Fereidan, Gulpaigan, Hapalak, Kezzaz, Khonsar, Khorey, Mahalat, Mushkabad, Chahar-ra.

The region of Burujird, from which the Seraband rug originates, is separated from the Arak district by a range of mountains. The population, of Turkish origin, makes a carpet which bears the very common design of the *boteh-miri*. Seraband rugs have their market in Burujird, a town of about 45,000 people, but they are made in some thirty villages of the region, including: Boneh, Gombad, Deh, Ali Morate, Galaj, Golezard, Gucheh, Haskian, Hendudar, Khoshkedar, Mir, Morate, Tabudaseht, Zaliun. Rugs from Mir are in a way a more refined replica of the Serabands. The early examples originated from the town of the same name, which is quite close to Burujird.

From the village of Lilihan in the Kemereh, comes another rug of the Arak district but which, at first sight, resembles more the rugs from the region of Hamadan. The Armenian population of this village uses a single warp, with a fairly tight knot. Their rugs almost always have a pink shade for the ground colour.

MAHAL

Origin: Iran, Arak region
Dimensions: 126 × 87 inches (320 × 222 cm)
Persian knot: 49 per sq. inch (75,400 per sq. metre)
Warp of six strands of undyed cotton
Double weft of thick blue cotton
Pile of two strands of wool of medium thickness, chemically washed
10 colours: 2 reds, 2 blues, 1 white, 1 black, 1 green, 1 yellow, 1 brown, 1 grey

Mahal rugs originally came from Mahalat, a place some 75 miles from Arak, but they are now made in several villages in the neighbourhood of Arak itself. Their style and knot relate them to Sarouk rugs, but they do not have the compact texture of these carpets. There exists an inferior type of Mahal, christened Mushkabad or Meshk Abad, from the name of the village situated some 18 miles from Arak, towards Qum.

The piece reproduced, with its central motif upon a plain red ground with elegant cut-out, is of the *kafzadeh* type, fashionable in the Arak region for some years. A pattern of stylized leaves and flowers of Herati type fills the corners and the grey ground of the central medallion. Three small bands, the largest of which bears the *boteh* motif, frame both sides of the main border, which is adorned with flowering tracery upon a dark-brown ground.

MIR

Origin: Iran, Arak region
Dimensions: 146 × 97 inches (371 × 273 cm)
Persian knot: 103 per sq. inch (159,600 per sq. metre)
Warp of twelve strands of undyed cotton
Double weft of blue cotton
Pile of two strands of wool of medium fineness, chemically
washed
9 colours

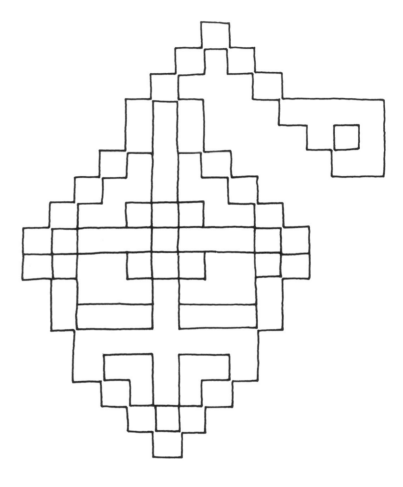

The *boteh-miri* design depicted is an old pattern which originated in India and which has been set into the form here by the weavers of Mir, a village of the Burujird region. Today as in the past, this type of rug is highly coveted.

A tiny seed-plot of *botehs* covers the whole field, of golden ground in this example, although more often red. Its many very fine borders give it an unusual air. The principal band also is decorated with the *boteh-miri* pattern, this time of more elongated form.

A feeling of restful delicacy emanates from this rug.

SAROUK

Origin: Iran, Arak region
Dimensions: 58 × 30 inches (147 × 78 cm)
Persian knot: 164 per sq. inch (253,800 per sq. metre)
Warp of seven strands of white cotton
Double weft of blue cotton
Pile of two strands of wool of medium fineness, chemically washed
8 colours: 3 blues, 2 reds, 2 browns, 1 yellow

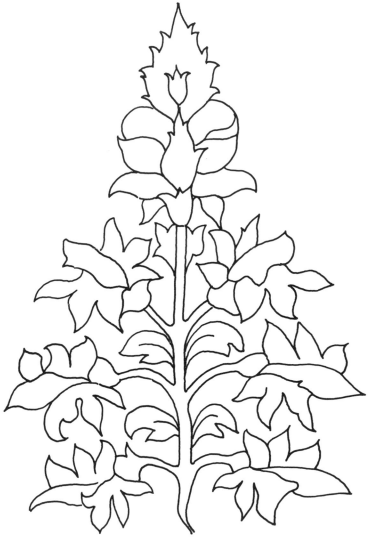

Small Sarouk rugs are often made in Arak itself.

Very large garlands of plant forms decorate the red ground of the field of this piece. The principal border of floral motifs is relatively narrow, accentuated by two small serrated bands.

This soft-coloured rug has a very dense weave which gives it great solidity.

SAROUK

Origin: Iran, Arak region
Dimensions: 128 × 85 inches (323 × 215 cm)
Warp of twelve strands of white cotton
Double weft of blue cotton
Pile of two strands of wool of medium fineness, chemically washed
8 colours: 2 reds, 2 blues, 2 beiges, 1 white, 1 green

The particular style of this carpet results in large part from the graceful indentation of the field of plain cream ground, against which stands out the central medallion, of diamond shape with two projections. Around the plain surface of the field is a blue ground with floral patterns.

The highly elaborate main border bears arabesques of leaves and flowers accentuated by two very thin bands of small flowers.

The overall refinement is evidence of a high standard of craftsmanship.

SAROUK

Origin: Iran, Arak region
Dimensions: 57 × 42 inches (146 × 103 cm)
Persian knot: 142 per sq. inch (220,800 per sq. metre)
Warp of five strands of undyed cotton
Double weft of undyed cotton
Pile of two strands of wool of medium fineness
10 colours: 3 reds, 2 blues, 1 yellow, 1 orange, 1 brown,
1 green, 1 beige

This rug of early manufacture with very dense pile has a very wide border in comparison to the field. At one end, the arabesques of the main border are interrupted to make way for the corner motifs, sure evidence that this piece was done without a pattern.

Against the very soft red ground of the large central hexagon floral motifs in blue tones stand out. These encircle a second smaller hexagon, but identical in form with the first; both have a stepped framework and a projection in the shape of a spearhead at the ends. A pattern of carnations and daisies fills the dark-blue ground of the corners of the field.

Two small borders of *boteh-miri* pattern frame the principal border. The colours throughout are very soft and mellowed.

SAROUK

Origin: Iran, Arak region
Dimensions: 122 × 86 inches (310 × 219 cm)
Persian knot: 119 per sq. inch (184,800 per sq. metre)
Warp of nine strands of undyed cotton
Double weft of blue cotton
Pile of two strands of rather fine wool, chemically washed
10 colours

Sarouk rugs are made throughout the region of Arak, especially in Arak itself, at Khonsar and Mahalat, and not only at Sarouk, as their name might lead one to suppose. Well known since about 1870, they have an excellent reputation for solidity. The weavers of the region are accustomed to working after a pattern, and can thus vary their designs.

In this example of classical style, the richness of the motifs and the skill of their arrangement strikes one immediately: the central rosette blends perfectly with the graceful tracery which links the flowers of every species which cover the field. An additional note of elegance is given by the rounding of the corners of blue ground. This is all framed by a main border of flowery arabesques, accentuated on each side by two narrow floral bands.

SERABAND

Origin: Iran, Burujird region
Dimensions: 82 × 52 inches (208 × 132 cm)
Turkish knot: 51 per sq. inch (78,400 per sq. metre)
Warp of nine strands of white cotton
Double weft of blue cotton
Pile of two strands of wool of medium thickness, chemically washed
8 colours: 2 reds, 1 black, 1 white, 1 green, 1 yellow, 2 blues

Seraband rugs are made in numerous villages in the neighbourhood of Burujird, a town of 45,000 inhabitants, situated in a verdant region, famous already in the fourteenth century for its orchards.

The Seraband rug has been known for almost a century and its design has always remained unchanged: the field, which here is red, is covered with *boteh-miri* motifs of slightly larger size than on Mir rugs. Examples with white and blue grounds are rarer. The main border, called *shekeri*, is typical of the Seraband and Mir type.

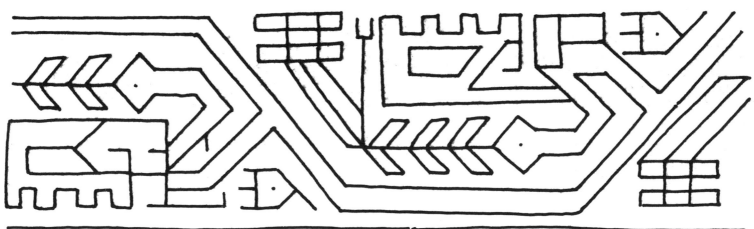

LILIHAN

Origin: Iran, Arak region
Dimensions: 46 × 26 inches (117 × 65 cm)
Persian knot: 68 per sq. inch (105,000 per sq. metre)
Warp of four strands of undyed cotton
Single weft of red cotton
Pile of two strands of wool of medium thickness
10 colours: 2 reds, 2 blues, 1 orange, 1 yellow, 1 gold, 2 browns, 1 white

Lilihan carpets bear less resemblance to others of the Arak region where it is produced than to carpets from the region of Hamadan, the single-weft knot, wool and style of which it has adopted.

Two sets of two bunches of flowers arranged face to face adorn the red ground of the field framed in azure blue and orange. The corners and sides are of dark blue patterned with leaves and big flowers. A blue line winds around small flowers upon the golden ground of the principal border. Two small serrated bands and an outer one with latch-hooks frame it.

Kirman, Yazd and Afshar Rugs

Often in the course of its long history the province of Kirman has known bloody times. Its difficult access made it the privileged refuge of the Zoroastrians, persecuted for their refusal to embrace the religion of Islam. Their community still exists today in the town of Kirman.

In area the province is about the same size as England. It is bordered to the north by the Great Desert, to the west by Fars, to the south by the Gulf of Oman and to the east by Pakistan. It is the poorest of the five large provinces of Iran because of its lack of water. Although only a few products grow there, those that do are of excellent quality: the pistachio nut, to name just one, is the finest in the country.

The town of Kirman, situated at an altitude of 6,100 feet enjoys a good climate and has about 130,000 inhabitants. There are several old mosques to be admired: the Masjid-i-Jomeh, which dates from the fourteenth century, the Masjid-i-Malek, built by the Seljuk sovereign Malek Turan in the eleventh century, destroyed in the sixteenth century and rebuilt in the same period, and finally the small Masjid-i-Bazaar-i-Shah, also from the Seljuk period, to be found in the bazaar. At Mahan, 25 miles from Kirman in the direction of Bam, can be seen what is undoubtedly the finest monument of the region, the tomb of the famous poet Nur-ud-Din-Nimat-Allah.

The first carpets from Kirman mentioned by historians date from the seventeenth century. We know that during his reign Akbar the Great (d. 1605) had two Kirman rugs brought to India. Afterwards and up to the end of the nineteenth century, no mention is made of Kirman carpets, whose production seems to have been superseded by embroidery. Towards the end of the last century, the dealers of Tabriz restored the weaving of Kirman rugs to favour, by passing orders to the weavers and by purchasing the pieces offered on the market. Between 1900 and 1929, the United States headed the list of buyers. American clients commissioned rugs still today called the American Kirman, of which the main characteristic is a very thick pile.

The town of Kirman largely depends on the carpet industry. The number of looms installed in the town itself is considerable and there are a number of factories making beautiful pieces. Some thirty neighbouring villages also exist from this industry, their output being indistinguishable from that of the town: indeed, the designs and materials are provided for them by the Kirman dealers, for whom they work exclusively.

Unlike those from other provinces, the pile of Kirman rugs is not clipped as the weaving proceeds, but only once the carpet is completely finished. The shearing is not done by the weavers, but by a specialist who does it after the rug has been taken off the loom. Usually, the rug is shown to the buyer before the shearing, which means that he must have a thorough knowledge of this type if he does not wish to be misled, since it is difficult to judge the quality, colours and design of an uncropped carpet.

The method of dyeing also differs from that of other regions of the country. It is done while the wool is still in the flock, that is to say before spinning, which guarantees a greater regularity of shade. Towards this end some factories go to the extent of doing the carding and the roving by machine, the spinning proper being carried out by hand: the appearance of hand-spinning is preserved, although the thread is more regular. For some years completely mechanized spinning has been in operation, but for knotted carpets machine-spun yarn cannot be considered an improvement.

Right from the outset Kirman rugs have their design reproduced upon paper squared into millimetres, which is the test of the ability of the workers. Thus in the workshops and villages which use this procedure, the designs can be varied, which is much more tricky, if not impossible, when the design is simply memorized. One can almost always distinguish a rug executed from a cartoon from one worked from memory because of the large outer border. If woven from memory, the rug usually has a border in which the motifs have been displaced.

When knotted after a cartoon, the covers are decorated with a motif at the point where the borders meet. The designers of the Kirman patterns have a reputation for being the best in the country.

The most common designs of Kirman rugs are:

Afshun		
Ardebili	=	Ardebil pattern
Bazobandi	=	bracelet
Kafzadeh	=	plain ground (medallion with a plain surround)
Kafzadeh morghi	=	plain ground with birds
Kheshiti	=	diamond shapes
Saadi dasteh goli	=	bunch of flowers of Saadi
Sel selei	=	flowery band

Shah Abbas		
Shah Abbas noghrei	=	silver Shah Abbas
Shah Abbas gole doroshte	=	Shah Abbas with big flower (large medallion)
Sotuni	=	with columns

There are on the market five qualities of Kirman rugs, determined by the number of warp threads and knots per *gireh* (a measure of about 2¾ inches or 7 cm). For example, for Quality 60, there are 60 warp threads per *gireh*, and theoretically, 30 lines of 30 knots each, one knot being made on two warp threads which gives 900 knots to 2¾ square inches (7 square cm), that is 83 knots to the square inch (128,600 knots to the square metre). The warp threads are of fourteen strands of cotton. For Quality 70, there are 70 warp threads, therefore 35 lines of 35 knots, that is 116 knots to the square inch (175,000 knots to the square metre) with warp threads of twelve strands. For Quality 80 there are 80 warp threads, thus 40 lines of 40 knots, that is 142 knots to the square inch (228,600 knots to the square metre) with warp threads of six strands. For Quality 90, there are 90 warp threads, therefore 45 lines of 45 knots, that is 186 knots to the square inch (289,200 knots to the square metre) with warp threads of eight strands. For Quality 100 there are 100 warp threads, thus 50 lines of 50 knots, that is 230 knots to the square inch (357,100 knots to the square metre), with warp threads of six strands.

In practice these standards are merely an indication and not always respected. The rug is sold by the piece, and if the work is not as tight as the standard prescribes, it is larger than expected. Still, in the bazaar of Tehran, the traders sell these rugs by the square metre, but the price varies according to the compactness and the beauty of the carpet.

Halfway between Kirman and Isfahan, Yazd is the metropolis of the Ghebers, distant followers of Zoroastra. Its inhabitants have the reputation for being hard-working and sober.

The output of carpets is not very considerable. The general appearance and design of Yazd rugs relates them to the Kirman type, whose motifs are frequently imitated but the workmanship of Yazd carpets has not the fineness of the true Kirman.

Afshar rugs take their name from the tribes of nomadic Turkish origin who eventually settled in the region of Bam, Rafsanjan, Shaebabah, Sirjan. In design and colour their carpets recall those of Niriz, in the Shiraz region, but the quality of Afshar rugs, or Kirman-Afshar, is infinitely finer. One also finds very well-made examples executed in the Soumak technique.

KIRMAN

Origin: Iran
Dimensions 157 × 115 inches (400 × 292 cm)
Persian knot: 201 per sq. inch (312,000 per sq. metre)
Warp of twelve strands of undyed cotton
Double weft of four strands of blue cotton
Pile of two strands of fine wool
14 colours in soft shades

The cartoon for this carpet is the work of an accomplished artist. The design called Shah Abbas, from the name of the seventeenth century ruler who patronized the rug-making art, consists of an elegant central medallion composed of several medallions superimposed upon an oval field of red ground. The floral decoration of the latter is of exquisite delicacy and forms a harmonious combination with that of the corners and principal border. This example of early manufacture belongs to the Quality 80 type. The fourteen colours are particularly beautiful and well chosen.

KIRMAN

Origin: Iran
Dimensions: 29 × 20 inches (74 × 51 cm)
Persian knot: 210 per sq. inch (324,500 per sq. metre)
Warp of eight strands of white cotton
Double weft of blue cotton
Pile of two strands of fine wool
12 colours: 3 reds, 3 blues, 1 mauve, 2 browns, 1 orange,
2 greens

This very fine piece is of early manufacture, with a floral decoration typical of Kirman rugs of the period between 1920 and 1930. The knotting is of type 90.

The field is a large bunch of flowers, with a design placed lengthwise. The border also bears floral patterns.

The colours are remarkable in their softness and harmony.

These small rugs were made originally to adorn the backs of armchairs, a similar little rug of square shape covering the seat.

KIRMAN

Origin: Iran
Dimensions: 123 × 81 inches (312 × 217 cm)
Persian knot: 168 per sq. inch (260,000 per sq. metre)
Warp of ten strands of undyed cotton
Double weft of blue cotton
Pile of two strands of fine wool, chemically washed
8 colours: 3 blues, 2 beiges, 2 greens, 1 white

The design of this carpet is called *Saadi dasteh gole* (Saadi's bunch of flowers) in homage to the great poet of Shiraz. The quality is of the most common type, 70.

The richness of the floral pattern denotes a very confident artistic sense. Only one very narrow band remains of the classical border, the decoration extending to the edges of the rug. The central medallion of elegant elongated shape is completely surrounded by small flowers, which stand out delicately upon a plain blue ground.

Arabesques forming graceful traceries of plant forms spring from the vases in the corners.

KIRMAN

Origin: Iran
Dimensions: 116 × 70 inches (295 × 178 cm)
Persian knot: 220 per sq. inch (342,200 per sq. metre)
Warp of seven strands of undyed cotton
Double weft of blue cotton
Pile of two strands of fine machine-spun wool, chemically washed
14 colours: 4 reds, 3 blues, 3 beiges, 3 greens, 1 gold

This example was woven in a factory which possesses both a mechanical spinning mill and a modern dye-works. The knotting is of type 90, therefore very dense.

The design, with floral motifs predominating, is called *patheh*. The field is covered with bunches of flowers, in the corners, large *jegai-boteh* motifs and in the centre, a medallion of rounded shape. The principal border is also richly decorated with floral motifs including vases of flowers. The small bands on each side are strewn with flowers.

The colours of this rug of pinkish-beige ground arc very soft.

KIRMAN

Origin: Iran
Dimensions: 129 × 84 inches (328 × 213 cm)
Persian knot: 148 per sq. inch (230,400 per sq. metre)
Warp of twelve strands of undyed cotton
Triple weft: one thread of two strands of blue cotton, two of ten strands of undyed cotton
Pile of two strands of wool, chemically washed, in bright colours
10 colours: 2 reds, 3 blues, 2 greens, 2 browns, 1 white

This pattern, of exclusively floral motifs, as is always the case in the production of this region, is called *sel selei* (flowery band). The central motif of elongated form stands out well against the plain surface of the field: one can recognize two trees encircled with formalized leaves, with bunches of roses at the ends. The flowered band which surrounds the field gives its name to the rug; this is separated by a plain area from the main border, which is very wide and richly decorated with various ornaments, with the palmette predominating. Note that it is devoid of the classical rectilinear frame.

The knotting is of type 70.

KIRMAN

Origin: Iran
Dimensions: 49 × 47 inches (125 × 120 cm)
Persian knot: 152 per sq. inch (235,000 per sq. metre)
Warp of twelve strands of fine undyed cotton
Double weft: one thread of undyed cotton of six strands, the other of six strands of blue cotton
Pile of two strands of wool of medium thickness, chemically washed
9 colours: 2 blues, 2 greens, 1 pink, 3 beiges, 1 red

Apart from standards of quality, there are two types of rug to be found at Kirman: the classical type and the American Kirman. The last term appeared between the wars to designate a rug of very pale colours and with a pile at least two-fifths of an inch thick (normally the pile is about half that thickness). One also encounters pieces with a dark-blue ground, such as this, with a pile nearly half an inch thick. This belongs to type 80, which, along with type 70, is generally used for the American Kirman. In contrast to the field, the tones of the border are very soft. The indentation of the latter is typical, rectilinear borders being reserved for classical pieces. This design is called *kafzadeh*, with the central medallion forming a star, towards which all else converges, with oval-shaped medallions in the corners.

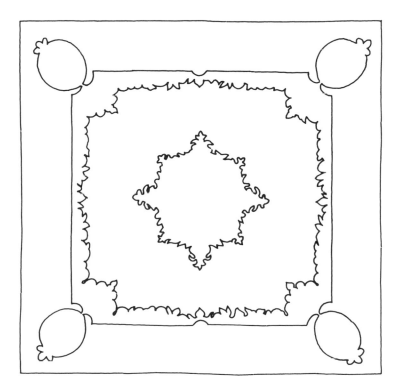

YAZD

Origin: Iran
Dimensions: 105 × 56 inches (267 × 142 cm)
Persian knot: 114 per sq. inch (176,400 per sq. metre)
Warp of twelve strands of undyed cotton
Double weft of ten strands of blue cotton
Pile of wool of two strands of medium thickness, chemically washed
12 colours: 3 blues, 3 greens, 3 beige-browns, 2 gold, 1 brown

Yazd, situated halfway between Isfahan and Kirman, was formerly famous for its cloths with gold thread: 'the *Zari* from Yazd', according to a Persian poet, 'are smoother than the petals of petunias'.

As with Kirman rugs, the pattern consists exclusively of floral motifs, the wool and the knot also recalling the rugs of that town.

In this example the field is covered with lines resembling vases filled with bunches of roses, leaves and ears of grain. One can distinguish five large rosettes, then four more half-rosettes in the middle of each side of the field, and in the corners, quarters of the same motif. In the principal border, flowers and leaves in pliant arrangement are framed by two small bands, also floral. The dominant tones are blue in different shades, and beige; the whole effect is very subdued.

AFSHAR

Origin: Iran, Kirman region
Dimensions: 70 × 49 inches (178 × 124 cm)
Persian knot: 103 per sq. inch (160,000 per sq. metre)
Warp of eight strands of undyed cotton
Double weft of six strands of blue cotton
Pile of two strands of wool of medium thickness, chemically washed
8 colours: 3 reds, 1 green, 1 blue, 1 orange, 1 white, 1 black

This pattern, of two large medallions on a field of *boteh* motifs, is called *do goleh Parizi* (two flowers of Pariz), from the name of the producing village situated between Sirjan and Rafsanjan.

A jagged line links the two medallions, which each enclose an octagon decorated with stylized flowers. Their sides, cut out into steps, are accentuated by a serrated band and a motif divided into nine sections, containing butterflies, stylized flowers and squares with nine compartments, occupies the centre.

Note that a displacement of the decorative motif (rosettes alternating with hexagons) occurs in the corners of the main border. The bands at the sides include stylized carnations.

KIRMAN-AFSHAR

Origin: Iran, Sirjan region
Dimensions: 78 × 62 inches (197 × 158 cm)
Persian knot: 76 per sq. inch (117,800 per sq. metre)
Warp of six strands of white cotton
Double weft of red cotton
Pile of four strands of wool, chemically washed
8 colours: 2 reds, 3 blues, 1 orange, 1 white, 1 brown

This design is called *khesti* in Iranian, which means 'boat'. Flower-patterned lozenges, encircled by a triple zigzag line, cover the whole field. The principal border is divided into two flower-strewn areas, one blue, the other red, by an irregular zigzag line. The two narrow bands on each side of this border also bear a floral pattern.

The colours throughout are fairly mellow, but dark.

KIRMAN-AFSHAR

Origin: Iran, Kirman region
Dimensions: 83 × 59 inches (212 × 154 cm)
Persian knot: 91 per sq. inch (140,800 per sq. metre)
Warp of four strands of undyed cotton
Double weft of red cotton
Pile of two strands of wool of medium thickness, chemically washed
8 colours

One can distinguish two sorts of Afshar rugs, those from the region of Niriz (Shiraz) and those from the region of Kirman (Sirjan and Bam). In Europe the latter are called Kirman-Afshar, in order to place them more correctly geographically speaking.

The design of this carpet is called *panj gole Parizi*, that is to say: five flowers from the village of Pariz. If it were not for this designation one would hardly guess that the five medallions which adorn the field of this piece represent flowers. The three bands of the same width which form the border are also floral patterned.

The overall impression of great simplicity does not lack charm.

AFSHAR

Origin: Iran, Kirman region
Dimensions: 81 × 57 inches (203 × 146 cm)
Warp of three strands of thick undyed cotton
Weft of red cotton
Soumak weave in two strands of wool
8 colours: 2 reds, 1 blue, 1 green, 1 white, 1 orange, 1 black, 1 brown

This is another rug of Soumak technique, and therefore has no pile. The design, of *khesti* type (boats), is also to be found on knotted rugs of the region.

Three rows of bright red, green and claret-coloured hexagons cover the complete surface of the field; these are surrounded by stepped lines. The main border has stylized flowers upon a white ground, framed by two narrow brown bands. Alongside the field is another flowered band, half claret-red, half sky-blue, which is bounded by a white stepped line in zigzags.

This example is of rustic appearance, with strong colouring.

AFSHAR

Origin: Iran, Kirman region
Dimensions: 75 × 58 inches (190 × 147 cm)
Warp of one strand of undyed cotton, mixed with a thread of
natural beige wool
Weft of red cotton
Soumak weave in two strands of wool
7 colours: 2 blues, 1 red, 1 green, 1 white, 1 black, 1 yellow

When woven like a Soumak with warp and weft threads and without pile, the Afshar usually has a thicker wool; its composition and design are the same as in knotted pieces.

The field of the example reproduced is covered with small crosses, arranged in such a way as to form lozenge shapes with white frames. The principal border is decorated with formalized trees and flowers, and both ends have an additional border with stepped fish-bone motifs.

This is a work of simple craftsmanship, of interest to the collector.

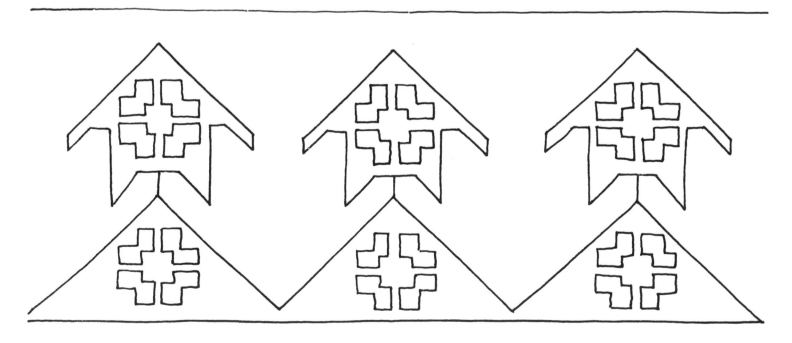

Hamadan

The town of Hamadan, the chief town of the province of the same name, stands upon the ruins of ancient Ecbatana, at an altitude of 5,600 feet at the foot of Kuh-i-Alwand (11,700 feet). It is the oldest royal town of Iran. According to Herodotus, it was founded by King Deioces about 700 BC. This monarch had his palace built in the form of seven superimposed and coloured fortresses, the first in white, the subsequent ones in black, purple, blue, orange, silver and gold. The sovereign occupied the highest floor, for reasons of security and comfort. The royal palace covered an area of 14,000 square feet and contained innumerable rooms. Ceilings and doors were sculpted and covered with gold and silver.

Today little remains of this ancient splendour. One of the oldest monuments is the stone statue of a lion, which according to historians dates from the Bactrian period; Sang-i-Shir, as it is called by the inhabitants of Hamadan, was supposed to have possessed magic powers, which enabled him to foretell the future, to grant wishes uttered in his presence, to cure the sick and to prevent famines. The Alavian Mosque, another ancient monument, dates from the end of the Seljuk period and resembles the Red Mosque of Maragheh. The historic tower of Burj-i-Qurban is a place of pilgrimage for Iranian Kurds. The mausoleum of Abu Ali, one of the great philosophers of Iranian Islam, dates from the eleventh century.

The Hamadan district is one of the largest in the country. It borders onto the districts of Zanjan and Bijar to the north, Qazvin to the east, Saveh and Arak to the south-east, Malayer and Tuisserkan to the south and Senneh to the west. Carpets so like Kirman rugs in style as to be mistaken for them are produced in the town itself, but their quality is thicker and heavier. In the bazaar one finds all the regional production, of which the principal names are as follows: Bagardeh, Burjalu, Dergezin, Injilas, Hosseinabad; others are: Assadabad, Bandi-Kurdi, Bibikabad, Comat, Gogarjin, Khamseh, Kabutarhang, Mehriban, Nensurabad, Nobaran, Tafrish, Tuisserkan, Wardewch, Zaheh and Zanjan.

Malayer, a small town situated 50 miles from Hamadan towards Arak, is one of the richest agricultural centres of Iran. The rugs of this region have more in common with those from the Arak district than those from Hamadan, and they are also occasionally confused in the trade with Sarouk rugs. The most beautiful examples of this region are those from the village of Josan; a double warp gives these rugs a fine appearance.

ASSADABAD

Origin: Iran, Hamadan region
Dimensions: 73 × 51 inches (186 × 130 cm)
Turkish knot: 48 per sq. inch (74,400 per sq. metre)
Warp of four strands of white cotton
Double weft of blue cotton
Pile of two strands of fairly thick wool, chemically washed
10 colours: 2 reds, 1 orange, 1 white, 1 black, 2 blues, 2 greens, 1 beige

Assadabad, a village of some importance on the road from Hamadan to Kirmanshah, produces fairly thick and sturdy rugs of small size.

The decoration is floral, with a field of warm red ground covered with leaves, flowers and diamond-shaped motifs.

A jagged line runs down the sides. The border is composed of three bands of almost equal width.

The simple style and the strong colours of this carpet show it to be a piece of rather rustic workmanship.

BURJALU

Origin: Iran, Hamadan region
Dimensions: 81 × 61 inches (215 × 154 cm)
Turkish knot: 71 per sq. inch (110,200 per sq. metre)
Warp of seven strands of undyed cotton
Single weft of blue cotton
Pile of two strands of wool of medium thickness, chemically washed, in pastel colours
10 colours: 3 reds, 1 blue, 1 yellow, 1 beige, 1 black, 1 white, 1 brown, 1 green

Burjalu is a region which, administratively, belongs really to Arak, but whose carpets are sold above all at Hamadan. The village of Komijan is the regional centre. The finest Burjalus come from the village of Kumbazan. Burjalu rugs are easily recognizable by their design of wavy lines, composed of large bunches of flowers and a fairly important central motif; this example has a large rosette of blue ground adorned with roses and leaves, which contains a smaller rosette, pink in colour, covered with flower petals. The two bunches of flowers at the ends emerge from vases while each corner is decorated with stylized flowers and leaves. The motifs of the principal border are also floral and include cypress trees. This carpet has very subdued colours on a white ground.

JOSAN

Origin: Iran, Malayer region
Dimensions: 80 × 52 inches (214 × 131 cm)
Turkish knot: 154 per sq. inch (239,200 per sq. metre)
Warp of six strands of undyed cotton
Double weft of blue cotton
Pile of two strands of wool of medium fineness, chemically washed
12 colours: 3 reds, 3 blues, 1 black, 1 yellow, 1 white, 1 brown, 1 green, 1 orange

Josan, a small village in the Malayer region, is justly famous for its fine carpets.

This piece shows a field of white ground patterned with flowers, with a central red medallion, in turn enclosing a second one of sky-blue, ornamented with a beige rosette. The orange-coloured corners are separated from the field by a dark-blue band. The main border is also decorated with flowers and is traversed by a line which doubles back upon itself at right angles. Three bands surround it on the inside, and two on the outside.

This is a very tightly woven rug, with rather thick pile, and of great solidity.

HOSSEINABAD

Origin: Iran, Hamadan region
Dimensions: 118 × 68 inches (300 × 173 cm)
Turkish knot: 71 per sq. inch (112,200 per sq. metre)
Warp of eight strands of cotton
Single weft of thick grey cotton
Pile of two strands of wool of medium thickness, chemically washed
8 colours: 2 reds, 2 blues, 1 white, 1 black, 1 orange, 1 green

long-stemmed glasses and pomegranates; the same motifs decorate the corners. In the main border, formalized tulips can be seen among other flowers; two small floral bands lie either side of this border. Hosseinabad rugs are among the finest on the Hamadan market.

In style the carpets of Hosseinabad are much less like those from the nearby settlement of Tuisserkan than those from the immediate vicinity of Hamadan or of Injilas. Jowkar, situated almost 40 miles from Hamadan towards Malayer, is another producer of rugs of the Hosseinabad type. The field is always composed of a bed of leaves and flowers upon a red ground, and in the centre of this example we find a cruciform rosette with

INJILAS

Origin: Iran, Hamadan region
Dimensions: 30 × 25 inches (75 × 63 cm)
Turkish knot: 93 per sq. inch (144,000 per sq. metre)
Warp of five strands of undyed cotton
Double weft of blue cotton
Pile of two strands of rather fine wool, chemically washed
11 colours: 2 reds, 1 black, 1 blue, 1 beige, 2 browns,
2 greens, 1 white, 1 orange

In the Hamadan market, the rugs from the village of
Injilas are considered to be of good quality.

The red ground of the field is invariably covered with
the *boteh-miri* motif.

In the border, two bands of floral pattern frame the
principal band of white ground, which is a variant of the
old carnation border.

The wool is fairly thick and of good quality.

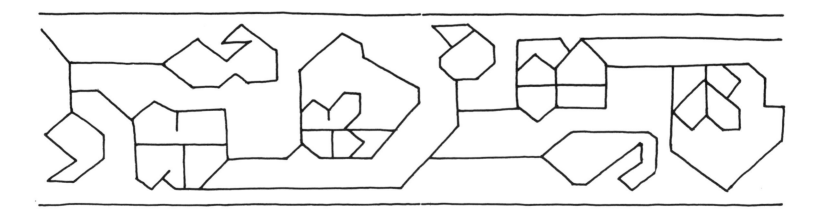

KHAMSEH

Origin: Iran, Hamadan region
Dimensions: 80 × 50 inches (202 × 126 cm)
Persian knot: 54 per sq. inch (84,000 per sq. metre)
Warp of eight strands of undyed cotton
Single weft of thick dark-grey cotton
Pile of two strands of wool of medium thickness
10 colours: 3 reds, 1 blue, 1 black, 1 white, 1 orange, 1 green, 1 yellow, 1 beige

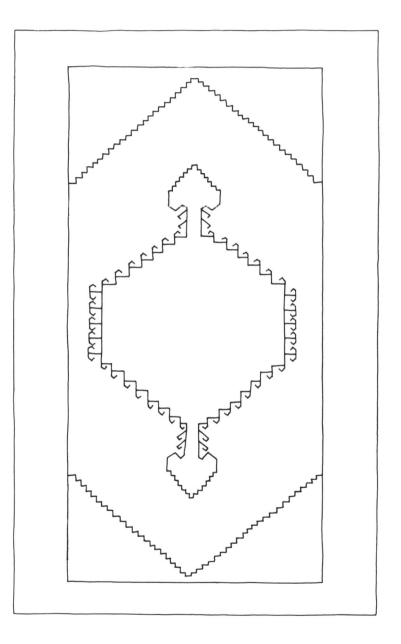

The region of Khamseh is to the north of the plain of Hamadan, and extends from the north-east of Ghorveh as far as the region of Zanjan. It is known for its Mussel rugs (approximately 40 by 80 inches) often incorrectly called Mosul, which misleadingly suggests that they come from the town of that name. Khamseh also produces *dozar* of about 47 to 49 by 79 inches. The example reproduced belongs to this second group.

The weaving is rather coarse, the design is fairly simple and the colours are bright. The wool is not of very high quality, so that Khamseh rugs, which are plentiful on the market, are modestly priced.

The hexagonal field is separated from the corners by a double stepped line. The central motif, also hexagonal, is furnished with latch-hooks. The decoration of the field is floral, like that of the corners; there are tulips, roses and *boteh* motifs. In the principal border is a variation of the old Anatolian border of tulips.

MALAYER

Origin: Iran, Hamadan region
Dimensions: 79 × 53 inches (200 × 134 cm)
Turkish knot: 113 per sq. inch (174,800 per sq. metre)
Warp of five strands of white cotton
Double weft of blue cotton
Pile of two strands of wool of medium fineness, chemically washed
12 colours: 3 reds, 3 blues, 2 greens, 1 white, 1 yellow, 1 black, 1 brown

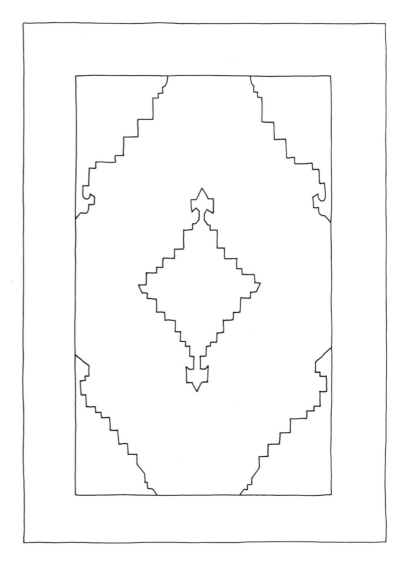

Malayer, a small city of 25,000 inhabitants, does not produce many carpets although a factory of the Iranian Carpet Company manufactures some fine pieces.

This example reminds one slightly of certain classical Sarouk rugs. Standing out against the blue ground of the field, is a central medallion with stepped outline, encircled with various flowers arranged in foliage. In the corners, flowers also decorate three stepped bands.

The main border of enormous roses and carnations is framed on both sides by two narrow floral bands.

MEHRIBAN

Origin: Iran, Hamadan region
Dimensions: 76 × 35 inches (192 × 89 cm)
Turkish knot: 118 per sq. inch (182,600 per sq. metre)
Warp of five strands of undyed cotton
Single weft of blue cotton
Pile of two strands of wool of medium thickness, chemically washed
12 colours: 3 reds, 2 blues, 2 beiges, 1 green, 1 yellow, 1 orange, 2 browns

The region of Mehriban, to the north of Hamadan, includes some forty villages, which produce rather elongated carpets and runners; the weaving is generally of a high standard and the pile is rather thick.

The decoration of the field of reddish-pink ground is mainly floral, but one can also see stylized trees. Three floral bands of almost equal width form a frame around it.

The softness of the colours make this a charming example, although its style is rather rustic.

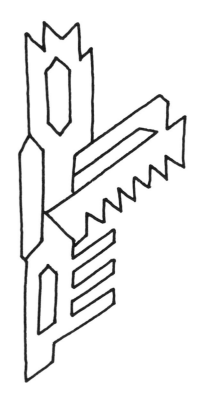

NOBARAN

Origin: Iran, Hamadan region
Dimensions: 75 × 51 inches (190 × 129 cm)
Turkish knot: 91 per sq. inch (140,800 per sq. metre)
Warp of five strands of undyed cotton
Single weft of nine strands of undyed cotton
Pile of two strands of fine wool
10 colours: 2 reds, 2 blues, 1 green, 1 yellow, 1 white, 1 black, 1 brown, 1 beige

Nobaran is a village in the Hamadan region, to the east of Dergezin. The carpets made there have a very interesting style. The field of very warm red is bordered by two fairly wide zigzag lines, one in yellow, the other sky-blue, which are repeated in reverse on the border of the medallion, right up to the diamond-shaped projections. The medallion is decorated with stars and flowers. On the field, a network of flowered fine lines forms hexagons round the two-coloured jagged *boteh* motifs linking them to each other and to the medallion. The azure blue corners are filled with a seed-plot of formalized flowers arranged in regular rows.

The composition of such a pattern might appear rather strange to the eyes of a Westerner, but it is the product of village traditions. The slightly displaced corner motifs of the principal border show also that the carpet has been made without a cartoon, simply from memory.

TUISSERKAN

Origin: Iran, Hamadan region
Dimensions: 66 × 44 inches (168 × 105 cm)
Turkish knot: 54 per sq. inch (84,000 per sq. metre)
Warp of five strands of undyed cotton
Single weft of grey cotton
Pile of two strands of wool of medium thickness
12 colours: 3 reds, 3 greens, 1 white, 2 blues, 1 beige, 1 orange, 1 yellow

Tuisserkan, situated at a distance of about 17 miles as the crow flies, from Hamadan, can be reached by a little road winding around the Kuh-i-Alwand, which reaches an altitude of 11,700 feet. The rugs of this village are made with a single weft, of good quality wool.

A large dark-blue hexagon strewn with flowers stands out upon the plain beige-brown ground of the field, framed by a serrated line. Two lozenges extend this central motif, each terminating in the sacred motif of two bustards, back to back.

In the corners are flowers upon the same dark-blue ground as that of the medallion. The main border of carnations is surrounded by two narrow bands of small round motifs, which are perhaps flowers.

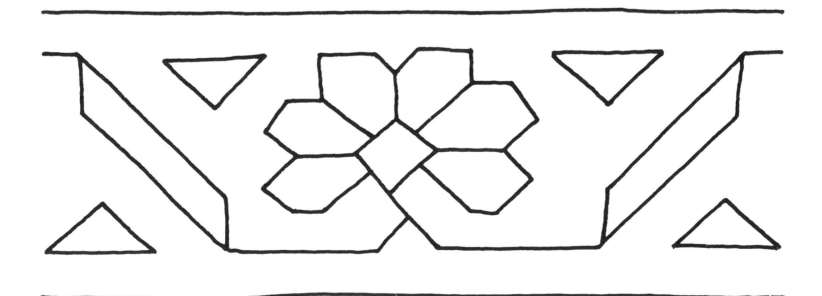

ZANJAN

Origin: Iran, Hamadan region
Dimensions: 89 × 56 inches (226 × 141 cm)
Turkish knot: 59 per sq. inch (91,000 per sq. metre)
Warp of seven strands of thick white cotton
Single weft of cotton with one grey and one blue thread
Pile of two strands of wool of medium thickness, chemically washed
10 colours: 3 reds, 2 yellows, 1 blue, 1 black, 1 white, 1 beige, 1 green

Zanjan, a small town with a population of 10,000, although situated at an altitude of 6,250 feet on the Qazvin-Tabriz road, sends its carpets to be sold at Hamadan and Kirmanshah. It is for this reason and also because of the style of the designs that they are mentioned as originating from the region of Hamadan. In the Sassanid period, Zanjan played an important role owing to its geographical situation between the Iranian plateau and Azerbaijan.

The pattern of this piece is rather interesting: a long hexagonal motif with a rounded corner at one end covers almost the whole of the field, which is edged with a serrated line. One end of the rose-patterned central motif repeats this same rounded shape. Flowers and leaves fill the corners. Stylized pomegranates can be seen among the flowers of the border.

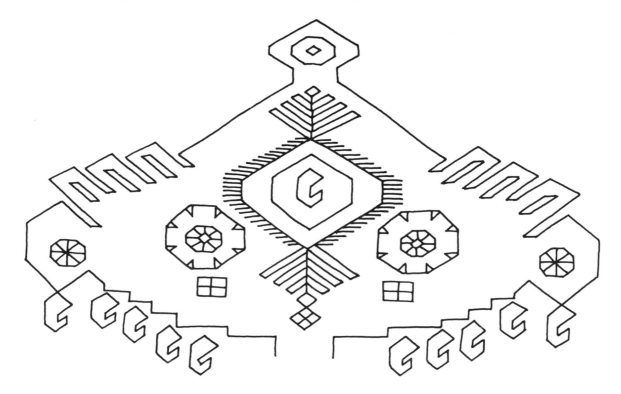

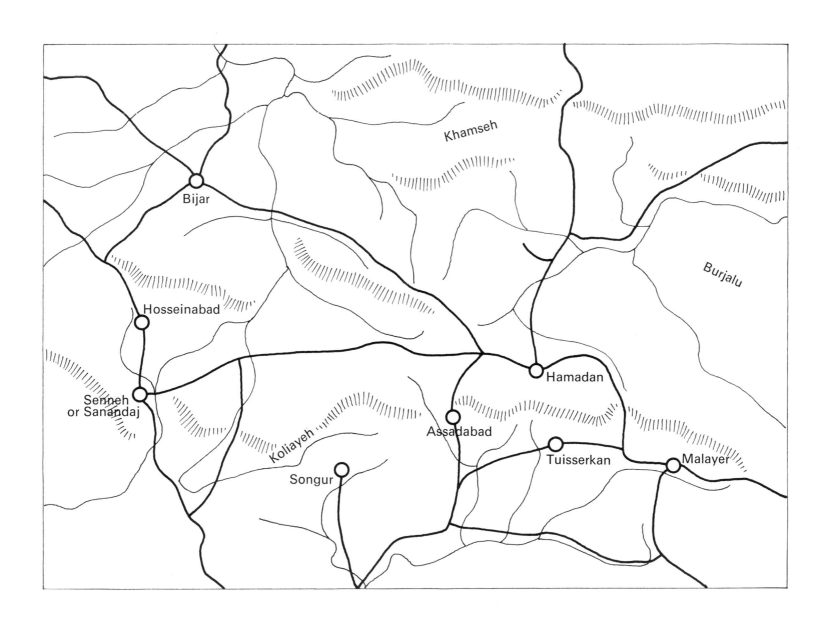

Kurdistan

The Kurds of Iran, a gay and hospitable people, speak a language which is a mixture of ancient Persian, elements of Indo-European and a dialect form of modern Persian. They are followers of the Sunni branch of Islam while the rest of the country is Shiite.

Bijar, a small town 118 miles to the north-west of Hamadan, was formerly under the domination of Shah Ismael, the first Safavid sovereign. In the last century, its inhabitants were able to buy back their lands and Bijar would have developed even more had it not suffered terribly from the First World War. Occupied first of all by the Russians, then by the Turks, as a crowning misfortune it had to deal with a famine as soon as the war was over. In 1914, the population stood at 2,000 but by 1918 only a small village remained; today its population is estimated at 10,000.

The weaving centre of Bijar involves all the neighbouring villages. Bijar rugs are highly esteemed by connoisseurs, because of their very heavy quality and their consistent strength; they have never been copied in other regions, and one can only hope that this will remain so in the future.

Senneh, also called Sanandaj, is a town situated 106 miles to the west of Hamadan. This attractive centre is the capital of Iranian Kurdistan.

For generations, the craftsmen of Senneh have been making rugs equally remarkable in texture as in patterns or colours. The knots of these rugs are often so fine that they are scarcely visible to the naked eye. The finest examples combine their unparalleled delicacy of workmanship with a design of naive originality that is full of charm. The design of Senneh rugs has varied very little throughout the centuries: the surface of the carpet is covered with an infinity of minute details which however does not distract from the subtle grace of the general lines. The use of colour is also characteristic, often with no plain areas. Examples which have a medallion with a plain surround are rare. The colour proportions are so perfect that one would not know how to say which is predominant. Upon a ground of ivory, red or blue, little touches of very bold colour, subtly balanced, combine to result in a slightly faded tone of great delicacy.

Koliayeh, Sirijabad and Songur are also Kurdish villages, but their output shows no resemblance to that of the two regions already mentioned. The rugs of these villages have large knots, that are reminiscent of the rugs of Hamadan in construction and colouring. Sometimes, in fact, in the trade they go under the name of Hamadan.

BIJAR

Origin: Iran, Kurdistan
Dimensions: 55 × 46 inches (140 × 116 cm)
Turkish knot: 78 per sq. inch (121,800 per sq. metre)
Depressed warp of two strands of natural beige goat's hair
Double weft of natural brown goat's hair
Pile of two strands of wool of medium thickness
10 colours: 3 reds, 2 blues, 1 brown, 1 black, 1 green, 1 yellow, 1 white

Bijar, a town in Kurdistan, is about 86 miles from Sanandaj, on the road to Zanjan. It was originally unique in making rugs with two levels of warp threads, but for some years other neighbouring villages have adopted this method, which results in rugs which are at the same time very thick and very heavy. Since their wool is usually of good quality, Bijar rugs are extremely strong.

The field and medallion of the example reproduced here are in the form of superimposed hexagons, and both have a pattern of flowers and leaves, with a cross at the ends of the central motif. On the dark-blue ground of the four corners, we encounter again the same motifs as on the field, which is surrounded by a fine jagged border. On both sides of the main border decorated with irises is a band of small flowers. All things considered, this is a classical and harmonious design.

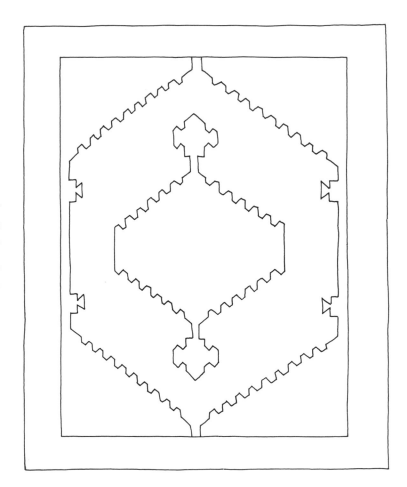

BIJAR

Origin: Iran, Kurdistan
Dimensions: 60 × 45 inches (153 × 115 cm)
Turkish knot: 247 per sq. inch (384,000 per sq. metre)
Double warp of three strands of wool, with applied cotton fringes at one end
Double weft: one of three strands of red cotton, the other of three strands of grey goat's hair
Pile of two strands of fine wool
12 colours

The design of this rug, called Herati, includes the *boteh* motif, the most classical of Iran: one finds it as often on Tabriz, Mashad or Arak rugs as on those from Bijar.

A restful seed-plot of flowers and leaves covers the whole field: it is composed of daisies arranged in lozenges and encircled either with four leaves or with four carnations, all upon a warm red ground. Flowered arabesques run along the dark-blue ground of the main border, which is framed by two narrow bands.

In spite of the two levels of warp threads usual in Bijar rugs, this piece is of great delicacy.

BIJAR

Origin: Iran, Kurdistan
Dimensions: 78 × 50 inches (197 × 128 cm)
Turkish knot: 85 per sq. inch (132,600 per sq. metre)
Double warp of six strands of white cotton
Weft of wool
Pile of two strands of medium fineness, in warm, slightly faded colours
12 colours: 2 reds, 3 blues, 2 browns, 1 yellow, 1 orange, 1 black, 1 green, 1 white

The decoration of Bijar rugs is always floral and this piece is no exception. The field is covered by two super-imposed hexagons both framed by a double line, the larger one in steps and the smaller in serrations. One can recognize the Herati motif, which is composed of two leaves inclined towards each other, with a flower in the middle, in this case a rose. There are also sunflowers and tulips. The main border of large flowers is separated from the two narrow bands which frame it by a striped line. Subdued in colour, this rug is harmonious and pleasing to contemplate.

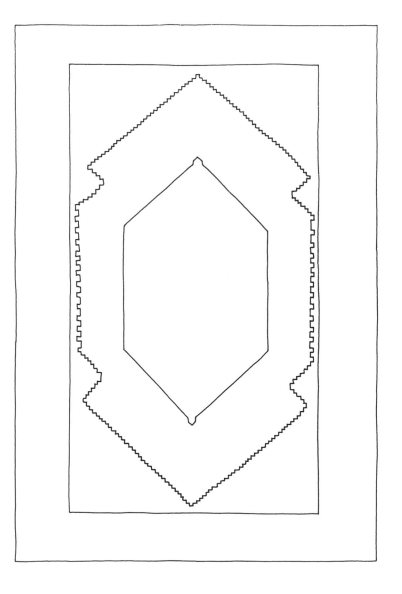

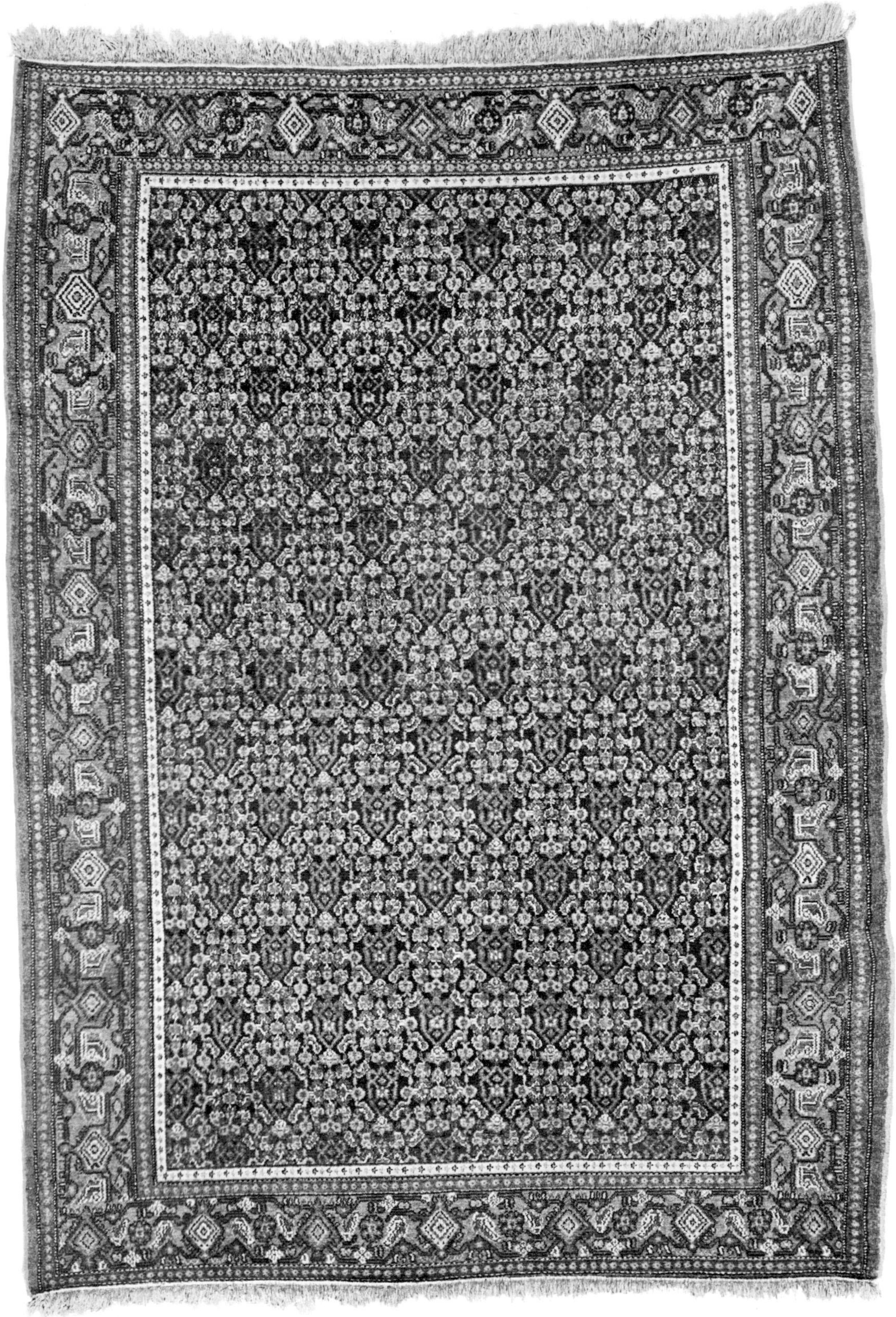

SENNEH (Sanandaj)

Origin: Iran, Kurdistan
Dimensions: 78 × 56 inches (198 × 143 cm)
Persian knot: 123 per sq. inch (193,200 per sq. metre)
Warp of six strands of undyed cotton
Single weft of white cotton
Pile of two strands of fine wool
12 colours: 2 reds, 3 blues, 1 yellow, 1 white, 1 green,
2 browns, 1 grey, 1 black

The town of Senneh, nowadays Sanandaj, has always produced rugs of exquisite fineness, quite different from other types of rugs from Kurdistan.

The field is covered with a regular pattern of flower seedlings, the largest being stylized tulips. A floral pattern alternates also with lozenges in the principal border. This is surrounded by two small bands, also of flowers, as is the light band which edges the field.

The successful choice of colours has been an important factor in creating this carpet's balanced harmony.

SENNEH (Sanandaj)

Origin: Iran, Kurdistan
Dimensions: 54 × 44 inches (137 × 109 cm)
Persian knot: 129 per sq. inch (200,000 per sq. metre)
Warp of five strands of undyed cotton
Single weft of undyed cotton
Pile of two strands of fine wool
9 colours: 2 reds, 2 blues, 1 black, 1 white, 1 yellow,
1 green, 1 brown

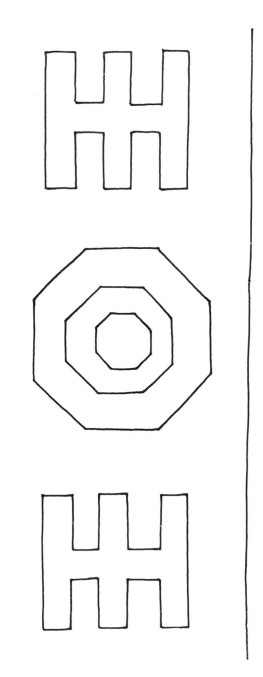

Senneh rugs are easily recognizable by their delicate floral decoration. This piece is no exception, with its large white hexagon patterned with flowers, as are the corners and the central dark-blue medallion; among the flowers one can distinguish large formalized tulips.

The main border is unusual in not having a consistent overall design. Along the length of the rug, rosettes alternate with combs, while across the width, the latter are replaced by motifs in the form of fir-trees. Two small flowered bands upon a sky-blue ground frame the main border.

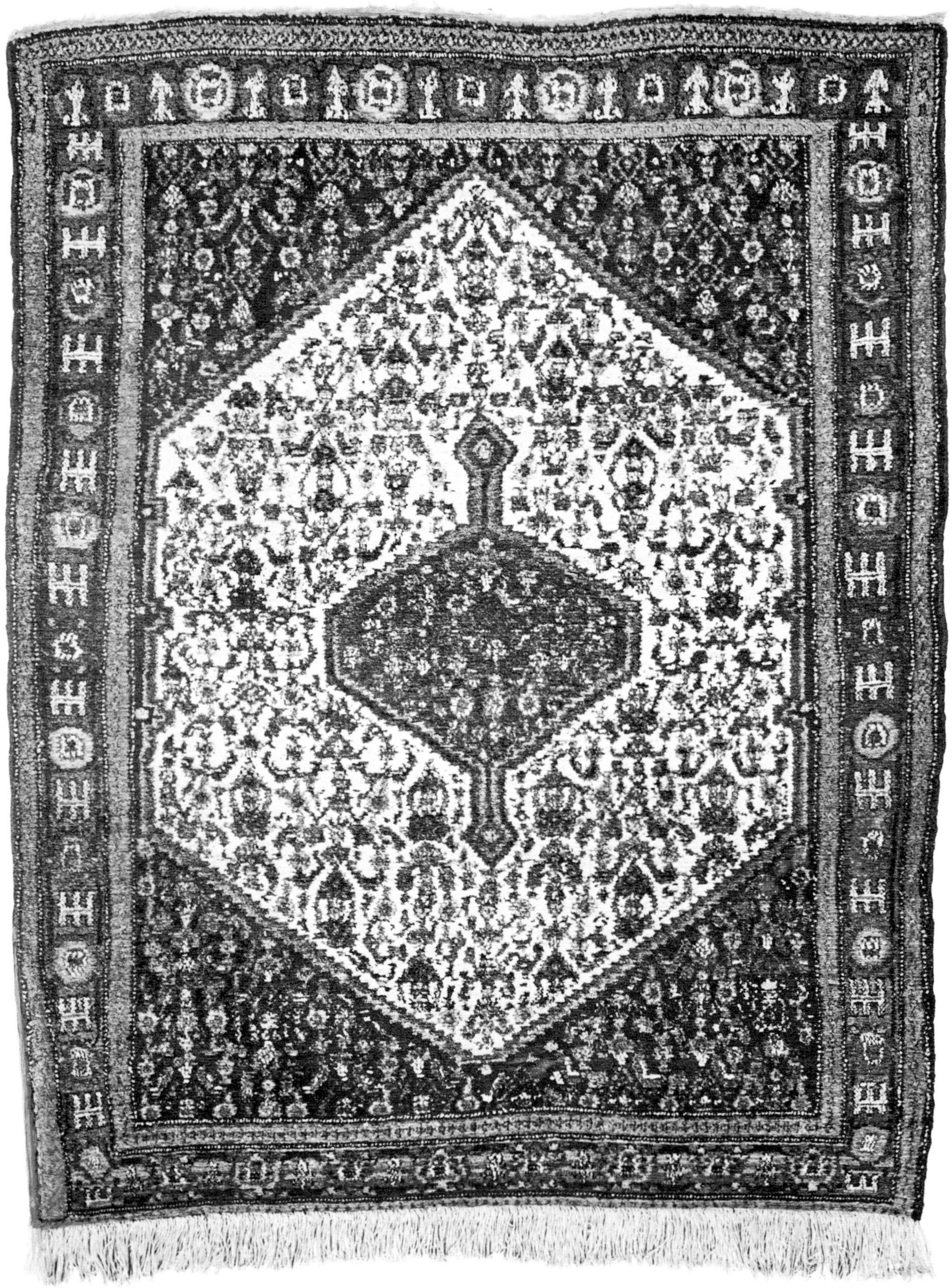

SENNEH (Sanandaj)

Origin: Iran, Kurdistan
Dimensions: 91 × 61 inches (232 × 155 cm)
Persian knot: 130 per sq. inch (201,400 per sq. metre)
Warp of six strands of undyed cotton
Single weft of blue cotton
Pile of two strands of fine wool
12 colours: 2 reds, 3 blues, 1 yellow, 1 white, 2 greens,
1 brown, 1 grey, 1 black

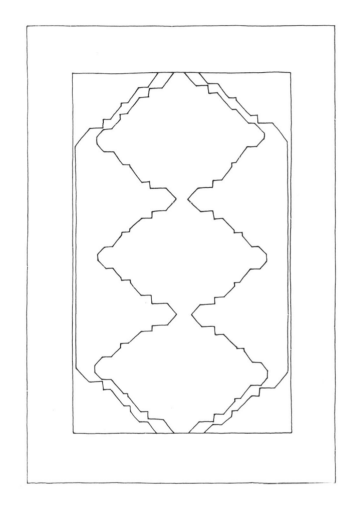

This is a variant of the Senneh rug, with three diamond-shaped medallions patterned with stylized flowers and fruits. There are also a number of crosses within conical motifs, perhaps a sign that this rug was made by Christians. The field scattered with flowers is typical of Senneh rugs. The corners repeat the motifs of the medallions. The small bands of flowers accentuate the arabesques of the principal border.

The tones of this example are very soft, as is usual in Senneh rugs. Indeed the weavers of this town have a highly developed colour sense.

SENNEH KILIM

SONGUR

Origin: Iran, Sanandaj (Senneh)
Dimensions: 79 × 50 inches (200 × 127 cm)
Warp of three strands of rather fine undyed cotton
Tapestry-weave carried out in two strands of wool of medium fineness
8 colours: 3 reds, 1 blue, 1 green, 1 white, 1 black, 1 yellow

The Kilims from Senneh are certainly to be included among the most beautiful of this type. Their designs, like their colours, are in exquisite taste, and their weave is tighter than that of other Kilims.

The carpet illustrated here is very representative. Its design is that of the knotted rugs from Senneh: four superimposed hexagons, the first red, the second white, the third dark blue and the last red, are delicately patterned with flowers, birds and dogs. The central hexagon is adorned with a diamond shape with four projections like a cross. It is edged, as are the other three, with a jagged line, like the knotted examples of the same origin. The corners are green, and the main border yellow.

The design and colours combine together to form a completely successful composition.

Origin: Iran, Hamadan region
Dimensions: 67 × 43 inches (170 × 108 cm)
Turkish knot: 50 per sq. inch (78,300 per sq. metre)
Warp of five strands of undyed cotton
Double weft of blue cotton
Pile of two strands of wool, chemically washed
12 colours: 4 reds, 1 blue, 2 greens, 1 black, 2 beiges, 1 white, 1 orange

This large Kurdish village situated on an arid plateau at an altitude of 5,512 feet has gained a reputation for producing rugs of high quality. In the example reproduced the field is decorated with a very large hexagon of beige colour, with a stepped border. It is covered with a kind of trellis formed of overlapping lozenges, between which are sandwiched horizontal rows of stylized roses.

It has sometimes been incorrectly believed that the beige colour used in these carpets comes from camel-hair, but this material is valued little by Persian weavers because it wears so poorly.

Floral motifs decorate the red ground of the corners. The pattern of the main border is not the same right round the rug: the stylized flowers and leaves down the sides differ from those across the width. It is framed by two small bands of flowers.

This rug has a deep pile and is, as a result, very solid.

KOLIAYEH

Origin: Iran
Dimensions: 92 × 58 inches (234 × 148 cm)
Turkish knot: 64 per sq. inch (99,000 per sq. metre)
Single warp of twelve strands of fine undyed cotton
Weft of four strands of red cotton
Pile of two strands of wool of medium thickness, chemically washed
12 colours

This is a carpet from Persian Kurdistan, which in construction bears more resemblance to Hamadan rugs than to the rugs of its own region.

The geometric style of the design recalls the Kazak rugs of the Caucasus. Its Persian name of *takhteh jamshid* ('throne of the King'), results from the central double motif. The principal border, of white ground, is divided lengthwise into compartments by wide red bands (except for one in blue) trimmed with two small motifs and a large double latch-hook, between which are depicted stylized trees. These bands are replaced across the width of the carpet by rosettes alternating with formalized animals. This border is enclosed by two narrow bands, the outer one consisting only of rosettes, and the inner one of rosettes and spots. The latter is separated from the field by a band of yellow ground patterned with rosettes, between which meanders an unbroken line. The field of dark-blue ground with large geometric motifs and the red central part with stylized ewers and

lines with latch-hooks are evocative of Kazak rugs. However, the wool and the weave are different: the Koliayeh rug being woven on a single warp and in a softer wool than a Kazak.

The charm of this rug lies in the very warm shades and the richness of the colour range.

Isfahan, Nain and the Carpets of Chahar Mahal: Bakhtiari and Joshagan

Isfahan is the second largest town in Iran, but undoubtedly the most beautiful and pleasant. Its origins go back, it appears, to the Achaemenian period (550–331 BC). It underwent numerous dominations, until 1598, when the great king Shah Abbas took up residence and created it capital of the country. It is to this ruler that we owe most of the splendid monuments still to be seen in Isfahan today. His sucessors, Shah Safi (1629–41), Shah Abbas II (1641–66), Shah Sulayman (1666–94), Shah Sultan Hossein (1694–1722), continued to beautify the town after him.

Apart from the Friday Mosque (Masjid-i-Jomeh), which dates from the eleventh century, the main places of interest in Isfahan are the Royal Square (Meidan-i-Shah), a vast rectangle measuring about 1,650 feet in length by 500 feet in width where one can see the Mosque of the Shah (Masjid-i-Shah), the Ali Qapu palace, the Mosque of Sheikh Luftullah and the main entrance to the Bazaar. This complex, unique in the East and constructed in accordance with an urban conception of exceptional grandeur, is the admiration of all visitors. The Chahar Bagh, a long, wide avenue shaded by plane trees, is one of the finest in Iran. Onto this avenue leads the Madraseh-ye-Madar-i-Shah or Madraseh-ye-Chahar-Bagh, a theological school set up at the beginning of the eighteenth century at the command of the mother of Shah Soltan Hossein. The Pavilion with Forty Columns (Chehel Sotun) now houses a museum. One can also see the Madraseh-ye-Imam Jyeh, a small school of theology, the mausoleum of Baba Qasim, with its little tower topped by a pyramidal roof, the Sareban minarets, 144 feet high, and Chehel Dokhtaran, the 'Minaret of the Forty Maidens'. Two of the most interesting bridges are the Hassan Beg and the Allahverdikhan. They span the Zayandeh Rud, which gushes down the eastern slopes of the Zagros, and crosses the town before finally losing itself in the desert.

The production centre of Isfahan is comparatively new. However, in the seventeenth century, Isfahan carpets were counted among the most beautiful in the world. The Afghan invasion at the beginning of the eighteenth century signed the death warrant of this production, which only began again about 1920. The contemporary rugs of Isfahan owe their renewed place among the finest of Iran to their extreme delicacy; the designs of these carpets, with their enchanting colour harmonies, are the product of deep reflection.

Nain is a town of approximately 10,000 inhabitants, situated 93 miles from Isfahan in the direction of Kirman. Although hardly known and scarcely mentioned on maps, Nain demands attention in more than one respect, particularly for its Friday Mosque (Masjid-i-Jomeh) which dates from 960 and which is devoid of the classical *iwans,* unlike mosques of typically Iranian plan of the Seljuk period. Its rugs are the finest in the whole of Persia. Nevertheless, the production is fairly recent: indeed, it began a short time before the Second World War. Until then, the craftsmen of Nain wove garments called *Aba*. The fashion for Western clothes put an end to this industry and obliged the inhabitants of Nain to take up another occupation, the carpet. The weavers, schooled in working with a fine yarn, right from the start made delicate rugs, the fame of which spread rapidly beyond the local markets.

Bakhtiari rugs, contrary to what is usually supposed, are not the product of the mountain-dwelling, nomadic tribe of the same name, but of a sedentary people, mainly of Turkish origin, settled in the region of Chahar Mahal, near Isfahan. Some of the villages of the district are peopled by races of Persian and Armenian origin and the Bakhtiari tribe is only sparsely represented.

Rugs of this name usually have a field divided into diamond shapes patterned with floral motifs: trees of life, pots, plants, flowering branches. There is also a 'garden' design which is a sort of mosaic, each compartment differing from its neighbour in ground colour, red, green, blue, yellow or white; the patterns are always lively. A third design, with central medallion, is less common. The borders consist of several bands, the central one rich in decorative plant forms. The warp and weft threads are of cotton.

There are about ten types of Bakhtiari rug, made in more than 300 villages. Among the better known ones, the finest are called Chalchotor, then comes Saman, Shalemgar, Kafero and Khorey. A Bakhtiari rug knotted by Armenian weavers is occasionally referred to as *Armenibaff* (Armenian knot).

Joshagan is located in the valley of the Kuh-i-Varganeh, 87 miles to the north of Isfahan. This village has steadfastly maintained its traditional design throughout the centuries. The fragment of an eighteenth-century Joshagan carpet in the Victoria and Albert Museum in London has exactly the same motifs as modern rugs.

This design is now reproduced in other villages of the region, particularly at Meymeh, a stopping-place situated 66 miles from Isfahan along the road which links this town with the capital. In the Bazaar at Tehran Meymeh rugs have replaced those from Joshagan, which they often surpass in quality. This same pattern is used by the craftsmen of Vazvan, a large village 2 miles to the south of Meymeh, which, curiously enough, also knots rugs of Kashan type, although quite different. Luristan rugs, the work of the Lur tribes, come from an area between Isfahan and Ahwaz.

ISFAHAN

Origin: Iran
Dimensions: 72 × 51 inches (183 × 130 cm)
Persian knot: 190 per sq. inch (294,000 per sq. metre)
Warp of eight strands of fine undyed cotton
Double weft of blue cotton
Pile of two strands of rather fine wool
12 colours: 2 reds, 2 blues, 1 pink, 2 yellows, 1 straw-yellow, 1 black, 1 white, 2 greens

This carpet depicts across its full width a map of Iran and surrounding territory. The names of Iranian provinces are shown upon a pinkish-beige ground, as well as those of some towns, including Tehran, Mashad, Isfahan, Shiraz and Kashan. At the top centre, in sky-blue, is the Caspian Sea, also called the Sea of Mazandaran. To the right of this, on a mustard-green ground, is Turkestan, with Bukhara marked beside it. To the left of the Caspian Sea, on a green ground, is the Caucasus, then on a yellow ground, Ottoman Armenia, Iraq, and Saudi Arabia. Below, one can see the Persian Gulf, followed by the Gulf of Oman, both in blue. Baluchistan is in red. The name of Afghanistan appears in red, and that of Ghazni in white, on a green ground.

Inscriptions in verse form arabesques on the red ground of the main border which is bordered by two floral bands.

This carpet dates from before the First World War, and was commissioned by Mr Saham Saltaneh and made in the school at Burujen.

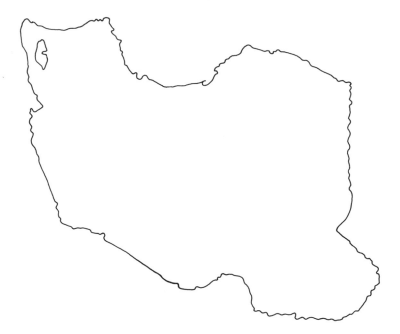

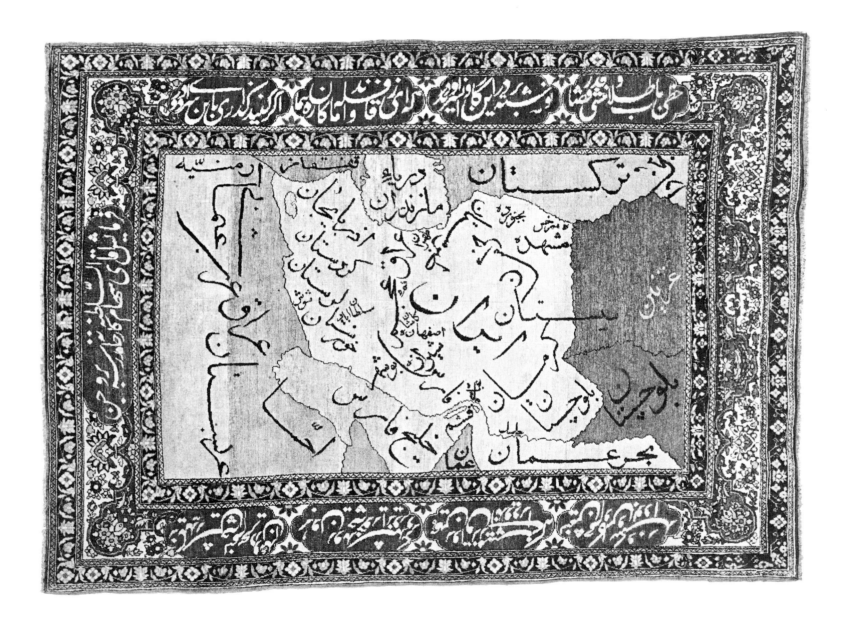

ISFAHAN

Origin: Iran
Dimensions: 78 × 49 inches (198 × 124 cm)
Persian knot: 414 per sq. inch (640,000 per sq. metre)
Warp of three strands of silk
Double weft of blue cotton
Pile of two strands of very fine wool, chemically washed
12 colours

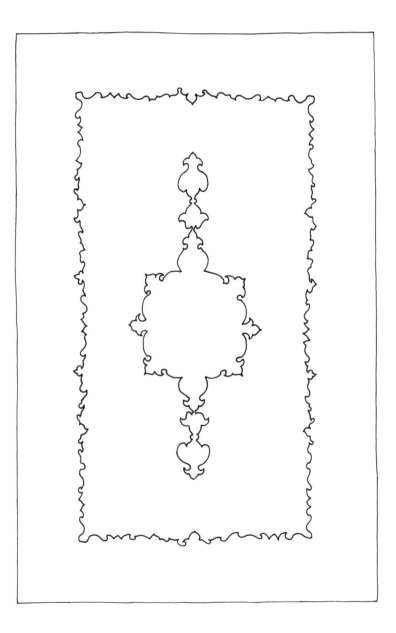

Today the rugs of Isfahan are among the finest to be found in Iran. Their prices are therefore high, as are those of Nain rugs, which are of closely related type.

The decoration of this piece again assumes the traditional floral motifs which already have figured in seventeenth-century rugs and in the early ceramics of the mosques.

The design of the central medallion, square-shaped with graceful projections, and that of the motifs set in the corners is evidence of much careful thought. Like the field, the three bands of the border are patterned with flowers among which one can recognize roses, tulips and daisies. The two bands of blue ground are narrower than the red one, and none of them have rectilinear sides.

One can scarcely imagine the patience necessary to create such a lovely example. Usually women and children are employed for this type of work, sometimes in difficult conditions.

NAIN

Origin: Iran, Isfahan region
Dimensions: 57 × 41 inches (144 × 103 cm)
Persian knot: 570 per sq. inch (883,200 per sq. metre)
Warp of three strands of natural silk
Double weft of blue cotton
Pile of two strands of very fine wool, chemically washed
12 colours: 4 blues, 1 copper-red, 1 red, 2 yellows, 1 white,
1 beige, 2 greens

The weavers of Nain knot the most delicate rugs possible, indeed in some of their creations the number of knots to the square inch exceeds 645 (one million knots to the square metre). The rug reproduced is a good example of their very fine workmanship.

The pattern of the copper-red ground of the field is floral and the central motif, a large star, is classic on Nain carpets. Very slender arabesques decorate the corners and the main border, which is framed by two identical pairs of little bands of floral motifs.

This rug is the product of a craft which has reached a very high artistic peak.

BAKHTIARI

Origin: Iran, Chahar Mahal (Isfahan region)
Dimensions: 94 × 51 inches (239 × 130 cm)
Turkish knot: 63 per sq. inch (97,200 per sq. metre)
Warp of four strands of white cotton
Single weft of natural grey goat's hair
Pile of two strands of wool of medium thickness, chemically washed
11 colours: 3 reds, 3 blues, 1 green, 1 white, 1 black, 1 mauve, 1 brown

The goat's hair weft of this rug leads one to suppose that this is the product of nomads or ex-nomads, for Bakhtiari rugs usually have warp and weft threads of cotton.

We are dealing here with a little known variant of the rug with lozenge decoration. Flowers and trees are formalized in a rather rudimentary fashion, but the number of colours is proof enough of some aesthetic efforts.

The principal border is decorated with large rosettes alternating with leaves. It is framed by two narrow strips. The tones of this rug are warm and the overall effect is rather harmonious.

BAKHTIARI

Origin: Iran, Isfahan region
Dimensions: 81 × 61 inches (205 × 155 cm)
Turkish knot: 71 per sq. inch (109,200 per sq. metre)
Warp of five strands of white cotton
Double weft of cotton: one thread white, one thread blue
Pile of two strands of wool of medium thickness, chemically washed
12 colours: 3 reds, 2 yellows, 1 white, 1 beige, 2 greens, 1 black, 1 blue, 1 brown

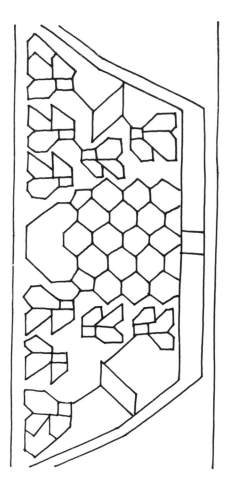

Bakhtiari rugs come from Chahar Mahal, a region in the province of Isfahan where the Bakhtiari tribes are settled. We are familiar with three main designs: the rug with a large medallion, the 'garden' pattern and the design with lozenges reproduced here.

The lozenges, patterned with tulips and pomegranates, are separated by roses and tulips. Edging the field are 'half-sunflowers', and in the corners, are 'quarter-sunflowers'. On the border are stylized carnations, large motifs like bunches of grapes and, in the corners, big leaves interlinked by a garland of flowers. Three very thin bands encircle this border on either side.

CHALCHOTOR BAKHTIARI

Origin: Iran, Chahar Mahal (Isfahan region)
Dimensions: 145 × 103 inches (368 × 262 cm)
Turkish knot: 88 per sq. inch (136,800 per sq. metre)
Warp of six strands of white cotton
Double weft of blue cotton
Pile of two strands of wool of medium thickness, chemically washed
12 colours: 3 reds, 2 blues, 2 yellows, 1 white, 2 greens, 1 brown, 1 black

A Chalchotor rug is the best and most compact of the Bakhtiari group. The style does not differ from other rugs of the same design except for the main border, which has a white ground. Among the arabesques, one can pick out the *boteh-miri* motif, as well as a rich scattering of flowers of all kinds.

The field is divided into squares patterned with various motifs such as weeping willows, peacocks, clusters of grapes, various birds and domestic animals.

This carpet seems the product of a lively imagination.

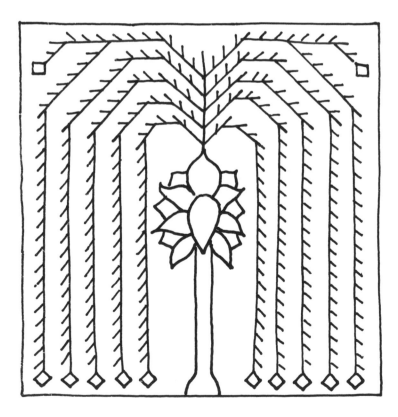 

SAMAN BAKHTIARI

Origin: Iran, Isfahan region
Dimensions: 126 × 85 inches (320 × 215 cm)
Turkish knot: 77 per sq. inch (118,800 per sq. metre)
Warp of two and four strands of undyed cotton
Double weft of blue cotton
Pile of two strands of wool of medium thickness, chemically washed
10 colours: 2 reds, 2 blues, 1 green, 1 black, 1 white, 1 yellow, 2 browns

After those from Chalchotor, the finest Bakhtiari rugs come from Saman, a village situated approximately 49 miles as the crow flies from Isfahan, not far from the Zayandeh Rud. Their double weft in general gives them a more compact and thicker weave than that of ordinary Bakhtiari carpets. The field is completely divided up into little squares, like a chessboard. The highly stylized floral pattern is typical of this type of rug. A wide main border adorned with flowered arabesques is enclosed by two narrow bands with a design of leaves and flowers.

Unlike other kinds of Bakhtiari rugs, which have bright colouring, those from Saman, as this example, are rather dark.

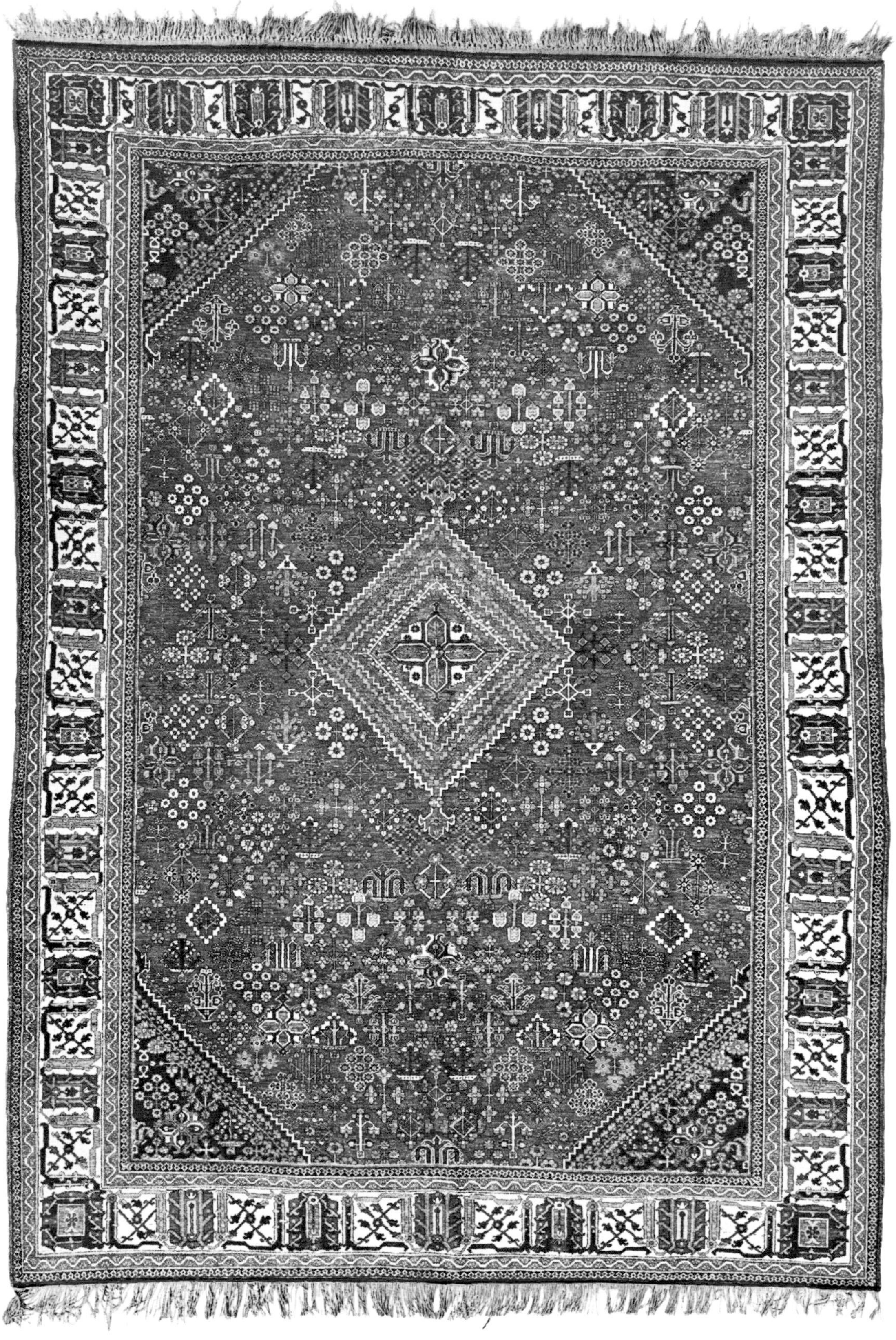

JOSHAGAN

Origin: Iran, Isfahan region
Dimensions: 118 × 80 inches (299 × 207 cm)
Persian knot: 166 per sq. inch (257,600 per sq. metre)
Warp of three strands of undyed cotton
Double weft of blue cotton
Pile of two strands of wool of medium thickness
8 colours: 2 reds, 2 blues, 1 yellow, 1 green, 1 brown, 1 white

This design is called *jangali* (of the jungle) because of the numerous floral motifs on the field and the corners. Note that the latter are not repeated in the centre of the field, as is usually the case in Joshagan and Meymeh rugs, but instead there is a medallion called *torrenj*: of

diamond shape, it encloses a cross of Islam with a flower called *puzaraki* in its centre.

All the floral motifs on the red ground of the field bear the names of flowers or trees, from which the title of the design is probably derived. They are of various colours — navy blue, yellowish-orange, green, white, blue, pink — arranged in a rather harmonious manner.

Tulips give their name (*laleh*) to the main border which is also decorated with cypress trees. Two bands encircle it on each side, the first decorated with zigzags and the second with sugar-loaves.

This design has been repeated, unaltered, for about 200 years.

LURISTAN

Origin: Iran, Luristan
Dimensions: 116 × 60 (295 × 152 cm)
Turkish knot: 59 per sq. inch (91,800 per sq. metre)
Warp of two strands of natural beige-brown wool
Single weft of natural brown wool
Pile of two strands of wool of medium thickness
10 colours

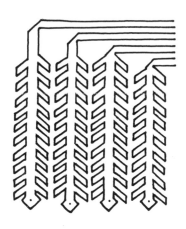

Luristan rugs are made by the Lur tribes, who still live partly as nomads. The region lies on the frontier with Iraq.

On the blue-black ground of the field, we find diverse large stylized motifs — willows, cypresses, roses, tulips — all arranged in the same direction. In the main border, cruciform motifs alternate with two confronted birds. Two floral-patterned bands, one with white ground, the other yellow, complete the border.

The design is simple, giving an impression of a primitive but captivating art.

272

Shiraz and the Carpets of Fars

Fars, one of the five main provinces of Iran, is the cradle of the Achaemenian kings. Cyrus was born there, and his tomb is at Pasargadae. Persepolis, the capital of the Achaemenian and Sassanid dynasties, is situated at a distance of 43 miles from Shiraz. Under the reign of Shah Abbas the Great, Shiraz was surpassed in splendour only by Isfahan, and the province enjoyed great prosperity.

Today, Shiraz is one of the finest towns of Iran, justly reputed for its gardens, wines and rugs. Despite its altitude of 4,900 feet it becomes hot in summer, while in other seasons the climate is temperate; snow is rare. An ultra-modern university and hospital are the pride of the town. For the person interested in the past there are not only the garden-surrounded tombs of the great Persian poets Saadi and Hafiz but also several mosques, the loveliest of which is the eighteenth-century Vakil Mosque, named after its builder, Karim Khan Zand, called Vakil-i-Raya (representative of the people).

The work *Hudud-al-Alam* points out that already in 892, carpets were being woven in Darabjerd, Fasa and Jahrom, which are still production centres of Fars today.

One would search in vain for looms in the actual town of Shiraz. Rugs of this name come from the villages of Bassiri, Bilverdi, Jarussa, Farukh, Fasa, Firuzabad, Kafretj and Seydan. Their relation with the Shiraz type is easy to see, owing to their typical colours and design, and to the fact that they all have warp and weft threads in wool.

The Kashgai rug, which has the reputation of being the finest of Fars, has often been named Turkish Shiraz or Mecca-Shiraz, because it was originally the work of Kashgai nomads of Turkish origin. Many of these nomads have now become settled, but they continue to use their nomadic horizontal looms just as before.

Behbehan is another centre in Fars which produces rugs knotted by the Lur tribes. The motifs resemble those of Shiraz rugs.

Baharlu carpets are the work of a Turkish-speaking tribe, which has settled in what was called the Khamseh confederation, between Persepolis and Abadeh. Warp and weft threads are of cotton, with a fairly thick weave.

Abadeh, a town with a population of 8,000 between Shiraz and Isfahan, produces characteristic carpets whose designs have not varied for decades. These are tightly woven rugs, with warp and weft threads in cotton.

Yalameh is the name of a rug which appeared on the market a few years ago, similar to the Shiraz rug, but with gayer colouring and more compact texture. These rugs, the work of the Kashgai tribe, some of whose members have settled at Aliabad some 43 miles from Isfahan, are nowadays also made by the inhabitants of Talkuncheh. The Yalamehs are knotted on a horizontal loom, often placed in front of the house, under the ancient black tent of the nomads. At Talkuncheh the dyes used are still mostly vegetable.

Niriz is quite close to the lake of the same name, between Shiraz and Kirman. This locality produces carpets of rather commonplace quality, in designs reminiscent of Afshar rugs from Kirman, but one cannot compare either materials or workmanship.

Gabbeh refers to a rug of recent production knotted by the Kashgai tribes of Fars, especially of Behbehan, with a natural undyed wool.

SHIRAZ

Origin: Iran
Dimensions: 106 × 73 inches (268 × 186 cm)
Persian knot: 51 per sq. inch (78,400 per sq. metre)
Warp of two strands of natural greyish-black goat's hair
Double weft of natural dark goat's hair
Pile of two strands of wool, chemically washed
7 colours

Though there are no stylized animals in this example they are commonly used as decorative motifs in carpets of this type.

The carpets known under the name of Shiraz all come from the neighbouring villages, for there are no looms in the town itself. They are characterized, as in the example reproduced, by a field of red of varying degrees of darkness, decorated with three medallions, or with a large hexagon. The warp and weft threads of goat's hair or wool give them more suppleness than those made on a cotton warp and weft.

The field is covered with bunches of flowers, four of which, in white, stand out particularly. At both ends, one can read the date of the year it was woven, 1338: repeated four times, this also is featured once on the reverse.

Entirely encircled by a serrated line, the field is bordered by nine bands of various widths which, starting from the inside working outwards, are as follows: a white dotted line, a variation of the Caucasian wineglass border, a band of *boteh* motifs, a little band of slanting stripes on either side of the main border, which itself is patterned with roses, a band of small *boteh* motifs and two spotted bands.

SHIRAZ

Origin: Iran
Dimensions: 46 × 35 inches (116 × 89 cm)
Persian knot: 47 per sq. inch (72,800 per sq. metre)
Warp of two strands of natural goat's hair
Double weft of wool, partly beige and partly red
Pile of two strands of wool of medium thickness
8 colours: 1 beige, 2 reds, 2 blues, 1 black, 1 white, 1 orange

It is rare to see a beige-brown ground such as this one on a Shiraz rug. All the decoration of this piece seems to be arranged irregularly over the field: the motifs are animals such as peacocks and grotesque birds. Squares of five compartments, each one studded with a spot of colour, are grouped in pairs here and there, each pair displaying a different colour. Stylized flowers complete the pattern.

This character of whimsical irregularity bestows a particular charm on this little piece.

The principal border is embellished with elongated motifs, with a bird's head at each end, forming a garland.

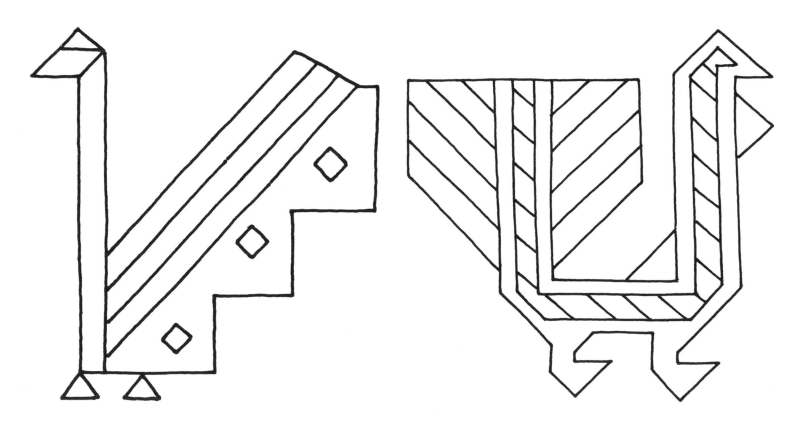

SHIRAZ

Origin: Iran
Dimensions: 59 × 45 inches (151 × 115 cm)
Persian knot: 40 per sq. inch (62,400 per sq. metre)
Warp of natural brown, black, grey and beige goat's hair and wool mixed together
Double weft of red cotton
Pile of two strands of wool of medium thickness, chemically washed
9 colours: 2 reds, 2 blues, 1 black, 1 white, 1 orange, 1 green, 1 brown

This is a rather curious design for a Shiraz rug: the whole field is divided into lengthwise bands, the widest ones bearing the motif of a two-handled vase, repeated one after the other, the narrowest ones with stripes. Against the natural white background, the vases and stripes are little splashes of varied colours.

The principal border repeats the design of the field, skirted on the outer edge by two small bands, one trimmed with triangles, the other with white squares with a coloured spot.

An amusing and charming piece.

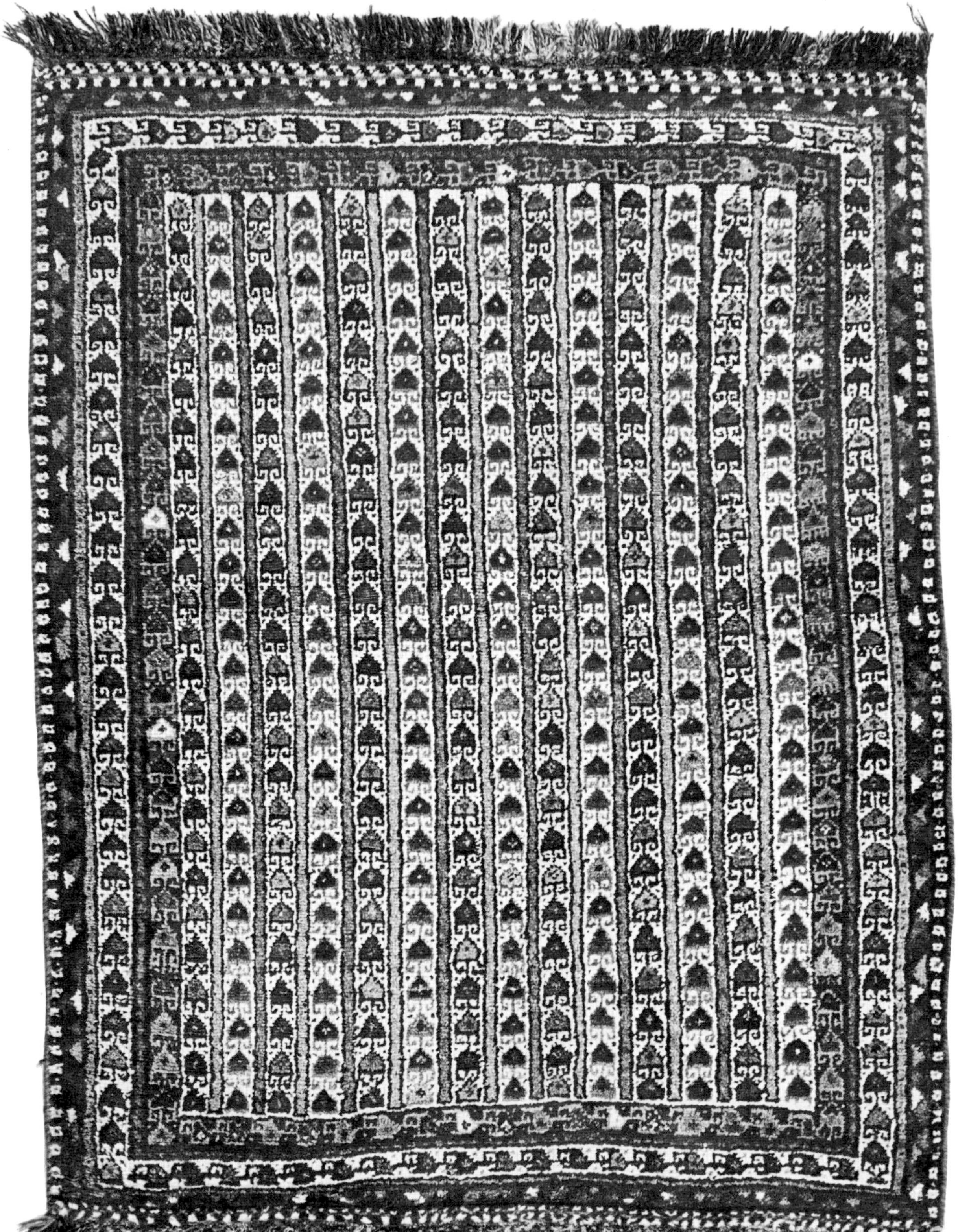

A HORSE BLANKET

Origin: Iran, Shiraz region
Dimensions: 57 × 39 inches (145 × 100 cm)
Kilim technique for the ground, with the motifs in pile, employ-
ing the Turkish knot
Wool of two strands of medium thickness
10 colours: 2 reds, 3 blues, 1 green, 1 orange, 1 white, 1 yel-
low, 1 black

The Persian name for these covers, which are the work of the Kashgai tribes, is *juleh asp*. The decoration—stylized figures, dogs and trees—stands out gaily on the white ground. The border, patterned with formalized trees, is not absolutely the same on all three sides; long fringes ending in tufts of wool add to its length. The two parts added to the fourth edge were fixed on either side of the saddle.

The *juleh asp* makes an extremely beautiful mural decoration. Regrettably this charming kind of weaving is doomed sooner or later to disappear.

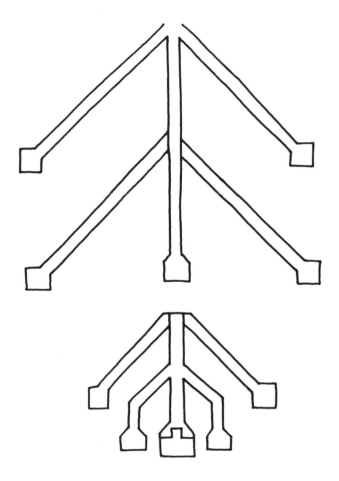

KASHGAI

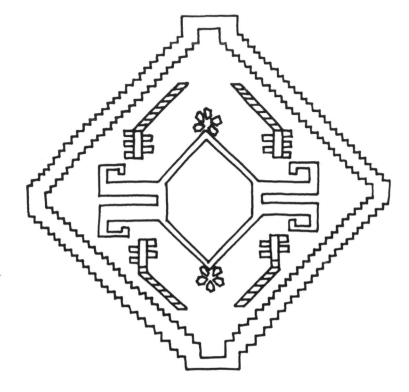

Origin: Iran, Shiraz region
Dimensions: 89 × 51 inches (227 × 129 cm)
Persian knot: 90 per sq. inch (140,400 per sq. metre)
Warp of two strands of goat's hair, one brown and one undyed
thread twisted together
Double weft of goat's hair: one brown and one red thread
Pile of one strand of wool of medium thickness
8 colours

The Kashgai people were originally Turkish-speaking nomads who lived in Fars, that is to say, in the region of Shiraz. This is why their rugs are often referred to under the name of 'Turkish Shiraz'. But nowadays, a good number of the now sedentary Kashgai race have settled in the villages of the region. They have, however, retained their habit of knotting their carpets on the horizontal looms of the nomads. During the fine season one sees women working on them in the garden or in the courtyard in front of the house.

The field is a large hexagon, inside which one finds a number of motifs in the form of leaves, notched on one side, and flowers. The diamond-shaped central medallion is encircled by two lines, the inner one jagged and the outer one cut out in steps. In the middle is a hexagon ornamented with two large lateral latch-hooks and a flower at each end. Four jagged motifs frame a big flower in each corner. Stars decorate the principal border which is flanked by two bands, one narrower than the other.

BAHARLU

Origin: Iran, Shiraz region
Dimensions: 67 × 50 inches (170 × 128 cm)
Turkish knot: 108 per sq. inch (166,600 per sq. metre)
Warp of natural wool: one brown and one undyed thread
Double weft of wool
Pile of two strands of wool of medium thickness, chemically washed
11 colours: 2 reds, 2 blues, 2 greens, 1 black, 1 white, 1 yellow, 1 beige, 1 brown

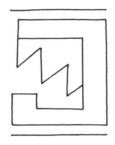

This is a little known variation of the rugs from the Shiraz region, which comes from the village of Baharlu. This piece, of a tighter and heavier weave than ordinary Shiraz rugs, also has bolder and more contrasting colours.

In the rather muddled pattern of two large hexagonal medallions with a jagged border, one can make out two sets of three combs, on either side of a light-coloured motif. There are flowers, including two large ones, on the red ground of the field.

An irregularly serrated border runs around the field. The principal border is patterned with large flowers and highly stylized leaves on a white ground; it is edged on each side by two little blue bands.

ABADEH

Origin: Iran
Dimensions: 60 × 42 inches (153 × 106 cm)
Persian knot: 109 per sq. inch (168,000 per sq. metre)
Warp of fourteen strands of undyed cotton
Double weft of blue cotton
Pile of two strands of wool of medium thickness, chemically washed
10 colours: 3 reds, 2 blues, 1 black, 1 white, 1 brown, 1 orange 1 green

Abadeh, which has a population of 8,000, is situated at an altitude of approximately 6,598 feet, 133 miles from Isfahan. Rugs are woven there in four traditional designs: *Mohamera* (a pattern with lines of the Shiraz type), *Jilli Sultan, Kaghasi* and *Keibathlu,* reproduced here.

This rug shows striking similarities to the products of the neighbouring region of Shiraz, with the difference that the hexagon, corner motifs, small central medallion and the pattern of stylized dogs have a more definite rectilinear character. This difference is intensified by the more rigid structure the cotton warp and weft give the Abadeh. The carpets of this village are usually finer in quality than those of Shiraz.

YALAMEH

Origin: Iran, Talkuncheh (Isfahan region)
Dimensions: 124 × 81 inches (315 × 205 cm)
Persian knot: 79 per sq. inch (121,600 per sq. metre)
Warp of two strands of natural black wool
Double weft of the same material
Pile of two strands of wool of medium thickness, chemically washed
10 colours: 1 red, 2 blues, 2 greens, 2 yellows, 1 white, 1 black, 1 brown

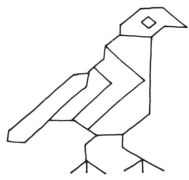

The style of this rug reminds one of the Shiraz type. However, it is very much a Yalameh rug, with different colours and tighter weave. It comes from the village of Talkhuncheh, where natural dyes are still used.

The design of the field, with its three medallions, is called *se hoze* (three basins); the motif decorating the small innermost medallions is called *gol-i-torunj* (central flower). And in the border of the field are four petals (in Persian: *shahar pareh pichi*).

The principal border, decorated with the *daste* (hand) motif, is framed by two narrow bands of latch-hooks.

YALAMEH

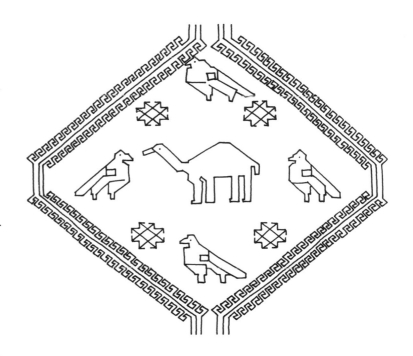

Origin: Iran, Aliabad (Isfahan region)
Dimensions: 120 × 85 inches (305 × 215 cm)
Persian knot: 87 per sq. inch (135,000 per sq. metre)
Warp of natural grey and brown wool, one strand of each colour twisted together
Double weft of two strands of natural brown wool
Pile of two strands of wool of medium thickness
8 colours

The rug reproduced opposite has a main border of white ground encircled by narrower borders, and a field of black ground, upon which are arranged four white hexagonal medallions, interlinked and bordered in red. The centre medallions include a camel, four birds and stylized flowers, and those at the ends have sheep (?), chickens and mice (?), in addition to a camel and stylized flowers.

The outlines of the medallions and the red framework are trimmed with a double row of latch-hooks of Caucasian origin, as are the little eight-pointed stars of the inner band, edged on the side nearest the field by a line of red latch-hooks. The field is embellished with animals, birds, crosses and closed latch-hooks. On both sides of the principal border two small bands are to be found with interesting motifs: the triangle, formerly symbol of divinity, and the motif underneath—of Chinese origin—called 'thunder border'. The latch-hook motifs of the main band are reminiscent of those on Yomud rugs of Turkestan.

Everything about this carpet points to influences from the Caucasus and Turkestan. The simplicity of the geometric shapes and the appealing gaiety of the colours make it an attractive piece.

NIRIZ

Origin: Iran, Shiraz region
Dimensions: 72 × 53 inches (183 × 133 cm)
Persian knot: 27 per sq. inch (41,800 per sq. metre)
Warp of three strands of white cotton
Double weft of thick red cotton
Pile of two strands of rather thick wool
8 colours: 1 red, 1 white, 2 greens, 2 blues, 1 orange, 1 black

The rugs of this name are not made in Niriz itself but in the villages of the region. In texture they resemble the Afshari rugs from Sirjan, but are of inferior quality.

Afshari rugs with such a small number of knots are only to be seen at Ghahestan, near Sirjan.

A large cruciform motif with red ground, the verticals cut out in steps, occupies a large part of the field. This motif is decorated with trees of life and outlined with several lines, of which one is serrated. In the centre is a large octagonal medallion trimmed with leaves and four eight-pointed stars enclosed within a lozenge of light ground.

Stylized birds, cockerels and dromedaries are arranged on the blue ground of the corners. The principal border is of the wine-glass type.

GABBEH

GABBEH

Origin: Iran, Shiraz region
Dimensions: 67 × 35 inches (171 × 90 cm)
Turkish knot: 35 per sq. inch (54,000 per sq. metre)
Warp of two strands of natural black and white wool
Double weft of natural white wool
Pile of two strands of wool of medium thickness, chemically washed
3 colours: 1 white, 1 beige, 1 brown

The nomadic Kashgai and their sedentary brothers of Behpahan knotted these rugs, occasionally called 'herdsmen's rugs'. Their natural colours remind one of the Berber rugs of North Africa.

But the four large jagged medallions of diamond shape, alternating with five smaller lozenges certainly belong to rugs of the Shiraz region. The decorative motifs stand out strongly against the plain white wool of the field. Small interlinked lozenges are arranged in the principal border, which is framed by two plain narrow bands. The simplicity of the carpet is not without a certain charm.

Origin: Iran, Shiraz region
Dimensions: 65 × 40 inches (165 × 102 cm)
Persian knot: 37 per sq. inch (58,000 per sq. metre)
Warp of two strands of greyish-black goat's hair
Double weft of natural brown goat's hair
Pile of two strands of wool of medium thickness, chemically washed
8 colours: 1 red, 2 blues, 1 orange, 1 yellow, 1 white, 1 black, 1 green

The large T-shaped motifs which project from either side of the central lozenge are, like the latter, entirely edged with latch-hooks, their red colour contrasting attractively with the bluish-black ground of the field, of which the remaining spaces are filled with little flowers.

The principal border comprises lozenges surrounded by triangles and this resembles the borders of the early Caucasian rugs. There are five more bands, four of which are plain.

This simply conceived piece in bright colours is the work of a Kashgai tribe.

GABBEH

Origin: Iran, Shiraz region
Dimensions: 68 × 48 inches (172 × 121 cm)
Persian knot: 39 per sq. inch (60,000 per sq. metre)
Warp of two strands of natural goat's hair
Double weft of red goat's hair
Pile of two strands of wool of medium thickness, chemically washed
8 colours: 2 blues, 1 red, 1 orange, 1 yellow, 1 white, 1 brown, 1 green

Gabbeh rugs with a red ground, such as this one, are usually of slightly earlier manufacture than those with white or beige grounds. They are made by the Kashgai nomads who live in Fars.

In the centre of the carpet, a lozenge with double latch-hooks at the sides is inscribed within a rectangle decorated with a cock in each corner. A narrow band like a cord encircles the rectangle and extends into two very large double latch-hooks. Very fine lines project at right angles from this band.

The main border of flowers is very simple and is framed by two bands of oblique lines in a variety of colours. This rug is the product of a rather rudimentary craft.

Kashan and Qum

Kashan lies 160 miles from Tehran and approximately 60 miles from Qum, in the direction of Yazd. It is an important town with a population of 70,000. According to legend the settlement was founded by Kashan, one of the sons of the mythological hero Faridun, but the Persian historian Mustaufi attributes the construction of Kashan to Zubaida, the wife of Harun al-Rashid. Be that as it may, it is almost certain that the city was already in existence in the Sassanid period. According to another legend, it was from Kashan that the Three Magi departed on their journey to Bethlehem.

Apart from its carpets, Kashan is also famous for its silks. The carpet industry flourished in the sixteenth and seventeenth centuries and it is probable that many an example from this period preserved today in museums and private collections originated from Kashan. Manufacture stopped completely during the eighteenth century and it was not till the end of the nineteenth century that it was resumed, and then on a large scale, owing to the initiative of an importer of merino wool, who had the idea of using imported wool in order to relaunch production. At the beginning of this century, Kashan was the sole town in Iran to use imported wool, but today, while this practice has become widespread elsewhere, the craftsmen of Kashan have started once again to use native wool. In 1940, according to a merchant in the town, there were four thousand carpet looms in Kashan itself and eight thousand in the neighbouring villages. This number of twelve thousand looms must still be in operation today. The quality of Kashan rugs continues to be excellent and there are known to be more than 80 producing villages, among which one

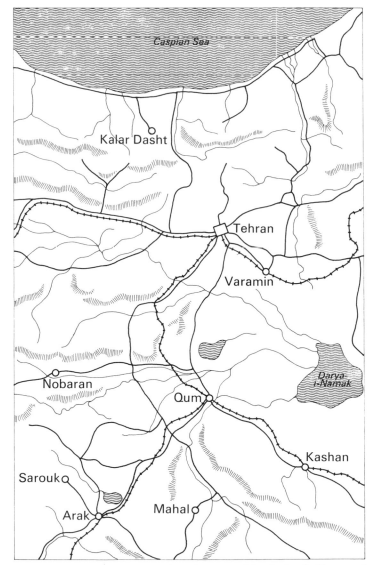

must mention Natanz, Fin, Armaq, Nushabad, Ravand, Tahirabad, Aliabad, Abuzaidabad, Qamsar, Mashad, Vazvan and Rahaq. Knotted rugs from Aron and Nasirabad are of inferior quality.

Qum, a city of approximately 100,000 inhabitants, is 100 miles from Tehran. Legend has it that its founder was King Tahmurath, of the legendary dynasty of the Peshdadids. According to the Arab geographer Yaqut, the existence of the town was supposed to have been prior to Islam, its name becoming abridged from Kumandan to Qum by the Arabs. The ancient town supposedly extended along the north bank of the river of the same name. The author of *The Book of Qum* maintains that the town was founded at the end of the first century AH (about 720). In 816, when Fatima, the daughter of Imam Musa al-Qacem and sister of Imam Reza, died a sanctuary was built for her, the *Hazrat-i-Mahsumeh,* whose fame has still not spread beyond the boundaries of the province. At the beginning of the seventeenth century Shah Abbas I had a splendid shrine erected in her honour to which many Persians come in pilgrimage. Qum also houses the tombs of Shah Safi (d. 1641), Shah Abbas II (d. 1666) and Shah Sulayman (d. 1694).

The carpet industry only began in the 1930s. The looms are to be found within the town itself, and not in the surrounding villages, as is usually the case elsewhere in Iran. The designs of these rugs show an original character: part of the floral motifs or all of the pile are executed in silk. Although the rugs of Qum do not match the delicacy of those from Kashan or Isfahan, they can still be included among the finest in the country.

KASHAN

Origin: Iran
Dimensions: 83 × 53 inches (211 × 133 cm)
Persian knot: 209 per sq. inch (324,000 per sq. metre)
Warp of three strands of three-ply undyed cotton
Double weft of blue cotton
Pile of two strands of fairly fine wool
14 colours: 3 reds, 3 blues, 3 greens, 1 white, 1 black, 1 yellow,
2 browns

ation of dark blue with the coral colour can be seen again in the corners. In the corners and in the principal border are flowers, leaves and various bouquets of flowing contours. On either side of this border are two pairs of identical narrow bands.

The richness of the colour and the harmony of the design are the mark of highly-skilled weavers.

This is a typical Kashan design, with a dark-blue central motif, decorated with a coral-coloured rosette, upon a red field patterned with floral arabesques. The associ-

KASHAN

Origin: Iran
Dimensions: 49 × 27 inches (124 × 68 cm)
Persian knot: 181 per sq. inch (280,000 per sq. metre)
Warp of eight strands of undyed cotton
Double weft of blue cotton
Pile of two strands of rather fine wool, chemically washed
12 colours: 2 reds, 2 blues, 1 green, 1 black, 1 white, 1 beige,
2 yellows, 2 browns

This pattern, with a star-shaped central motif standing out on a plain field (of red, in this example), is called *kafzadeh*. The decoration is completely floral, with corners of blue ground and the main border of cream adorned with roses, carnations, daisies and leaves. Three lines separate it from each of the two narrow bands surrounding it.

This small example is proof of the taste and skill of the Kashan weavers.

KASHAN

Origin: Iran
Dimensions: 97 × 61 inches (246 × 155 cm)
Persian knot: 274 per sq. inch (422,400 per sq. metre)
Warp of three strands of fine undyed cotton
Double weft of two strands of blue cotton
Pile of two strands of fine wool, with silky sheen accentuated
by chemical treatment.
12 colours

Kashan, a town renowned for its textiles, produces rugs of exceptional quality. The famous carpet from the mosque at Ardebil, now in the Victoria and Albert Museum in London, is the work of a Kashan weaver. Even though some experts cast doubt upon its place of origin, it is probable that it was woven in this town.

The example reproduced opposite has a pattern of extraordinary richness. Certainly designed by an artist of talent, it reminds one of the carpets of the great seventeenth-century period. The border, with stylized flowers predominantly in blues of various shades, surrounds the fine red field which is richly decorated with floral tracery. The interlinked corner pieces repeat and develop the motifs of the border without a break. The different bands of the border cannot be clearly defined, the motifs of the central strip encroaching upon the adjacent ones. All the lines of the pattern, simultaneously graceful and vigorous, converge on the central medallion. This almost circular form has two lengthwise projections and is decorated with formalized vases and flowers in a very varied range of colours. The virtuosity of the design is enhanced by the skilful use of twelve different colours. This very beautiful piece is evidence that Iran still produces rugs of high quality.

QUM

Origin: Iran
Dimensions: 80 × 53 inches (204 × 134 cm)
Persian knot: 216 per sq. inch (333,500 per sq. metre)
Warp of four strands of undyed cotton
Double weft of the same material
Pile of two strands of rather fine wool, chemically washed
12 colours: 2 reds, 2 blues, 2 greens, 1 black, 1 white, 1 gold,
2 browns, 1 grey

The design with large *boteh* motifs is typical of the rugs of Qum; it covers both the ivory field and the border. Note that on the field there is a smaller *boteh* between each of the large ones, and that they are turned towards the left, while the large ones face the right. Again one finds flowers on the field and bouquets in the border, which is encircled by two small identical bands.

This is a fine rug, knotted with a good wool in soft and harmonious colours.

QUM

Origin: Iran
Dimensions: 126 × 84 inches (319 × 214 cm)
Persian knot: 187 per sq. inch (290,000 per sq. metre)
Warp of three strands of three-ply undyed cotton
Double weft of red cotton
Pile of two strands of fairly fine wool
12 colours: 2 reds, 2 blues, 2 greens, 2 browns, 1 gold, 1 black
1 white, 1 yellow

either side. The colours are well chosen and soft. The fineness and good workmanship make this an attractive rug.

It is only recently that carpets have been manufactured in Qum and as there are no traditional designs, patterns have been borrowed from neighbouring regions. The pattern used here, one of the loveliest in Iran, can be found in sixteenth-century carpets from Isfahan.

The white ground of the field is completely covered with flowering arabesques, repeated in the border, which is also white and surrounded by two narrow bands on

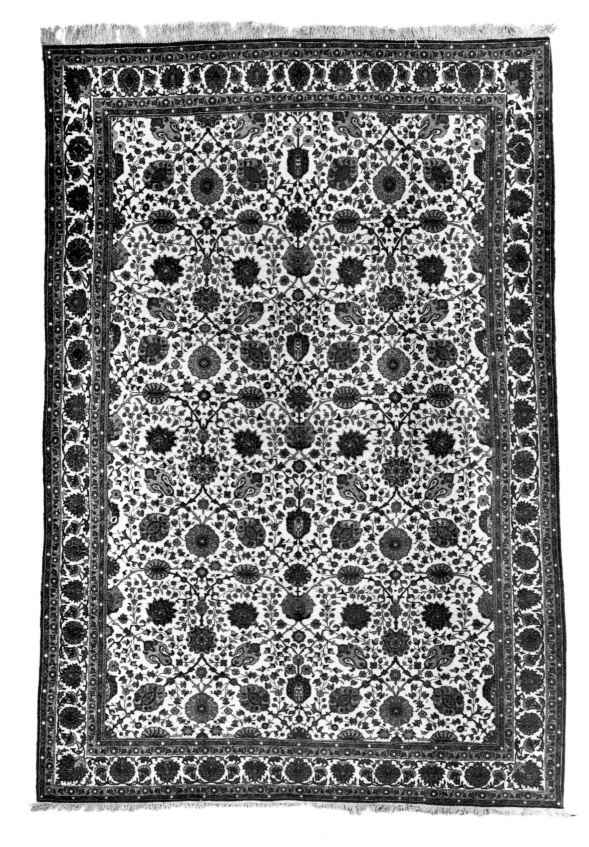

QUM

Origin: Iran
Dimensions: 80 × 53 inches (204 × 134 cm)
Persian knot: 422 per sq. inch (653,600 per sq. metre)
Warp of three strands of natural white silk
Double weft of natural silk
Pile of two strands of natural silk
12 colours

Qum, a holy town of Shiite Islam, is situated beside a basin filled in the centre by the Darya-i-Namak, a salt lake. Though its carpet industry has developed only recently the products are of good quality. The natural silk rugs which are at present manufactured there enjoy a high reputation among buyers.

The example reproduced is in very subdued tones, of a design which relates it to Bakhtiari rugs, with a field divided into twenty-eight compartments, each one representing a garden. The decoration is therefore exclusively floral, including that of the framework, which is composed of two slender bands encircling the principal border, on which vases alternate with rosettes.

The Rugs of Mashad, Khorasan and of the Turkoman Tribes

The town of Mashad ('Place of Martyrdom') is the capital of Khorasan and one of the two holy towns of Iran. Situated at an altitude of 3,180 feet, its population is normally 190,000, but it increases to 300,000 in times of pilgrimage, that is to say during the months of Moharram, Soffar and Ramadan. The area of the holy places cannot be visited by non-Moslems, regrettably since several of the mosques are extremely beautiful. The town was founded in 817, on the death of the Imam Reza, poisoned, so it is said, by the Caliph Mamun, the son and successor of the famous Harun al-Rashid, who is also buried in the town. The mausoleum of another great Persian, the poet Omar Khayyam, is located about two miles to the south-east of Mashad. At the beginning of the eighteenth century, under the reign of Nadir Shah, Mashad was the capital of the country. Even today the town is still unwesternized; to the visitor its charm lies in its typical Persian character. It is famous in Iran for the quality and excellence of its fruits.

One can assume that the carpets formerly called Khorasan were knotted at Mashad or in the immediate neighbourhood. Herat, which is now part of Afghanistan but which was until the middle of the nineteenth century the capital of Khorasan, gave its name to carpets of a typically Persian style: the province was then called Herat and the design of its 'Herati' rugs became widespread, not only in the region of Sultanabad (present-day Arak) but also as far as Tabriz.

The rugs of Mashad are made with both Persian and Turkish knots. This peculiarity originated at the beginning of the twentieth century, when the dealers of Tabriz installed factories at Mashad in which the Tur-

kish knot was used, while local preference was for the Persian knot. These new rugs were christened Turkbaff, which means 'Turkish knot'; they were of the best quality owing to a double warp which imparted a denser weave. In addition, rugs made with the Persian knot often had four warp threads per knot, as against two for the Turkish knot: their pile was thus less compact and became worn more quickly. Until the Second World War, the dyers of Mashad had the disastrous habit of dipping their wool in lime, in order to obtain better shades, but this process seriously impaired the strength of the wool. This practice, as well as the use of the knot on four warp threads, has however been abandoned, so that now one can have confidence in all carpets from Mashad, provided their weave is compact.

Rugs classified as Qain formerly came from the province of the same name, which included a large number of villages. Today, the village of Qain no longer produces rugs: they are knotted at Birjand, Bohluri, Dorukhsh, Ghaen, Keibar, Mud, Sarbished and Zirhuh.

In spite of their name, Baluchi rugs do not come from Baluchistan, a region straddling Iran and Pakistan, but from the neighbourhood of Mashad and from Herat in Afghanistan. Nowadays these rugs no longer merit their old title of 'nomad rugs', for the craftsmen who knot them are today sedentary and settled in the localities of Turbat-i-Haidari, Turbat-i-Shaikhjam, Turshiz, Sarakh, Nishapur, Seistan, and Firdaus. Turbat-i-Haidari, the former Bisheh, also known under the name of Zaveh, has been famous since the thirteenth century, with the foundation of a sect of Dervishes. The loveliest examples are made in the villages of Ali Mirzai and

Ghassemabad; Abravaneh, Bayk, Bezgue, Jahanbeigui, Hassanabad, Nhaf, Kolah-derazi, Maadan, Mussabad, Salar Khan, Chechmegol, and Turbat-i-Shaikhjam provide second-class examples, while the products of Firdaus are of poor quality.

Kurd rugs have a design and texture of Turkoman type and originate from Bajguiran, Bojnurd, Bavanluh, Emamgholi, Gantchan, Kalat, Mesh-Kanlu, Shirvan, Tukanluh and Zaferanluh.

Turkoman rugs are made in the region of Gombad-i-Qabus, a town of some 10,000 inhabitants, situated quite close to the Caspian Sea on the road linking Gurgan with Mashad, at an altitude of 250 feet. For a long time it was the capital of the province of Gurgan, under the name of Jorjan. Ibn Hauqal, who visited it in the tenth century, described it as a town surrounded by gardens and orchards. In the year 1006 (397 AH), the Ziyarid Qabus who ruled Tabaristan and Jorjan from 976 to 981 and from 998 to 1012, constructed the Mausoleum to which the town owes its present name. Its brick tower, 167 feet high, dominates the whole town. There is no staircase, exterior or interior, to give access to the upper part of the tomb.

Turkoman rugs are made in the town itself and in the neighbouring villages. Five types are known, which are the work of tribes who have kept their traditions intact: Aghkhal, Tekken, Yomud, Nokhalli and Gharawalli.

At Pahlavi Dej, 12 miles from Gurgan, there is a market every Thursday to which the Turkomans of the whole region bring their rugs and other products to sell to the dealers of Gurgan and elsewhere.

Many Turkomans established themselves in Mashad itself, after fleeing from Russia in 1917. They continue to knot their traditional rugs, particularly those in the Bukhara design. Recently, the Turkomans have been reproducing also the Zaher-Chahi pattern, originally from the region of Herat, but with modifications in colouring.

Although similar in style, Turkoman carpets can be distinguished from those from Russian Turkestan and Afghanistan by their texture, materials and colours.

MASHAD

Origin: Iran
Dimensions: 97 × 64 inches (246 × 163 cm)
Persian knot: 78 per sq. inch (120,000 per sq. metre)
Warp of three strands of beige cotton
Single weft of the same material
Pile of two strands of wool of medium fineness
10 colours: 2 reds, 2 blues, 2 greens, 1 white, 1 brown, 1 beige, 1 orange

The lion holding a sabre, his paw resting on a serpent, with the rising sun appearing over his back, is the motif of the arms of Iran, and appears here four times on the warm red ground of the field. The corners, in a rather lighter shade of red, have a jagged edge, similar to the central diamond-shaped motif. They are decorated with stylized leaves and flowers. There are numerous borders: the main one is patterned with a tracery of flowers and is flanked on the inside by five bands, two with a floral pattern and three plain, and on the outside by three bands of identical design separated by four plain bands.

This early piece owes its interest to its unusual design. The colours are warm and the wool has a natural sheen.

MASHAD

Origin: Iran
Dimensions: 76 × 49 inches (194 × 125 cm)
Turkish knot: 109 per sq. inch (168,000 per sq. metre)
Warp of two strands of four-ply undyed cotton
Double weft of cotton: one fine brown thread and one thick undyed thread
Pile of two strands of wool of medium fineness
12 colours: 2 reds, 3 blues, 2 greens, 1 orange, 1 brown, 1 beige 1 white, 1 grey

small one of red. The flowered arabesques of the principal border are accentuated by two small floral bands of white ground.

The rather dark key of the colours is typical of Mashad rugs.

As this rug employs the Turkish knot, it could be called Turkbaff-Mashad.

Flowers and leaves form harmonious curves on the blue ground of the corners and the claret-red field. The colours are cleverly mixed, with some flower petals containing four shades. In the centre, the two superimposed rosettes are patterned with big flowers. The large one has a ground-colour of dark blue and the

MASHAD

Origin: Iran
Dimensions: 72 × 51 inches (183 × 130 cm)
Persian knot: 155 per sq. inch (240,000 per sq. metre)
Warp of four strands of undyed cotton
Single weft of red cotton
Pile of two strands of fine, soft wool
12 colours: 1 red, 3 blues, 2 greens, 1 coral, 1 grey, 1 white, 2 browns, 1 orange

The soft, warm red of the field is covered with palmettes, leaves, daisies and carnations. On the main border, leaves and flowers form arabesques upon a dark-blue ground. Two small bands of white ground frame it.

This is an early example of fine quality, which owes its attractive appearance to its extremely soft wool and mellowed colours.

MUD

BALUCHI

Origin: Iran, Mashad region
Dimensions: 85 × 54 inches (215 × 136 cm)
Persian knot: 185 per sq. inch (286,000 per sq. metre)
Warp of seven strands of undyed cotton
Double weft: one of two strands of fine grey cotton, the other of four strands of thick grey cotton
Pile of two strands of rather fine wool, chemically washed
12 colours: 2 reds, 1 pink, 1 orange, 1 black, 2 blues, 2 browns, 1 green, 1 white, 1 yellow

This is a classic example of the Mashad type, often incorrectly called Meshed (after the English pronunciation). In the centre is a large star, richly decorated with flowers, towards which converge all the curved lines which link the flowers and arabesques of the field. The corners are elegantly cut out and trimmed with flower-surrounded motifs on a red ground.

Two bands of stylized leaves and flowers frame the main border of dark-blue flower-patterned ground with a floral pattern. The rather sombre tonality is typical of this type of rug. The harmonious design is the work of an artist who is master of his craft.

Origin: Iran, Mashad region
Dimensions: 67 × 36 inches (171 × 92 cm)
Persian knot: 67 per sq. inch (104,000 per sq. metre)
Warp of five strands of white cotton
Double weft of grey cotton
Pile of two strands of wool of medium fineness
5 colours: 2 reds, 1 black, 1 violet, 1 white

The simple but charming decoration of this Baluchi rug comprises a field completely covered with a classical design of diagonal stripes, in a restrained number of colours.

A small band bearing the running-dog motif on a white ground encircles the field. The main border, which has a lozenge pattern, is enclosed by two bands decorated with trapezia, and a white zigzag line decorates the edge.

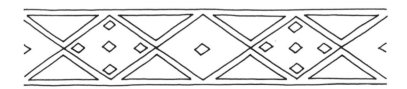

BALUCHI

Origin: Iran, Mashad region, Turbat-i-Haidari
Dimensions: 64 × 34 inches (164 × 85 cm)
Persian knot: 148 per sq. inch (230,000 per sq. metre)
Warp of two strands of wool
Double weft of natural brown goat's hair
Pile of two strands of rather fine wool, with natural sheen
5 colours

Turbat-i-Haidari is a town of some 20,000 inhabitants, situated at an altitude of 4,300 feet. The best Baluchi carpets are made in the surrounding villages, like this example. Its design is extremely simple as it has very few colours, which is rare in Iran where some carpets have as many as fourteen colours.

The field is covered by two rows of large stylized flowers in light colours which alternate with the same, more subdued, motifs in red. The main border, which is very broad, includes large floral motifs linked by bands of double latch-hooks. Between the field and the border is a double serrated line with, outside it, a small zigzag border.

BALUCHI

BALUCHI

Origin: Iran, Turbat-i-Haidari
Dimensions: 63 × 36 inches (160 × 91 cm)
Turkish knot: 112 per sq. inch (173,900 per sq. metre)
Warp of two strands of natural white wool
Double weft of brown wool
Pile of single spun wool, with natural sheen
7 colours: 3 reds, 1 orange, 1 white, 1 blue, 1 black

The best quality Baluchi rugs are made at Ali Mirzai and Ghassemabad. The rug shown comes from this region, and is of early manufacture. Stylized roses dominate the bluish-black ground of the field, but one can also find fir-cones and birds. The border consists of seven bands, including two with double latch-hooks and a central band of crosses alternating with stylized trees.

Origin: Iran
Dimensions: 71 × 31 inches (180 × 80 cm)
Persian knot: border only, 71 per sq. inch (110,000 per sq. metre)
Warp of two strands of natural beige wool
Single weft of two strands of natural wool, in black in the knotted area
7 colours: 2 reds, 1 blue, 1 beige, 1 yellow, 1 white, 1 green

This is a rather interesting piece, for while the border is knotted in the traditional manner, the centre of the rug is in the Kilim technique, without pile, with stitching on the triangles which project on to the field. These have little tufts of wool at each tip. There is also a band of Kilim weaving at both ends of the rug. The ground is beige-brown.

This carpet is the work of an imaginative craftsman, who has deliberately avoided the usual.

KURD

KACHLI-TURKOMAN

Origin: Iran, Mashad region
Dimensions: 105 × 60 inches (267 × 153 cm)
Turkish knots: 32 per sq. inch (49,400 per sq. metre)
Warp of two strands of natural beige wool
Single weft of red wool
Pile of wool of medium thickness, chemically washed
8 colours: 2 reds, 2 blues, 1 yellow, 1 brown, 1 white, 1 green

In make-up Kurd rugs are related to the rugs of Luristan or to those of the Kurds of Turkey; the warp and weft threads are of wool, with a fairly deep pile and a rather coarse weave. In decoration, however, they show the influence of Turkoman or Afghan motifs.

In the example reproduced, the two octagons at the ends are typically Afghan, while the two large central motifs, also octagonal, are in Persian style. In the centre of the larger one a star of David stands out conspicuously. The other motifs which adorn the reddish-brown ground of the field particularly include rectangles framed with latch-hooks, but there are also some slightly distorted Afghan motifs. An irregular zigzag line edges the field, followed by a band of multicoloured triangles. The decoration of the main border consists of interlinked lozenges on a white ground. The outer band is of interlinked squares divided into quarters (two white and two red) on a yellow ground.

This carpet, which perhaps lacks uniformity in the design, is typical of the Kurd type.

Origin: Iran, Gonbad-i-Qabus
Dimensions: 55 × 39 inches (140 × 98 cm)
Persian knot: 167 per sq. inch (258,400 per sq. metre)
Warp of two strands of undyed goat's hair
Single weft of the same material
Pile of two strands of rather fine wool
7 colours: 2 reds, 1 black, 1 white, 1 orange, 1 blue, 1 green

Turkoman rugs are the work of tribes living in that region of Iran which borders on Russian Turkestan, hence a certain similarity in design and colouring in these two groups.

The carpet reproduced, with no *mihrab,* is a modern variation of the Kachli. The field is divided into four rectangles covered with *sarghola* motifs, a kind of jagged hexagon patterned with birds' feet.

The bands which divide the field bear jagged latch-hooks (of Z-shape on the longitudinal band) called *sarchian.*

The main border is of *ghiri* pattern, with delicately outlined hexagons, which look like insects. This is framed by two narrow bands trimmed with small multicoloured bars.

At the end with the longest fringe, one can see a little band of stars *(chuchehboran),* like the beaks of tiny birds.

The predominant white colour is a modern variation of this type of rug, red being the traditional Turkoman preference.

Turkestan

Former Russian Turkestan is today divided into five republics of the USSR: Turkmenistan, Uzbekistan, Tadzhikistan, Kirghizia and Kazakhstan. There is also Chinese Turkestan (Sin-Kiang) and Afghan Turkestan.

Turkestan covers an area of 74,000 square miles with approximately 14 million inhabitants, principally Turkomans, Uzbeks and Kazaks. A large part of the country is composed of semi-desert steppes, where sheep are bred to produce astrakhan fur or wool for rugs. The production of cotton is also important.

Throughout its history, Turkestan has seen a succession of invading races: Iranians, Indo-Scythians from Bactria, Epthalite Huns, Chinese. The Uygurs occupied the country in the ninth century and imposed their civilization and Turkish dialect, followed in the twelfth and thirteenth centuries by the Mongols. In 1853, the Russians subdued the Kazaks and in 1868 extended their protectorate over Bukhara. After the revolt of the Turkish population between 1915 and 1917, the Soviets regrouped the inhabitants by race and thus created the five present autonomous republics.

The carpets of Turkestan have the reputation of being among the best and most beautiful in the East, and most collectors hope to possess an example at some time or other. The best known groups are the Beshir, Bukhara, Kerki (also called Russian Afghan), Kizyl Ayak, Pendeh and Yomud rugs.

Bukharas are made in Turkmenia in the following regions: Mary, Bakharden, Geok Teppe, Kizyl Ayak and Tedzhen.

Pendeh rugs are so called from the name of the oasis situated in the region of Jolostan and Takhta-Bazar, to the south-east of Turkmenia. The Kizyl Ayak derives its name from the village of the same name, in the Amu Dar'ya region, 25 miles from the town of Kerki, which has also given its name to a type of carpet. Yomud rugs are produced in the regions of Gassan Kuli and Tachauz.

BESHIR

Origin: USSR, Republic of Turkmenia
Dimensions: 54 × 64 inches (264 × 162 cm)
Persian knot: 114 per sq. inch (176,000 per sq. metre)
Warp of two strands of natural beige wool
Double weft of grey goat's hair
Pile of two strands of wool of medium thickness, chemically treated to make it glossy and to tone down the brightness of the colours
6 colours

Beshir rugs can be distinguished from other Turkoman rugs by the attempt to balance the ground and the pattern harmoniously while retaining, however, a predominance of the latter.

Beshir rugs, from the village of the same name situated in the Amu Dar'ya region, follow one of three designs: the first is composed of medallions varying from one to five, the second is called *guerat* with a field covered with stylized plants, and the third, called *ilan* is reproduced here. The field is filled with coiled curvilinear motifs like formalized serpents.

On the main border, medallions with a central flower alternate with cypress trees. The latter, of conventional appearance on the two bands at the ends, take on the form of a crook at the sides.

BUKHARA

Origin: Russian Turkestan
Dimensions: 115 × 85 inches (292 × 216 cm)
Persian knot: 222 per sq. inch (344,000 per sq. metre)
Warp of two strands of fine natural beige wool
Single weft of two strands of fine natural brown wool
Pile of two strands of fine wool, chemically washed and faded
8 colours

Bukhara, a town in Uzbekistan (USSR) with a population of approximately 70,000, has had a particularly glorious past. In the seventh century, it was already a famous cultural centre. In the tenth century, it fell under Turkish domination, then in the fifteenth century was taken by the Mongols. After many vicissitudes, it became Russian in 1868.

The town has always had a caravan market for carpets, astrakhan skins and cotton. Like Shiraz in Iran, Bukhara has given its name to a rug, without being the centre of its production. The rugs of this region are more properly called Tekin, a name which is a reminder that their weavers are of the Turkoman race.

Bukhara rugs have been copied very often in other regions, but their beauty has never been equalled. The classic design has remained unaltered. Of recent years the output has dropped; particularly uncommon today are carpets about six feet by nine feet.

In the example reproduced opposite, we rediscover the classical and especially typical Turkoman carpet, in a design which has not changed for centuries. On a ground of old rose colour octagons of consistently rectilinear shape are repeated. One would search in vain for a curved line.

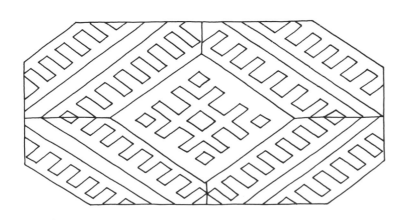

BUKHARA

Origin: USSR, Republic of Turkmenia
Dimensions: 53 × 32 inches (135 × 81 cm)
Persian knot: 184 per sq. inch (284,000 per sq. metre)
Warp of two strands of natural goat's hair, partly grey, partly white
Double weft of two strands of pink goat's hair
Pile of two strands of fine wool, in pastel shades
7 colours: 2 reds, 1 blue, 1 brownish-black, 1 brown, 1 white, 1 yellow

This Bukhara or 'Tekin' is of the double weft type; at first sight its weave appears no less fine than that of the usual Bukhara with the single weft. In fact, the reverse side shows a less compact surface, since half of the knot cannot be seen. One becomes aware of its extreme fineness when checking the number of knots.

The narrowness of the field allows for a pattern of only two rows of octagons, of the classical type known as *tekke-gul*, with birds' feet and a second octagon inside. The motifs between the octagons, called *chemcheh-gul*, are patterned with crosses and ram's horns at the ends. The two lateral borders, with multiple frames, are almost twice the width of the field. Of the seven bands, the one running alongside the field has octagons, three have tapering motifs, one has rosettes, the main border bears small lozenges like those in the octagons on the field and the last one has diagonal stripes. Each end of the rug has another border patterned with large lozenge shapes with serrated edges, which are called *ener-dychi*. Note that there are three of these motifs on one side, and three and a half on the other. A plain band of Kilim-weaving separates this border from the fringe.

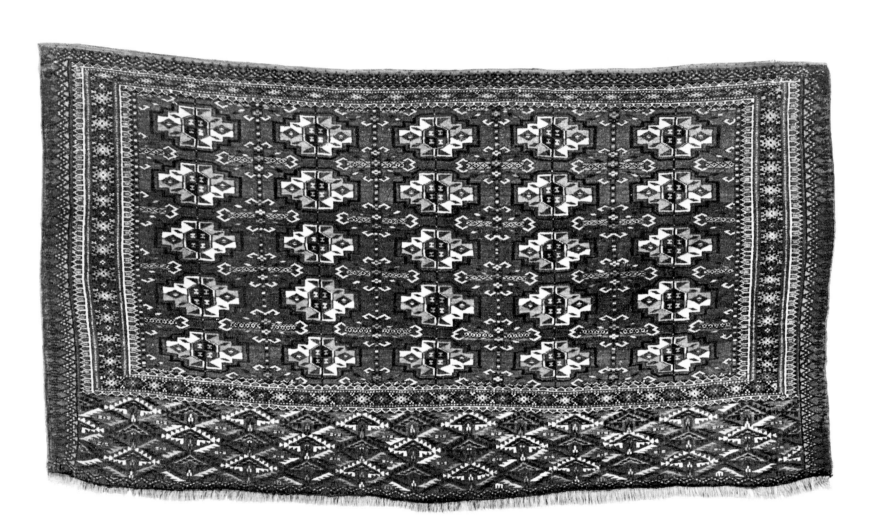

BUKHARA CHUVAL

Origin: USSR, Republic of Turkmenia
Dimensions: 55 × 27 inches (127 × 68 cm)
Persian knot: 222 per sq. inch (344,000 per sq. metre)
Warp of two strands of natural white goat's hair
Single weft of the same material
Pile of two strands of fine wool, lustreless, but in very warm tones
6 colours: 2 reds (one containing several shades), 1 blue,
1 brown, 1 white, 1 yellow

The octagons of this small-sized piece have a simpler pattern than those on larger examples. This pattern is called 'three leaves'. Between the octagons, one finds the *chucheh-gul*, a cruciform shape with sheep's hooves.

The border surrounding the field bears octagonal motifs with latch-hooks and the skirt at one end has crenelated motifs.

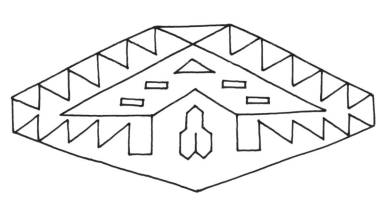 

The term *Chuval* denotes a particular form of rug in which the design runs across the width and not lengthwise, as is usually the case. The two ends do not have an identical pattern and the rug was originally woven in the form of a bag. A Kilim is attached to the back of the rug.

The *Chuval* was formerly knotted by young girls of marriageable age in order to prove their skill. This is why one finds some extremely fine examples among this type.

BUKHARA JOLLAR

Origin: USSR, Turkmenistan
Dimensions: 33 × 9 inches (83 × 25 cm)
Persian knot: 342 per sq. inch (528,000 per sq. metre)
Warp of two strands of fine goat's hair, of natural colour
Long separate wool fringes
Single weft of the same material
Pile of two strands of very fine wool, of soft tones
8 colours: 3 reds, 1 brown, 1 white, 1 black, 1 yellow, 1 dark blue

The *jollar* is a narrow band which served to adorn the camel of the bride, during the marriage procession. These strips are usually very finely woven, and the example reproduced is no exception.

The decoration of the field includes jagged hexagons and rectangles bearing a ram's horn or a latch-hook.

The border has wavy lines and, at the sides, a row of small lozenges. Ram's horns appear again at the outer edge of the upper border, and below, the same jagged motifs as used on Kachli-Bukharas.

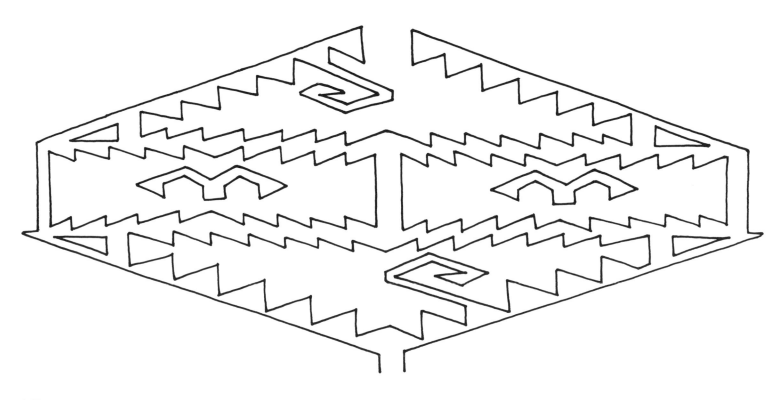

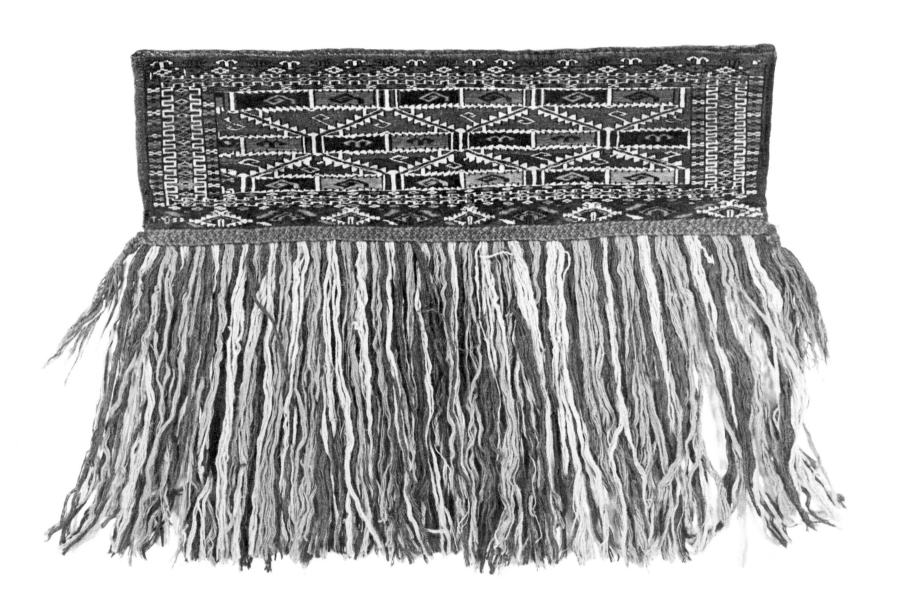

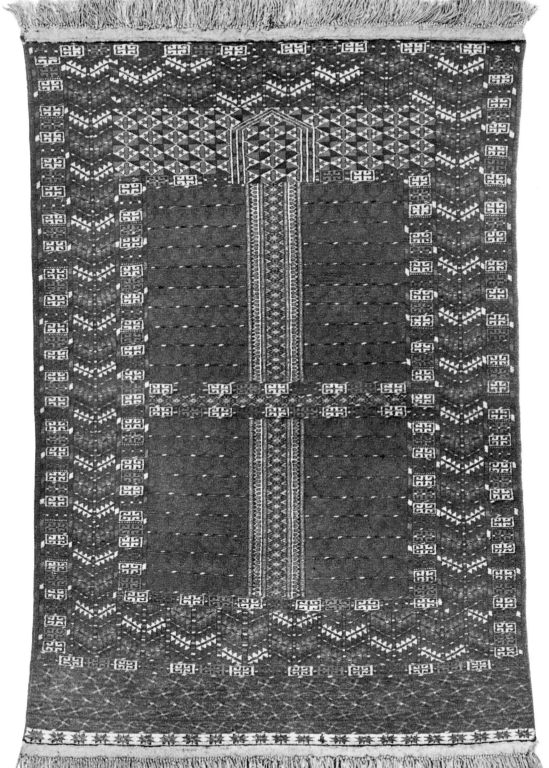

KACHLI-BUKHARA

Origin: USSR, Republic of Turkmenia
Dimensions: 57 × 39 inches (145 × 98 cm)
Persian knot: 191 per sq. inch (295,200 per sq. metre)
Warp of two strands of natural wool
Single weft of two strands of black goat's hair
Pile of two strands of fine wool, chemically washed
8 colours: 2 reds, 1 blue, 1 beige, 1 white, 1 black, 1 green,
1 orange

Kachli means 'Cross' and this design was originally reserved for prayer rugs; it is to be found among the Yomud, Iranian Turkoman and Afghan peoples. The Russians call it Tekke Ensi, for their name for a Bukhara is a Tekke or Tekin, which are at any rate the more correct names. The Kachli-Bukhara comes from the same regions as the octagon-patterned type: Mary, Bakharden, Geok Teppe, Kizyl Ayak and Tedzhen.

It differs in format from other prayer rugs, whether Turkish, Persian or Afghan. Those are rather elongated in form ranging from approximately 40 to 47 inches in width by 70 to 78 inches in length, while this kind does not exceed 63 inches in length, with a width between 37 and 47 inches, which results in an almost square look.

The field, with the usual tulip-covered red ground, is divided into quarters by two perpendicular bands: the transversal one decorated with paired latch-hooks and flowers, the other with formalized flowers. The *mihrab* is barely visible, lost among a series of diamond-shaped decorative motifs. The wide border is composed of two bands which repeat the pattern of pairs of latch-hooks, and a central band with the 'fishbone' pattern.

KERKI

Origin: USSR, Turkmenia
Dimensions: 80 × 47 inches (203 × 119 cm)
Persian knot: 92 per sq. inch (141,900 per sq. metre)
Warp of two strands of natural white goat's hair
Double weft of natural brown goat's hair
Pile of two strands of wool of medium thickness
7 colours: 2 reds, 2 browns, 1 white, 1 blue, 1 yellow

Kerki rugs are not made in the town of the same name, but in the Amu Dar'ya region. The octagons of this rug resemble slightly those on Bukharas, but the ornamentation, stylized trees and animals, is typically Kerki.

The principal border and its flowering garlands are set off on either side by two similar bands with a lozenge pattern. On the outer edge, there are three more small bands. This early example radiates an impression of absolute harmony because of the softness of its slightly purplish-red tones.

The modern Kerki, which resembles Afghan rugs with plainer borders, usually has bright colours, often on a reddish-orange ground.

PENDEH CHUVAL

YOMUD CHUVAL

Origin: USSR, Republic of Turkmenia
Dimensions: 60 × 26 inches (152 × 67 cm)
Persian knot: 267 per sq. inch (412,800 per sq. metre)
Warp of two strands of natural white goat's hair
Double weft of natural brown goat's hair
Pile of two strands of fine wool, in beautiful warm shades
8 colours: 3 reds, 2 blues, 1 white, 1 brown, 1 green

Origin: USSR, Republic of Turkmenia
Dimensions: 50 × 30 inches (127 × 75 cm)
Turkish knot: 123 per sq. inch (190,400 per sq. metre)
Warp of two strands of natural grey goat's hair
Double weft of natural brown goat's hair
Pile of two strands of fine wool, chemically washed
10 colours: 1 red, 1 pink, 1 white, 1 mauve, 1 black, 2 blues, 2 greens, 1 brown

This carpet derives its name from the Pendeh oasis which is situated in the region of Jolostan and Takhta-Bazar in south-eastern Turkmenia. Like the Bukharas, it has retained its traditional decorative motifs.

The field is covered by six large octagons called *salor-gul* which frame a pattern of twin horns called *kochak* or *buinuze*.

The border is of the multiple frame type with large rosettes on the main band. The large skirt at one end is thickly patterned with several rows of lozenges.

The Yomud Turkomans give a distinctive appearance to their Chuval rugs, three sides bearing a trimming of tassels, with the fourth of triangular form. These pieces were intended to serve as saddle covers.

The design of jagged diamond shapes on the field is called *achiq*. This is repeated on the principal border, which is enclosed on three sides by two narrow floral bands. The arrow-head motif which alternates with the *achiq* pattern is currently used in North Africa. It represents the bustard, the symbol of protection.

YOMUD

Origin: USSR, Republic of Turkmenia
Dimensions: 81 × 46 inches (203 × 116 cm)
Turkish knot: 149 per sq. inch (230,400 per sq. metre)
Warp of eight strands of fine undyed cotton
Single weft of natural beige wool
Pile of two strands of fairly fine wool
7 colours: 1 red, 1 purplish-brown, 1 green, 1 blue, 1 white,
1 orange, 1 dark brown

Yomuds are principally made in Turkmenia in the regions of Gassan Kuli and Tachauz.

This design, with elongated diamond-shaped motifs trimmed with stylized anchors, is called *kapseh-gul*. Two small bands of trapezia surround the main border of pairs of formalized birds on a spotted ground.

The rug is terminated at both ends by a wide band of ornaments called *kabyrga*.

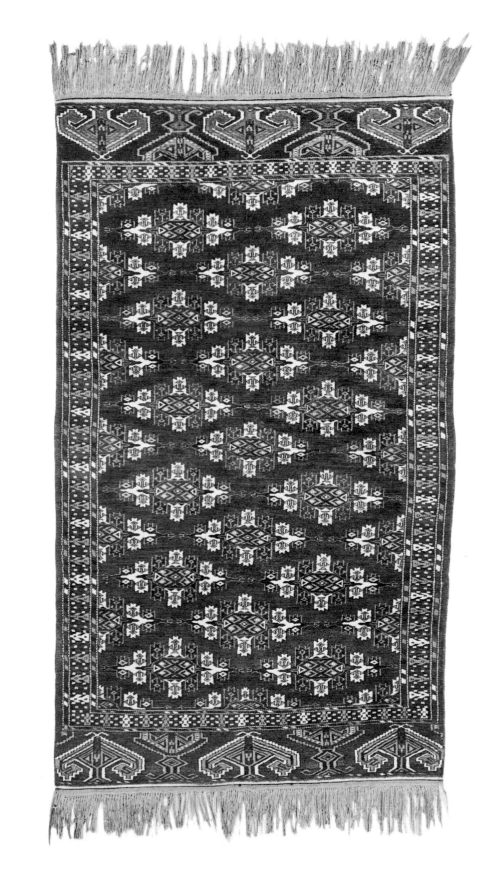

Afghanistan

This constitutional kingdom, which has common frontiers with Iran, the USSR and Pakistan produces a very well-known rug, with a pattern of octagons on a red ground. Approximately 14,000,000 inhabitants are distributed over a territory of 250,000 square miles; they speak Persian and Pushtoo and, like the Iranians, belong to the Shiite branch of the Moslem religion.

Afghanistan has known an eventful past. We know that Alexander the Great led an expedition there. Converted to Islam since the ninth century, the country was divided by quarrels of feudal dynasties. It had often to fight for its independence, especially against Persia. In the eighteenth century, the Iranian province of Khorasan was Afghan. After lengthy resistance, it became an English protectorate for some years (1907 to 1921). Since that date, it has been independent.

Afghan rugs are the work of Turkomans living in the north of the country, in the region of Maymana and at Daulatabad, Aktsha, Mazar-i-Sharif and Kunduz. Their resemblance to Turkoman rugs from the USSR and Iran is great; however Afghan rugs are usually less fine than those of the other two provenances. They have won over a considerable clientele in the West, owing to the simplicity of their style and colouring.

In the region of Herat, which was Iranian until 1850, rugs of the Baluchistan type are made, but of a different construction and design. In the trade, to distinguish the Afghan Baluchi from the Iranian, one often calls the first by the name Herati Baluchi. Another very delicate kind, with the Zaher-Chahi pattern, is the work of the Tekke tribes of the region of Herat. Among the Turkoman tribes settled in Afghanistan, we again find the names of Kizyl-Ayak, Beshiri, Tekke, as well as the Ersari. Baluchi rugs are knotted by the Dokhtar-i-Ghazi-Baluchi, who live in the north of Herat.

The Turkish knot is as common in Afghan rugs as the Persian knot. The best known production centres are Daulatabad (with a good quality rug of the same name), Maymana (where the Mauri rugs are made, also of high quality), then Andhkui, Aktsha, Mazar-i-Sharif, Kunduz (which produce rugs for everyday use), and finally Karkin whose rugs are of inferior quality.

AFGHAN

Origin: *Afghanistan*
Dimensions: *57 × 46 inches (145 × 118 cm)*
Persian knot: *107 per sq. inch (165,600 per sq. metre)*
Warp of *two strands of natural white goat's hair*
Double weft of *natural grey goat's hair*
Pile of *two strands of rather fine wool, with natural sheen*
8 colours: 3 reds, 2 blues, 1 brown, 1 white, 1 yellow

It is difficult, if not impossible, to locate exactly the provenance of a Pendeh rug like this one, for the Turkoman Kizyl-Ayak tribes who knot them are scattered in diverse regions of Afghanistan, at Andkhui, Aktsha, and Mazar-i-Sharif. They resemble those of the same name made in the USSR.

The octagonal motifs which decorate the field are called *mar gul*. The main ornamentation of this piece is provided by its numerous borders, as is usual on Turkoman rugs; note the principal band with tulips, typically Afghan. Of the remaining nine, the one surrounding the field is the same basic type as the outer one, but the small diamond shapes on each tip are replaced on the latter by double latch-hooks.

The ground of the rug is a purplish-red of very warm tone, which imparts a restful tranquillity.

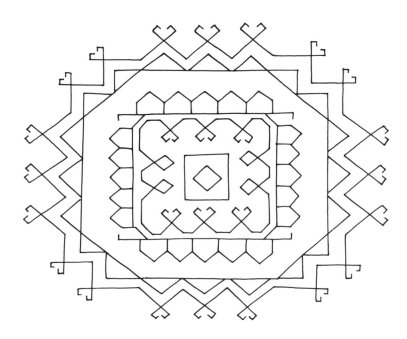

AFGHAN

Origin: *Afghanistan, Aktsha region*
Dimensions: *123 × 93 inches (313 × 236 cm)*
Persian knot: *74 per sq. inch (114,000 per sq. metre)*
Warp of two strands of brown goat's hair
Double weft of the same material
Pile of two strands of rather fine wool
8 colours

The whole field of the piece is decorated with *guls* of the Ghazan tribe, who live in the Aktsha region. These are octagons of large size, each patterned with four sets of three stems sprouting three leaves, with fairly wide borders. Between these octagons are diamond-shaped motifs with eight flowers.

The principal border consists of lozenges with inscribed crosses and is framed by two narrow bands decorated with formalized tulips.

AFGHAN

Origin: Afghanistan, Daulatabad region
Dimensions: 81 × 46 inches (205 × 123 cm)
Persian knot: 86 per sq. inch (133,300 per sq. metre)
Warp of two strands of brown goat's hair
Identical double weft
Pile of two strands of wool of medium thickness, chemically washed
5 colours: 2 reds, 1 blue, 1 black, 1 white

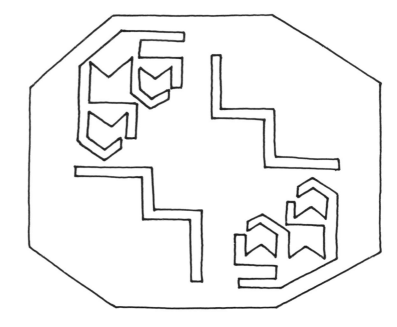

Although the number of colours in this example are rather limited, the glowing red gives an impression of a rich tonality.

The design is of Bukhara type: three rows of octagons with bird's feet motifs covering the red ground of the field.

The seven bands of the border (three narrow and four wide) are also decorated with Turkoman motifs: spidery stars, geometric notched lozenges and arabesques.

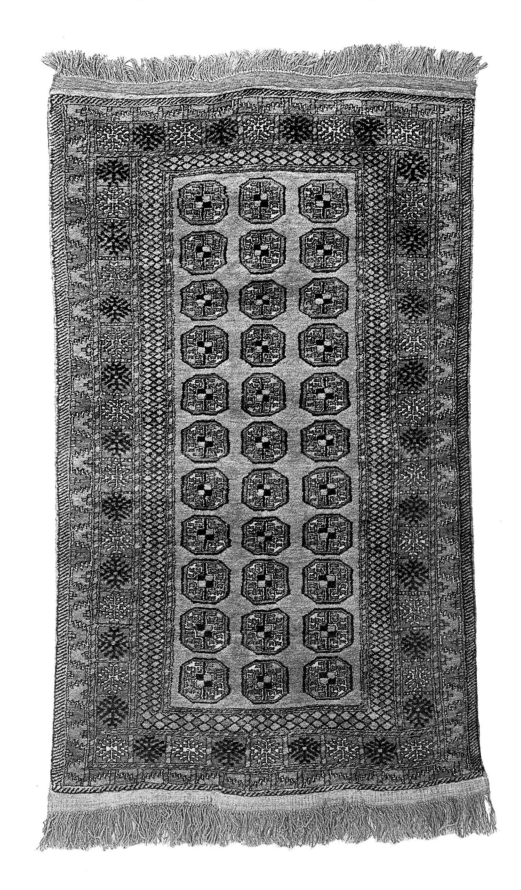

AFGHAN

Origin: Afghanistan
Dimensions: 76 × 51 inches (194 × 130 cm)
Persian knot: 59 per sq. inch (91,000 per sq. metre)
Warp of two strands of undyed goat's hair
Double weft of brown goat's hair
Pile of two strands of wool of medium thickness, chemically washed
7 colours: 3 reds, 1 yellow, 1 white, 1 blue, 1 black

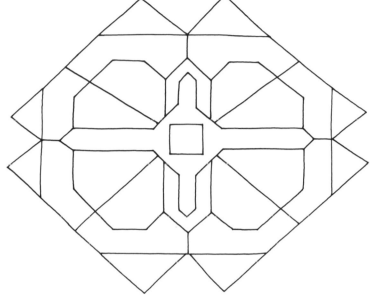

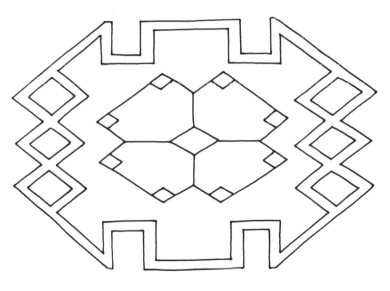

The design of this rug, the work of the Beshiri tribes, differs slightly from that of the classical Afghan with octagons. Here the field is filled with lozenges, alternating with motifs framed partly in bright yellow.

On either side of the main border of diamonds and leaves is a band of small flowers and two others with S- or Z-shaped motifs.

BESHIR CHUVAL

Origin: Afghanistan
Dimensions: 39 × 63 inches (100 × 159 cm)
Persian knot: 94 per sq. inch (145,200 per sq. metre)
Warp of two strands of natural brown goat's hair
Single weft of the same material
Pile of two strands of wool of medium thickness, with natural sheen
6 colours: 2 reds, 1 blue, 1 black, 1 yellow, 1 white

The Beshiri tribes live at Andkhui, Shurtepa, Kunduz and Herat. The *chuval* was originally intended, like the *jollar*, to adorn the camel of the bride during the marriage procession.

Three octagons patterned with ram's horns occupy the centre but the jagged white motif inside them is the most striking. At each side of the octagons are four zig-zag bands. Directly round the field is a band of rather curious motifs, which precedes another wider one at one side with ram's horns, and a narrow band on the other side.

The general colour key is of a very warm, restful and attractive red.

ZAHER-CHAHI

Origin: Afghanistan, Herat region
Dimensions: 62 × 43 inches (157 × 110 cm)
Persian knot: 266 per sq. inch (412,800 per sq. metre)
Warp of two strands of natural wool
Single weft of natural wool
Pile of two strands of fine wool
9 colours: 2 reds, 2 blues, 1 white, 1 beige, 1 orange, 1 black, 1 grey

The border with multiple frames, a decorative method dear to the Turkomans, includes no less than twelve very fine bands. These constitute the beauty of this piece, which blends with any setting, because of its well-balanced colouring.

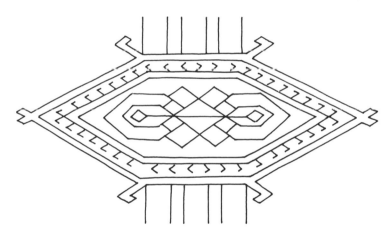

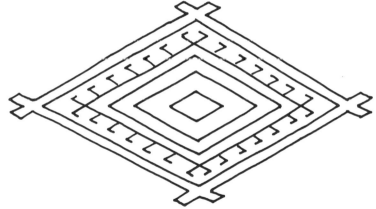

Zaher-Chahi rugs, called after the Afghan ruler Zaher-Chahi who inspired the Akhal Tekkes with this design, are the finest in Afghanistan.

This example, although devoid of the traditional octagons of the Afghan or Bukhara, is quite within the Turkoman style. Furthermore, the Iranian Turkomans use this same design.

Two rows of hexagons alternating with complete lozenges, in the centre, and with half-lozenges, at the edges, cover the whole field.

Pakistan

An independent country since 1947, Pakistan is divided into two parts, West and East Pakistan, 1,056 miles apart. This is the most populous Moslem country in the world, with a population over 100,000,000.

The carpet manufacture centres are all situated in West Pakistan, in the Lahore and Karachi regions. The production is only a few years old but is of fairly fine quality. The most widespread design is the Bukhara; one does also see other patterns, but much more rarely, often of Persian provenance. The wool used comes from Kashmir or is imported from Australia or New Zealand.

PAKISTANI BUKHARA

Origin: Karachi, Pakistan
Dimensions: 140 × 111 inches (355 × 282 cm)
Persian knot: 154 per sq. inch (237,600 per sq. metre)
Warp of four strands of natural white wool
Single weft of the same material
Pile of two strands of wool of medium fineness, chemically washed
6 colours: 2 reds, 2 blues, 1 black, 1 white

Since the end of the Second World War, a prosperous production of knotted carpets has developed in Karachi, which complements the older manufacture of Lahore.

This rug is the successful replica of a Bukhara, thicker than the original. The field is covered with five rows of octagons, *tekke-gul*, and crosses with ram's horns at the ends, called *chemcheh-gul*. In the thirteen borders are octagonal motifs, ram's horns and crenelated ornaments. The zigzag motifs *(ener dychi)* at the ends and the bands of diamonds complete the rich ornamentation of this refreshingly harmonious piece.

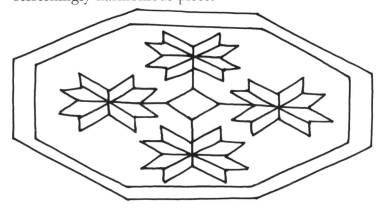

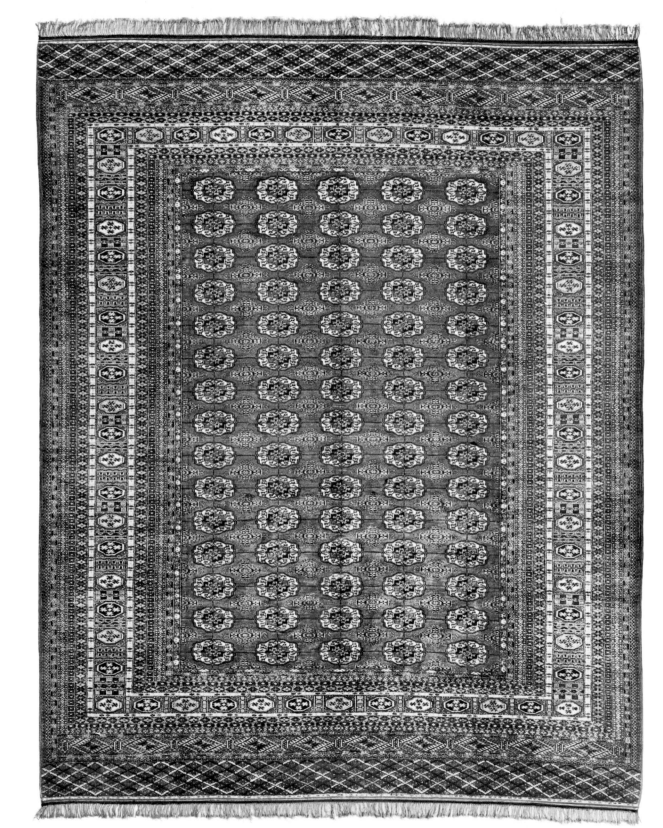

India

The introduction of the knotted carpet into India dates back to the reign of Akbar, who, in the second half of the sixteenth century, brought Persian rugs and their weavers to Agra. The famous Indo-Persian rugs date from this period, which equal in beauty the Persian models, which they copied unslavishly.

As the production developed, a characteristic style was fashioned, of clearly Indian character; the artisans were inspired by local flora, quite different from that of Iran. Until 1850, the quality of Indian carpets was excellent. Unfortunately, from 1860, it started to deteriorate as a result of the government decision to have rugs made by prisoners throughout the country, as much to occupy them as to compensate partly for the costs of their incarceration. The prison governors and warders were not qualified to direct such craft workshops, and the result was disastrous: this output was of such inferior quality that it could only be disposed of with great difficulty, and at derisory prices.

The modern production of India suffers still from this bad reputation. A conscientious dealer sometimes hesitates to include Indian rugs in his selection, although at the present time there are number of carpets of good quality.

Another handicap of the modern Indian carpet is its lack of a distinctive style. Carpets with truly indigenous decoration are rare while those following Persian and Chinese designs are common. The Kashmir workshops use native wool to make very delicate rugs which follow Persian or Turkoman patterns. Of the other centres the best known are Agra, Amritsar, Bhadohi, Jaipur, Mirzapur, Bangalore, and Madras.

AGRA

Origin: India
Dimensions: 84 × 48 inches (213 × 122 cm)
Persian knot: 98 per sq. inch (152,000 per sq. metre)
Warp of eight strands of undyed cotton
Double weft of red cotton
Pile of two strands of wool of medium thickness, chemically washed
12 colours: 2 reds, 3 blues, 2 browns, 1 yellow, 1 white, 1 orange, 2 greens

This design is reminiscent of the Kashgai rugs of Iran but the tones are softer. Three large lozenges, (the outer two of white ground, and the central one with sky-blue ground), interlinked by smaller lozenges, are arranged on a dark-blue field, covered with dense rows of stylized flowers. The border framing the field consists of no less than eight bands.

It is regrettable that this high quality rug, with the texture of an early Agra, in beautiful soft colours, is devoid of any individual character.

KASHMIR

Origin: India
Dimensions: 71 × 48 inches (181 × 123 cm)
Persian knot: 223 per sq. inch (345,600 per sq. metre)
Warp of five strands of undyed cotton
Double weft of undyed cotton
Pile of two strands of fine wool, chemically washed and faded
12 colours

The design and colouring of this example remind one of the early Agra carpets, greatly admired by collectors. On the field strewn with flowers and animals is a central motif of rounded form decorated with plant-form arabesques and surrounded by a circle of animals and flowers. The floral motifs appear again on the gold ground of the corners.

The red of the main border is that found on early rugs. The decoration of this border, and that of the two narrow surrounding bands of white, is floral.

Although antique in appearance, this carpet is of recent manufacture.

KASHMIR

Origin: India
Dimensions: 84 × 54 inches (213 × 138 cm)
Persian knot: 151 per sq. inch (234,000 per sq. metre)
Warp of sixteen strands of fine undyed cotton
Single weft of four strands of undyed cotton
Pile of one strand of rather fine wool, chemically washed
7 colours: 2 reds, 2 blues, 1 white, 1 yellow, 1 green

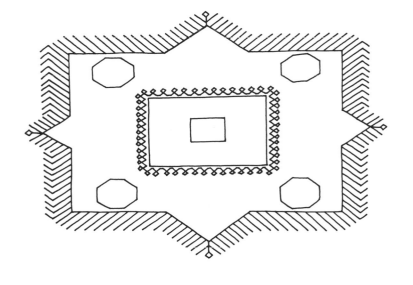

This is a fairly finely knotted rug, but the design in the Caucasian manner has been treated in too regular a fashion. The three medallions of blue ground which cover the field are filled with various motifs so thickly arranged that they almost touch each other. The rather strange latch-hook framework of the medallions throws them into relief. The remainder of the red ground of the field is patterned with flowers and double latch-hooks.

The principal border is decorated with large motifs of Turkoman style, and is surrounded by two narrow floral bands.

This is a rather attractive example, in spite of its lack of unity, because of the softness of the colours. It was produced in a region lacking in tradition, whose weavers content themselves with adopting and modifying foreign motifs.

EMBROIDERED RUG

KILIM

Origin: India
Dimensions: 109 × 55 inches (278 × 139 cm)
Yarn of two strands of wool
14 colours: 3 pinks, 2 blues, 2 greens, 2 beiges, 1 grey, 2 mauves, 2 gold

Origin: India
Dimensions: 72 × 43 inches (184 × 110 cm)
Warp of six strands of undyed cotton and two strands of natural beige wool
Tapestry-weave carried out in two strands of wool
3 colours: 1 red, 1 black, 1 white

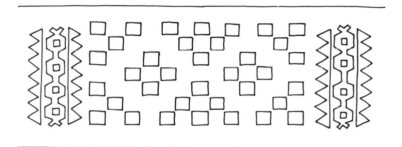

This is a hand-embroidered rug, reinforced with a thick jute cloth to make it suitable for use as a rug for the floor. This type is not very widespread.

The pattern, carried out in very soft colours, is the replica of an early Isfahan piece with floral decoration.

This example will blend particularly well with silk-covered antique furniture.

The Indian Kilim is still fairly unknown and is only rarely encountered on the market. It differs from the classical Kilim in that the wool of the pattern continues to the back of the rug, as in jacquard weaving, instead of doubling back so as to present two identical faces. Unlike most Kilims, it has enough body to be suitable for use as a floor rug.

In design this piece is reminiscent of the early Kilims of North Africa, especially Tunisia. However, its colours are darker and less lively, in a mid-brown key. The weave is compact and well executed.

Tibetan Rugs

Tibetan rugs are still barely known in the West, since Tibet has always been closed to foreigners. It was only in 1964, with the settlement in India and Nepal of refugees fleeing the Chinese occupation, that Tibetan carpets actually made their début on the market. It was first of all the International Red Cross, then Swiss technical aid to developing countries which allowed these refugees to work at a production which at once assured their material well-being and the survival of their traditions. The author has had the privilege of collaborating in this enterprise and thus has been able to study on the spot the very characteristic technique of these people. The simple vertical loom is identical with that used in other regions of Asia but the method of knotting the

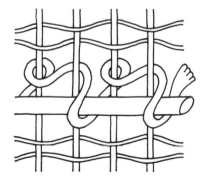

Tibetan knot

wool is unique to the Tibetans. For this operation, the weaver uses a round metal rod on which he makes the knots without cutting the wool at each knot, but only when he arrives at the end of a row of knots of the same colour. This method permits very rapid working and avoids wasting wool. It results in a fairly tight knotting, but less fine, since the Tibetan uses six to eight strands of wool per knot, as opposed to two elsewhere.

The disadvantage of the process is that if the weaver does not pull his thread very tightly, the resulting carpet will suffer from irregularities. Most Tibetan rugs can be recognized by this characteristic.

The motifs are fairly close to those on Chinese carpets, the main ones being the dragon and the 'lion of the snows'. In some early pieces, one finds embossed patterns, but this method has been completely abandoned nowadays.

The wool comes from Tibet, the Nepalese having normal commercial relations with their large neighbour. There are in Nepal three production centres, at Katmandu, Chialsa and Pokhara. The latter can be reached by regular air flights, while Chialsa, ten days' walk from the capital, is without any air or land links.

Other production centres of Tibetan rugs are found in India at Darjeeling, Dalhousie and Chandaghiri in the state of Orissa. Since India has another kind of wool, the Tibetan rugs of that country have a different appearance from those of Nepal. At Darjeeling, under the direction of the wife of the elder brother of the Dalai Lama, the carpets produced by the refugees are of a fairly high standard. When the author visited this region in 1964, the dyeing was carried out with the aid of vegetable colourings, which gave these carpets an added charm.

TIBETAN

Origin: Nepal
Dimensions: 39 × 39 inches (98 × 98 cm)
Persian knot: 48 per sq. inch (74,000 per sq. metre)
Warp of five strands of white cotton
Double weft of the same material
Pile of six strands of wool of medium thickness, chemically washed
9 colours: 3 reds, 2 blues, 1 orange, 1 white, 1 beige, 1 green

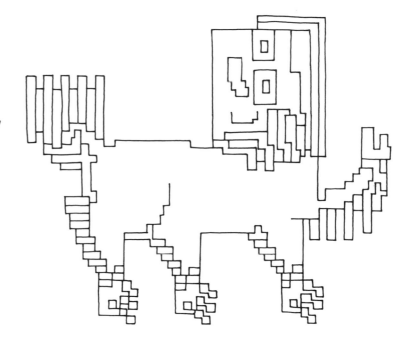

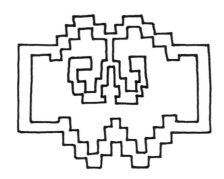

The rugs knotted by the Tibetan refugees in Nepal are of higher quality than those made in India. The wool comes from Tibet.

The decoration of this very simple piece shows two 'lions of the snow' and three clouds freely arranged upon a plain red ground.

In spite of the low number of knots, due to the use of a six-ply wool, the fabric is firm and compact.

This is an example of rustic craftsmanship, the charm of which lies in its simplicity and warm colouring. It looks particularly attractive as a wall-hanging.

TIBETAN

Origin: Tibet
Dimensions: 58 × 31 inches (147 × 78 cm)
Persian knot: 27 per sq. inch (42,000 per sq. metre)
Warp of five strands of rather fine undyed cotton
Single weft of thick natural white wool
Pile of six strands of wool of medium thickness, with natural sheen
9 colours: 2 reds, 1 pink, 3 blues, 1 yellow, 1 brown, 1 green

This rug of early manufacture was brought to Nepal by the refugees. It is sewn to a piece of grey cloth and framed with a red cloth band.

Three red octagonal medallions are arranged on the blue ground of the field. These are decorated with four animal masks (perhaps yaks?), flowers and a central rosette. On the field are vases placed side by side with stylized flowering trees.

With its lotus blossoms and some of the traditional fourteen *ssu-shih-pao*, the principal border of green ground resembles those on the early Ning-hsia rugs. A Greek key border of T-form and a little band of white peas on a blue ground separate the main border from the field.

This is a most charming rug, with bright, warm colours.

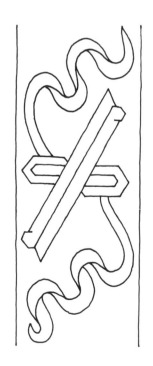

TIBETAN

Origin: India, Dalhousie
Dimensions: 80 × 46 inches (203 × 118 cm)
Persian knot: 5 per sq. inch (8,000 per sq. metre)
Warp of six strands of white cotton
Single weft of the same material
Pile of four strands of wool of medium thickness, chemically washed
12 colours: 3 reds, 2 blues, 2 greens, 3 beiges, 1 orange, 1 black

Dalhousie is situated in the mountains of the Punjab, above Pathankot, not far from Dharmsala where the Dalai Lama lives. A Tibetan colony continues to make rugs there which have remained typical, in spite of the use of the local wool of Amritsar. The designs are always composed of very simple large motifs.

In the example reproduced, a large part of the field of patchy bluish-black ground is occupied by a parrot perched upon a branch, surrounded by lotus blossom.

TIBETAN

TIBETAN

Origin: Nepal, Katmandu
Dimensions: 67 × 35 inches (169 × 89 cm)
Persian knot: 43 per sq. inch (66,000 per sq. metre)
Warp of seven strands of undyed cotton
Double weft of the same material
Pile of four strands of wool of medium thickness
7 colours: 1 red, 2 blues, 1 white, 1 orange, 1 straw-yellow,
1 brown

This piece was made by Tibetan refugees at Katmandu. It has a quite distinct character, with pairs of dragons around a central single dragon on a field of red. The border, predominantly of orange, recalls the early Peking and Ning-hsia rugs. This example is classical in style and has very beautiful colours.

Origin: Nepal
Dimensions: 67 × 36 inches (171 × 92 cm)
Persian knot: 110 per sq. inch (170,000 per sq. metre)
Warp of six strands of undyed cotton
Single weft of six strands of undyed cotton
Pile of four strands of wool
7 colours: 2 yellows, 2 browns, 2 reds, 1 black

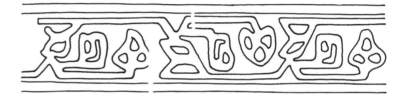

This carpet is the work of Tibetan refugees settled in Nepal. It is close in style to the Khotan rugs of Chinese Turkestan. The author has had the privilege of collaborating in fixing the design and of supervising the early stages of the production on the spot. This is a classical early Khotan pattern, reproduced faithfully in the particular technique of the Tibetans (see page 377). The colourings are unfortunately imported, since it is too complicated to obtain natural colours.

In general style this piece can be placed between the rugs of China and Eastern Turkestan. The double key pattern stands out clearly on the golden yellow ground of the field, which is framed by three borders. The middle one of white ground is adorned with rosettes alternating with bunches of carnations, interlinked by garlands. The two bands on each side of this border are a variation of the carnation border, which is very widespread on early Anatolian rugs.

China

The early carpets of this historic country are not as well known in the West as those of the Middle East. It is only since the beginning of the century that the Chinese rug has made a significant appearance on the market. However, modern carpets are quite different from the early Peking, Pao-t'ou and Ning-hsia types. Large factories are now established at Tientsin, Shanghai, Peking, Tsingtao, Shantung and Sinkiang, where hand-made rugs are manufactured according to exact standards. The standard weave, which is practised in Shanghai and Peking uses four strands of hand-spun wool for the pile: this can be carried out in two ways, either of 70 lines per 11 inches or of 90 lines per 11 inches ('open back'). For the 'closed back' technique, a speciality of Tientsin, the pile is of five strands of machine-spun wool and is to be found in a choice of three thicknesses: 0.36 inches, 0.5 inches and 0.62 inches. The 'open back' weave is the classical type with double weft. In the 'closed back' technique, the two warp threads around which the knot is tied are positioned one above the other, which results in a very dense weave.

There are four styles of pattern: the classical Peking design with a field of typically Chinese motifs surrounded by a wide border; the 'aesthetic' pattern imitating early Aubussons; the floral pattern with bunches of flowers at the ends or the sides of the carpets; and lastly, the tint-upon-tint pattern, with embossed motifs.

Less known in the West are carpets manufactured in Sinkiang, which are replicas of Persian rugs. Copies are also made in Peking of early Chinese models. These pieces are often more beautiful than the originals and one needs an experienced eye to recognize them. However, it should be made clear that they are sold as imitation ('antique finished') by the Chinese.

The author was able to visit several factories in Peking in 1968, and could verify the high standard of their organization. All aspects of the manufacture of carpets are in the hands of qualified people. The modern equipment includes looms on which it is possible to stretch the warp threads after assembly, an operation which is carried out most carefully.

A designer outlines the pattern on the warp threads. The wool, dyed according to modern processes with chrome colourants, is measured, and the number of knots, the tightness and depth of the pile are strictly controlled.

When the carpet is complete, it is chemically washed. The Chinese, experts in this particular procedure, can make their wools so lustrous that the layman could mistake them for silk. After the washing, the outlines

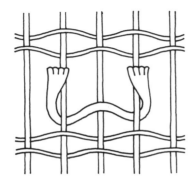

Chinese knot

386

of the motifs on the rug are trimmed with electric scissors, in such a way as to throw the design into relief. This rather delicate operation requires great skill.

Apart from the production of knotted rugs, in the last few years one also has found Kilims and woven rugs, identical in appearance to the knotted examples. In these rugs, the wool is simply passed over the ground, on three weft threads. The wool is as solidly anchored as in a knotted rug. This process makes for a much simpler and quicker manufacture, and is used by the Shantung manufacturers, in an embossed tint-upon-tint pattern.

CHINESE

Origin: China, Shanghai
Dimensions: 116 × 94 inches (294 × 238 cm)
Persian knot: 50 per sq. inch (78,000 per sq. metre)
Warp of sixteen strands of undyed cotton
Double weft of white cotton
Pile of five strands of rather fine wool, chemically washed
10 colours: 3 reds, 2 blues, 2 greens, 1 grey, 1 beige, 1 mauve

This is an interesting example, dating from the 1930s. Its design is a blend of the classical style of early pieces and the modern. The traditional motifs are not yet carved out in relief, but the absence of the classical border indicates an attempt at innovation, which has materialized in the contemporary 'aesthetic' pattern.

Red lotus blossoms, grey and green leaves and little blue flowers stand out against a green ground, with a mauve border.

Origin: China, Sinkiang
Dimensions: 74 × 48 inches (188 × 121 cm)
Persian knot: 79 per sq. inch (122,400 per sq. metre)
Warp of five strands of undyed cotton
Double weft of blue cotton
Pile of two strands of wool of medium thickness, of rather lustreless appearance
9 colours: 2 reds, 2 blues, 1 orange, 1 yellow, 1 green, 1 brown, 1 white

Origin: China, Sinkiang
Dimensions: 161 × 88 inches (410 × 210 cm)
Persian knot: 77 per sq. inch (118,400 per sq. metre)
Warp of six strands of white cotton
Double weft of blue cotton
Pile of two strands of wool of medium thickness, chemically washed, in bright colours
8 colours: 2 blues, 1 red, 1 black, 1 white, 1 yellow, 1 grey, 1 beige

Khotan production is not very considerable and the carpets are not often found on the market. The texture of this piece links it with early Chinese rugs, whilst its decoration could well be Persian. Flower seedlings cover the whole field, including the central motif, arranged in an almost too regular fashion. In the corners, one can distinguish lotus and iris blossoms.

The framework of multiple borders consists of eight bands.

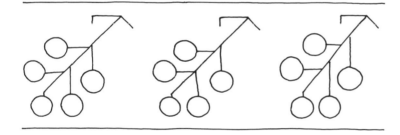

Although naturally influenced by Chinese art, the Khotan rug from Chinese Turkestan has its own motifs. In the trade the Khotan sometimes incorrectly goes under the name of Samarkand, a town which in fact produces no carpets.

The claret-coloured field is covered with trees, rudimentarily stylized. The red principal border bears bunches of flowers. While very little thought appears to have been given to the very simple decoration, the same could not be said for the colours, which are all extremely attractive.

MONGOL

Origin: China, Mongolia
Dimensions: 65 × 35 inches (165 × 88 cm)
Persian knot: 28 per sq. inch (44,000 per sq. metre)
Warp of four strands of fine grey cotton
Double weft of brown goat's hair
Pile of four strands of rather thick wool
6 colours in pastel shades

Mongol rugs are little known in the West and are only rarely found on the market. They are distinguished from other Chinese rugs by their slightly different decorative motifs but even more by their colours, which utilize the whole range of browns.

The three medallions arranged on the white ground of the field have a floral decoration containing (except in the central motif) four swastikas, in crosswise formation. An inner border patterned with globes precedes the main border, which is richly decorated with pomegranates, grapes, flowers and, halfway down either side, a variation of the motif called 'the knot of destiny'.

The outlines of the pattern are finely embossed.

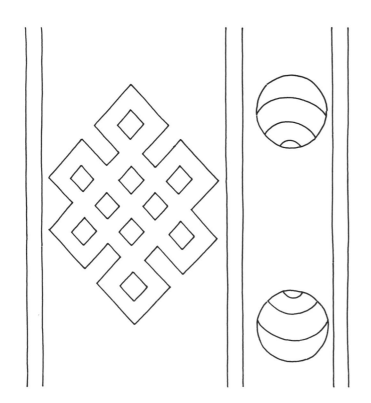

NING-HSIA

Origin: North-west region of China
Dimensions: 28 × 26 inches (70 × 67 cm)
Persian knot: 37 per sq. inch (57,500 per sq. metre)
Warp of three strands of undyed cotton
Single weft of the same material
Pile of four strands of wool of medium thickness, with naturally mellowed colours
7 colours: 2 reds, 2 blues, 1 green, 1 white, 1 brown

Even a few years ago, Ning-hsia rugs were very little known on the Western market. Now, these carpets, all at least one hundred years old (production has long since ceased), are being sold in fairly large quantities to foreign buyers.

Their weave is not fine, but since the knotting was carried out with a four-ply wool, it was difficult to obtain a greater density of knots.

The extremely simple floral decoration of this example comprises lotus flowers and pomegranates. The predominant colour is golden yellow.

The particular shape of this rug indicates that it was intended to cover the back of an armchair.

Origin: North-west region of China
Dimensions: 100 × 31 inches (255 × 79 cm)
Persian knot: 29 per sq. inch (45,000 per sq. metre)
Warp of three strands of undyed cotton
Single weft of natural wool
Pile of five strands of fine wool in soft colours
7 colours: 2 blues, 1 yellow, 1 brown, 2 reds, 1 white

This example dates from about 1860. The predominant colour is a lemon yellow, which is frequently encountered in rugs of this type. The decoration is very simple: three pairs of elegantly stylized blue dragons, each framed by four lotus blossoms, occupy the field, which is bordered by a garland of flowers, also in simple style. Nevertheless, the whole effect is not without charm.

Origin: China
Dimensions: 63 × 32 inches (160 × 81 cm)
Persian knot: 64 per sq. inch (99,200 per sq. metre)
Warp of six strands of fine undyed cotton
Single weft of thick undyed cotton
Pile of four strands of rather fine wool
11 colours: 3 reds, 3 blues, 2 yellows, 2 greens, 1 white

This interesting rug, composed of two squares, seems to have been intended to adorn an armchair. In the centre of the red ground of each square are two dogs of Fô, one yellow, the other blue, and in the corners, the head of a lion. The very varied pattern on the golden-yellow ground of the principal border, consists of flowers (pomegranates, chrysanthemums, and lotus blossoms), serpents and other motifs (knots of destiny, daggers). The carpet is very finely embossed.

CHINESE

Origin: China, Shanghai
Dimensions: 146 × 102 inches (370 × 268 cm)
Persian knot: 55 per sq. inch (84,000 per sq. metre)
Warp of sixteen strands of undyed cotton
Double weft of cotton
Pile of four strands of wool, chemically washed
12 colours

The Chinese rug shown here is in the pattern called 'aesthetic', and comes from Tientsin, Peking or Shanghai. Since the production is standardized throughout the country, it is difficult, without the certificate of origin, to locate the exact provenance of a carpet. This one, which comes from Shanghai, belongs to the 'open back' type, and its pile has a depth of almost half an inch. The outline of the designs in Aubusson style is accentuated by a special clipping to throw them into relief. This soft and harmoniously-coloured rug will blend perfectly with furniture of the French style.

PEKING

Origin: China
Dimensions: 81 × 48 inches (206 × 122 cm)
Persian knot: 34 per sq. inch (52,800 per sq. metre)
Warp of nine strands of grey cotton
Single weft of white cotton
Pile of two strands of wool of medium thickness, in dull colours
7 colours: 2 beiges, 2 blues, 1 yellow, 1 grey, 1 beige-brown

Peking rugs of early manufacture like this piece, which dates from about 1890, are often of very simple style.

A modest central rosette, two bunches of flowers, and cloud bands in the corners, form the entire decoration of the gold ground of the field. A border of blue ground with leaves and flowers, also in a very simple pattern, surrounds this.

The general effect is of elegant restraint.

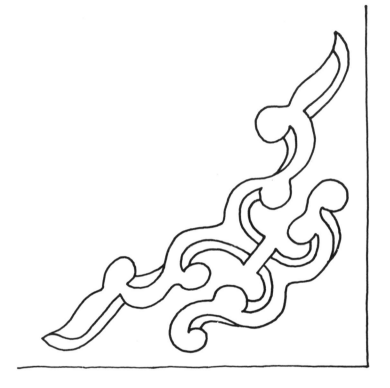

PEKING

Origin: China
Dimensions: 73 × 40 inches (185 × 91 cm)
Persian knot: 54 per sq. inch (83,200 per sq. metre)
Warp of five strands of undyed wool
Double weft of five strands of undyed cotton
Pile of two strands of rather thick wool
8 colours

The Peking rug is of the classical Chinese type. Large areas of the field are free of decoration, with the pattern reduced to a few floral motifs, surrounded by a Greek key border. The series of six motifs at the left-hand side is repeated at the right, in reverse order, the first motif at the top left becoming the first at the bottom right.

In spite of the simplicity of the pattern, the piece contains no less than eight different colours, evidence of the mastery of the Chinese in the use of shades.

This carpet, about 80 years old, is rather thin in texture, unlike the rugs of present manufacture, of which the warp and weft threads are no longer of wool. The texture of the classical Chinese rug is always rather coarse, compared with that of the Persian rug, and so this rug is characteristic of its period.

Its charm lies, above all, in the discreet freshness of its shaded colours and in the simplicity of its decoration.

PAO-T'OU

Origin: China
Dimensions: 73 × 49 inches (185 × 124 cm)
Persian knot: 54 per sq. inch (83,200 per sq. metre)
Warp of five strands of fine grey cotton
Double weft of the same material
Pile of three strands of wool of medium thickness
5 colours: 4 blues, 1 white

Pao-t'ou carpets, which are no longer made under this name, come from the Suiyuan region, in the north of China. The carpets produced in the Peking region under the name 'Peking, antique finish' reproduce the early Pao-t'ou rugs and are often lovelier than the originals. For the uninitiated it is difficult to distinguish the modern from the earlier carpets.

The example illustrated dates from the end of the last century. Its field is covered with a flower-decorated trellis. The sign depicted in the centre, within a circle, is called *shou,* the symbol of longevity. In the corners are clouds and the main border has a decoration of swastikas.

The predominant blue shade imparts a characteristic note to this piece.

KILIM

Origin: China
Dimensions: 53 × 28 inches (134 × 70 cm)
Warp of five- and two-ply strands of undyed cotton twisted together
Tapestry-weave carried out in two strands of hand-spun wool
5 colours: 2 blues, 1 brown, 1 beige, 1 white

The Chinese Kilim has only recently appeared on the Western market. In design, it resembles the Shiraz Kilim, but differs however in that the tapestry-weave is carried out in a wool which is at the same time brighter and more drab. In size they barely exceed 55 by 79 inches or 59 by 87 inches.

The example reproduced is the size of a bedside rug. Three of the lozenges with jagged edges which decorate the dark-blue field are in azure, brown and beige tones with the remaining two in brown, white and azure. The small lateral motifs are beige, like the ground of the main border.

North Africa

The carpet, invented in Asia, must have been introduced at an early date into North Africa. Already in the thirteenth century Ibn Yaqut points out that sumptuous rugs of strong weave were being made in the neighbourhood of Tebessa. Carpet-making therefore, has a long-standing tradition in North Africa.

Of the Algerian rugs, the most widely known are of the Berber type, a rug with large knots, ranging from 8 to 13 knots per square inch (12,000 to 20,000 knots per square metre), and with a plain ground or decorated with some rare motifs. They are made with natural sheep's wool in light colours.

Morocco also produces Berbers and a type called 'High Atlas' (see p. 417).

Tunisia has a wider range of carpets. First and foremost comes the classical rug originating from Kairwan, remarkable for the originality of its script, with a variable fineness ranging from 13 to 160 knots per square inch (20,000 to 250,000 per square metre), then the Bizerta rug with traditional motifs, with 58 knots per square inch (90,000 knots per square metre).

The National Office of Crafts of Tunisia makes special efforts to improve the quality of Tunisian rugs; it employs full-time a great number of craftsmen and weavers who enjoy good living conditions. Den Den, a pilot workshop, creates carpets from early motifs of embroidery or weaving, which can have up to 160 knots per square inch (250,000 knots per square metre).

Apart from knotted rugs, Tunisia produces Kilims from the island of Djerba and Gafsa, and Merghums, a type of Soumak, some of which are very beautiful. The charm of the Kilims of Gafsa lies in the gaiety of their colours and simplicity of their designs.

The United Arab Republic specializes in flat-woven rugs of the Kilim type, but thicker; made with natural wool of good quality, they can be used as floor coverings. Of rustic style, they look best in simple settings.

EL DJEM

Origin: Tunisia
Dimensions: 115 × 77 inches (293 × 196 cm)
Technique: Soumak
Warp of twelve-ply undyed cotton
Soumak weave of single wool
5 colours: 1 white, 1 beige, 1 brown, 1 black, 1 grey

This rug with smooth weave, also called Merghum, is a product of the Tunisian National Craft Centre.

All the colours are natural. The white ground emphasizes the design of traditional motifs. The large central hexagon and the border with large zigzags are found also on some Kairwan pieces.

This rug has a very tight Soumak weave and so is quite suitable for use as a floor covering.

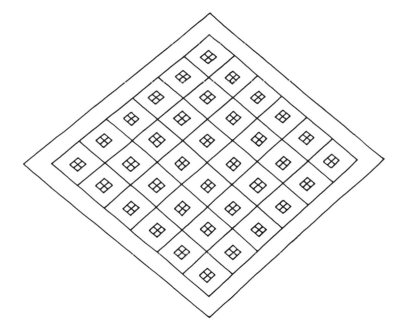

GABÈS

Origin: Tunisia
Dimensions: 113 × 78 inches (287 × 198 cm)
Turkish knot: 28 per sq. inch (44,000 per sq. metre)
Warp of three and four strands of undyed cotton twisted together
Double weft of blue cotton
Pile of four strands of wool of medium thickness
2 colours: 2 blues

This carpet was produced by the Tunisian National Craft Centre, which is a guarantee of the quality of its materials. It was designed to fit in with a modern interior.

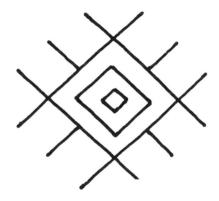

Gabès, which today has a population of 30,000, was probably a Phoenician warehouse before becoming the Roman colony of Tacapae.

The decoration of this piece is extremely sober, both in motifs and colouring: indeed, the plain blue ground of the field is simply framed with three borders of a more subdued blue.

KAIRWAN

Origin: Tunisia
Dimensions: 74 × 48 inches (188 × 121 cm)
Turkish knot: 101 per sq. inch (156,900 per sq. metre)
Warp of six strands of white cotton
Double weft of red cotton
Pile of four strands of wool of medium thickness, chemically washed
7 colours

The mosque of Darbiès, one of Kairwan's ancient religious buildings, is decorated with faience in Asiatic style. But although the potters were inspired by Oriental models, the weavers do not seem to have submitted to any foreign influences.

The classical decoration of the field in this piece is called *ûbaquel* (jars). In the points of the central red hexagon are arranged *qamra uni tmânia* (medallion with eight branches). At the sides are two pairs of lozenges *qamra sgira* (small medallion), and in the centre, an elongated motif composed of carnations.

Of the four borders, the first one surrounding the field is called *njum* (stars), and the next one *mongâla* (watch). The principal border which follows is a variation of the *njum* motif, and the outer band is called *hzama suri* (European girdle).

414

HIGH ATLAS

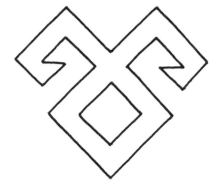

Origin: Morocco, Marrakesh
Dimensions: 71 × 47 inches (180 × 120 cm)
Turkish knot: 9 per sq. inch (13,200 per sq. metre)
Warp of two strands of yellow wool
Weft of the same material
Pile of two strands of thick wool
5 colours: 1 red, 1 blue, 1 white, 1 yellow, 1 brown

Moroccan rugs of the High Atlas type have a rustic weave with large knots, with four or five shoots of weft between each row of knots. The depth of the pile is intended to compensate for the low number of knots.

The lozenge pattern completely covers the field. The predominant colour is brown, with a border of golden-yellow ground.

This type of rug fits in well with a modern or rustic interior; the wool is of good quality.

KILIM

Origin: United Arab Republic
Dimensions: 32 × 25 inches (81 × 63 cm)
Warp of three strands of undyed cotton
Tapestry-weave carried out in wool of one strand of medium
fineness
13 colours: 1 red, 2 blues, 3 greens, 1 pink, 1 orange, 1 yellow,
1 grey, 1 brown, 1 black, 1 white

As well as woven rugs, the United Arab Republic also exports Kilims.

The pattern and construction of this carpet makes it particularly suitable for use as a wall-hanging. On it are depicted several scenes of rural life: a shepherd leading his sheep, two men on a donkey, labourers making their way to their work, a herdsman seated under a tree, watching his grazing animals.

The great simplicity, coupled with the rich colouring, produces a most attractive result.

HAND-WOVEN RUG

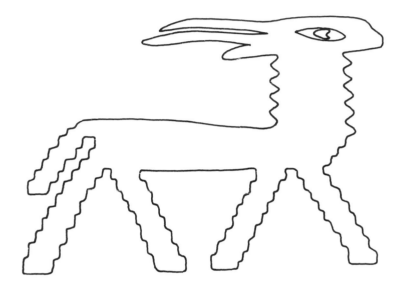

Origin: United Arab Republic
Dimensions: 24× 30 inches (62×75 cm)
Technique: Kilim
Warp of two strands of natural wool, one brown, the other white
Tapestry-weave carried out in one strand of rather thick wool
3 colours: 2 browns, 1 white

The use of a thick strand of wool for both warp and weft makes this carpet suitable for use as a hard-wearing floor rug just as if it were a knotted carpet. For this reason these carpets are not referred to in the trade as Kilims but rather as 'hand-woven rugs'.

As in the example reproduced, this kind of rug is always made with natural wools, hence its rustic appearance, further emphasized by the extreme simplicity of the design. Here, in the centre of the white ground of the field, is a large stag, surrounded by a border of lozenges.

Rugs of the Balkan Countries

These rugs are to be found in the trade under the name of 'Macedonian' rugs and come from Yugoslavia, Albania, Romania, Bulgaria and Hungary. The manufacture of knotted and woven rugs has been carried on in these countries since Turkish domination, and the output has developed in an astonishing manner since the Second World War.

The designs are replicas of Persian and Turkish originals, often well executed, in good materials. These carpets are fairly reasonably priced.

Knotted rugs are also produced in Greece resembling Turkish Ispartas, and often sold under this denomination, too. The shaggy Flocati, also called 'herdsmen's rugs', are not knotted.

BALKAN RUG

Origin: Romania
Dimensions: 104 × 70 inches (265 × 178 cm)
Persian knot: 149 per sq. inch (230,400 per sq. metre)
Warp of seven strands of undyed cotton
Double weft of blue cotton
Pile of two strands of wool of medium fineness, chemically washed
8 colours: 2 blues, 2 reds, 2 greens, 1 beige, 1 grey

The Romanian, Bulgarian, Yugoslav, Hungarian and Albanian rugs which one encounters on the market under the name of 'Macedonian' rug, are all hand-knotted, and are mostly replicas of classical Iranian or Turkish originals. Their knotting is compact and the quality of their wool and colours is good. Considering their quality, their prices are attractive: of late years they have gained favour with buyers.

This example reproduces a Kirman design, with a dark-blue ground, patterned with a large elongated central motif. In each corner is a large rosette. The principal border deviates from the chosen model. The motifs all stand out very clearly.

The number of knots of this fairly compact rug corresponds with that of a good quality Tabriz or Kirman rug, but it is more modest in price.

KILIM

Origin: Romania
Dimensions: 16 × 28 inches (40 × 70 cm)
Warp of nine strands of undyed cotton
Tapestry-weave carried out in two strands of wool, mixed with staple fibre
4 colours: 1 red, 1 blue, 1 black, 1 white

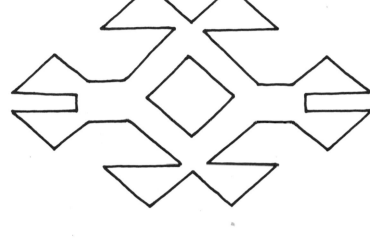

A motif with ram's horns is to be found in the three rectangular red medallions which adorn the white ground of the field. These horns are repeated in each of the jagged-edged lozenges on the field, which together form a frame for the medallions.

The colours are bright and the weaving rather slack— a rustic, but pleasing, rug.

BIBLIOGRAPHY

Beccaria, G. *Una pirateria e un inventario di stoffe veneziane* Palermo, Vena 1894.

Bode, W. von and Kühnel, E. *Antique Rugs from the Near East* (trans. Ellis, C.G.), London 1970

Campana, P.M. *Il tappeto orientale*, Milan 1945

Edwards, A.C. *The Persian Carpet*, London 1953

Erdmann, K. *Oriental Carpets: an account of their history*, London 1960

Erdmann, K. *Seven Hundred Years of Oriental Carpets*, London 1970

Feuvrier, *Trois ans à la cour de Perse*, Paris

Grote-Haselbalg, *Der Orientteppich, seine Geschichte und Kultur*, Berlin 1922

Haack, H. *Oriental Rugs* (trans. Digby, G. and C.W.), London 1960

Hawley, W.A. *Oriental rugs, antique and modern*, New York and London 1913

Hopf, A. *Oriental Carpets and Rugs*, London 1962

Hubel, R. *Ullstein Teppichbuch*, Frankfurt and Vienna 1965

Jacoby, H. *Eine Sammlung Orientalischer Teppiche*, Berlin 1923

Jacobsen, C.W. *Oriental rugs, a complete guide*, London 1966

Negro, S. *Seconda Roma 1850–1870*, Milan 1943

Orendi, *Das Gesamtwissen über antike und neue Teppiche des Orients*, Vienna 1930

Pope, A.U. *A Survey of Persian Arts*, London and New York 1939 and 1970

Raznoexport Moscow *Tapis d'art de l'URSS*

Ropers, H. *Les tapis d'Orient*, P.U.F. 1967

Sarre, F. and Trenkwald, U. *Altorientalische Teppiche*, Leipzig 1926 and 1928

Schlosser, I. *Tapis d'Orient et d'Occident*, Fribourg 1962

Schuermann, U. *Caucasian rugs: a detailed presentation of the art of carpet weaving in the Caucasus in the eighteenth and nineteenth centuries*, Brunswick

Soulier, G. *Les influences orientales dans la peinture toscane*, Paris 1924

Vegh, J. de and Layer, C. *Tapis turcs provenant des églises et collections de Transylvanie*, Paris

Index

Abadeh 275, 288
Abravaneh 315
Abuzaidabad 300
Adana 77
'aesthetic' pattern 388, 399
Afghan carpets 13
Afghan invasion 10
Afghan, Russian *see* Kerki
Afghanistan 351–63
Afshar, 187, 203, 207, 208, 211, 295
Aghkhal 315
Agra 367, 368
Ahar 112, 125
Ahis 53
Ahmedabad 126
Akbar 367
Aktsha 351, 352
Albania 27, 422
Algerian rugs 409
Aliabad 275, 300
Ali Mirzai 314, 327
Amritsar 367
Amu Dar'ya 331, 332, 344
Anatolia 9, 13, 17, 24, 32
Anatolian carpets 27, 31, 38, 41, 49, 53, 70,
   77, 78, 81
Ancyrona 46
Andalucia 10
Andhkui 351, 352, 360
Ankara 53, 70, 73
Antalya 42
Antioch 37
antique finished 26, 386
Arak (Sultanabad) 16, 27, 167, 168–79, 183,
   217, 314
Ardebil carpet 19, 20, 306
Ardebil region 112, 153
Armaq 300
Armenia, Republic of 83, 107
Armenibaff *see* knot, Armenian

Aron 300
Asia Minor 10, 17, 27
Assadabad 214
Austria 11
Avanos 33, 34
Azerbaijan 83, 108, 112–61

Baharlu 275, 287
Bajguiran 315
Bakharden 331, 343
Bakhshayesh 129, 133
Bakhtiari rugs 118, 255, 263–8, 313
Balkan countries 7, 422
Baluchi rugs 314, 323, 324, 327
Baluchistan 13, 24, 314
Bangalore 367
Bassiri 275
Bavanluh 315
Bayk 315
Behpahan 275, 296
Berber rugs 409
Bergama 17, 33, 37, 45
Berlin 28
Beshir 331, 332
Beshir Chuval 360
Beshiri tribe 351, 359, 360
Bezgue 315
Bhadohi 367
Bijar 237, 238, 241
Bilverdi 130, 275
Birjand 314
Bisheh *see* Turbat-i-Haidari
Bizerta rug 409
Bohluri 314
Bojnurd 315
Book of Qum, The 301
Bor 73
boteh motif 73, 167, 168, 171, 176, 180, 203,
   222, 230, 241, 267, 276, 309
buinuze motif 347

Bukhara rugs 13, 331, 335, 336
Bukhara Chuval 339
Bukhara Jollar 340
Bulgaria 27, 422
Burjalu 217
Bursa 33
Burujird 171, 180
bustard motif 233
Byzantium 83

Caesarea *see* Kayseri
Cairo 10
Cal 33, 38
Camel-hair 13, 14
Canakkale 33
Cappadocia 34
Caspian Sea 83
Caucasus, the 22, 24, 27, 31, 81, 292
Caucasian rugs 17, 18, 45, 83–111, 153
Central Asia 13, 17, 18, 27, 31
Chahar Mahal 255
Chalchotor 255, 267
Chandaghiri 377
Chechmegol 315
Chekh Rajab 133
chemcheh-gul motif 364
Chialsa 377
Chichi 83
China 7, 10, 20, 22, 27, 31, 386–407
chuchehboran motif 328
chucheh-gul 339
chuval 339, 360
'closed back' technique 386
conservation of carpets 28
Cordoba 10
Cufic script 10

Daghestan 83, 91, 108
Dalhousie 77
Damascus 10

dating of carpets 19
Darabjerd 275
Darjeeling 377
Darya-i-Namak 313
daste motif 291
Daulatabad 351, 356
Dazkiri 33, 41
Demirci 33
Denizli 38
Derbent 24, 83, 91
Designs of carpets 16–17
Djerba 409
do goleh Parizi motif 203
dogs of Fô motif 396
Dokhtar-i-Ghazi-Baluchi 351
Dorukhsh 314
Dosemealti 42
dragon motif 377, 385, 396
dyes 14–15, 314

El Djem 410
Emamgholi 315
embossing 387, 392, 396, 399
embroidered rug 375
ener dychi motif 364
Erivan 83
Ersari tribe 351
Erzurum 70
Ezine 33, 45

Faridun 300
Fars 275, 284, 299
Farukh 275
Fasa 275
Ferahan 167
Fereidan 167
Fethiye 62
Fin 300
Firdaus 314, 315
Firuzabad 275

fish-bone motif 211, 343
flat weaving 81
'flight of eagles' motif 18
Flocati carpets 422
Florence 28

Gabbeh 275, 296, 299
Gabès 413
Gafsa 409
Gantchan 315
'garden' design 255, 264
Gassan Kuli 331
Gendja 83, 92
Genoa 28, 83
Geok Teppe 331, 343
Georgia 83
Ghaen 314
Ghahestan 295
Gharawalli 315
Ghassemabad 315, 327
Ghazan tribe 355
Ghiordes prayer rugs 32, 33
ghiri pattern 328
goat's hair 13
gol-i-torunj 291
Gombad-i-Qabus 315
Granada 10
Greece 27, 422
Greek key motif 18, 381, 403
guerat motif 352
gul 355
Gurgan 315

Hafiz 275
Hamadan 16, 213–34, 250
Hamburg 27
hand-woven rug 421
Harun al-Rashid 300, 314
Hassanabad 315

Herat 314, 315, 351, 360
Herati Baluchi 351
Herati design 241, 242
Hereke 27, 33, 46
Heriz 112, 122, 133, 137, 141, 142, 145, 146, 149
High Atlas rugs 409, 417
Holbein carpets 10, 28
Horse-blanket 283
Hosseinabad 221
Hudud-al-Alam 275
Hungary 11, 422
hzama suri motif 414

Ibn Hauqal 315
ilan 332
Incesu 33
India 7, 10, 22, 31, 367–75, 377
Injilas 222
Iran 7, 22, 24, 31, 50, 112, 130, 275, 316, 351; *see also* Afshar, Arak, Azerbaijan, Chahar Mahal, Fars, Hamadan, Isfahan, Kalar Dasht, Kashan, Khorasan, Kirman, Kurdistan, Mashad, Nain, Qum, Seraband, Shiraz, Varamin and Yazd
Iranian Carpet Company 27
Isfahan 27, 254, 256–71, 275, 288, 291–2, 310
Isparta 33
Istanbul 27, 46

Jahanbeigui 315
Jahrom 275
Jaipur 367
jangali design 271
'jewel of Mohammed' motif 99
Jilli Sultan design 288
Jin-Jin 161
jollar 340, 360
Jolostan 331, 347
Jorjan *see* Qabus

Josan 218
Joshagan 255, 271
juleh asp, *see* horse-blanket

Kachli 343
Kachli-Bukhara 340, 343
Kachli-Turkoman 328
kadradomes motif 162
Kafretj 275
kafzadeh design 168, 199, 305
Kughusi design 288
Kairwan 28, 408, 414
Kalar Dasht 162
Kalat 315
Kalinska 83
Karabagh 83, 103
Karachi 364
Karaja 112, 134, 137
Karakechi 33, 49
Karamani *see* Kilim
karim khani motif 162
Karim Khan Zand 275
Karkin 351
Kashan 300–6
Kashgai rug 275, 284, 368
Kashgai tribe 275, 284, 296, 299
Kashmir 371, 372
Katmandu 377, 385
Kayseri 33, 50, 53, 61, 66, 69
Kazak 83, 95, 96, 99, 100, 253, 331
Kazakhstan 331
Keibar 314
Keibathlu design 288
Kerki 331, 344
Khamseh confederation 275
khesti design 204, 208
Khila 83
Khorasan 13, 314, 351
Khorey 167
Khotan 385, 391

Kilim 9, 22–4, 33, 37, 41, 45, 54, 77, 78, 104,
    111, 250, 327, 339, 375, 387, 407, 418, 425
Kirghizia 331
Kirman 20, 27, 50, 118, 185–99, 203, 207–11
Kirsehir 33, 53
Kizyl Ayak 331, 343, 351, 352
knot: Armenian (Armenibaff) 255, Ghiordes
    (Turkish) 21, Senneh (Persian)
    21–22, Spanish 10, Tibetan 377
'knot of destiny' motif 392, 396
kochak motif 347
Kolah-derazi 315
Koliayeh 253
Kolvanaq 112, 138
Konya 33, 54, 77
Kuba 83
Kula 33
Kunduz 351, 360
Kurds 57, 58, 77, 328
Kurdistan 237–49, 253
Kurdlar 141

Ladik 33, 42
Lahore 364
lamp motif 33
Lanbaran 150
Leningrad 27
Lilihan 167, 183
'lion of the snows' motif 377, 378
London 27, 28
looms: horizontal 20, vertical; village loom
    20, Tabriz loom 20, loom with rollers 20
lotus flower motif 18
Lur tribes 275
Luristan 13, 272

Maadan 315
Macedonian (Spartan) rugs 27, 422
Maden 33, 61
Madras 367

Mahal 167, 168
mahi-tu-huse motif
Malatya 33
Malayer 213, 226
Maltese cross 18
Marco Polo 9, 54
mar gul 352
Marrakesh 417
Mary 331, 343
Marzanabad 162
Mashad 300, 314–23, 328
Mauri rugs 351
Maymana 351
Mazar-i-Sharif 351, 352
Mecca-Shiraz *see* Kashgai rug
medahil motif 74
Megri 33, 62
Mehriban 112, 134, 146, 149, 229
Meina 142
Merghum 409, 410
Merkit 149
Mesh-Kanlu 315
Meymeh 255
mihrab 19, 32–33, 34, 42, 53
Milan 28
Milas 33, 65
mina khani motif 165
Mir 167
Mirzapur 367
Mishkinshahr 154, 157
Mohamera design 288
mongâla motif 414
Mongols 83, 331, 335
Mongol rug 392
Morocco 417
Moscow 27
Mud 314, 323
Mujur 33
Mushkabad 167
Mustaufi 300

Muzaffar-ud-din 15
Mylasa *see* Milas

Nain 27, 254, 260
Nasirabad 300
Natanz 300
Nepal 21, 27–28, 31, 377, 378, 381
Nhaf 315
Ning-hsia rugs 381, 385, 386, 395, 396
Niriz 275, 295
Nishapur 314
Njum motif 414
Nobaran 230
Nodge 33
Nokhalli 315
North Africa 7, 31, 408–21
Nushabad 300

'open back' technique 386
Ortakoy 33, 41, 66

Pahlavi 315
Pakistan 7, 31, 351, 364
Pakistan Bukhara 364
Palas *see* Kilim
Palermo 28
Palmette motif 18, 196, 320
panj gole Parizi motif 207
Pao-t'ou rugs 386, 404
Paris 28
Pasargadae 275
patheh design 195
Pavia 28
Pazyryk carpet 9
Peking 386
Peking rugs 385, 386, 403
Pendeh 331, 347
Pendeh Chuval 347
Persepolis 275
Persia 10, 13, 16, 17, 18, 28, 112

Persian carpets 31
pialeh motif 162
Piatigorkin 83
Pile 13, 21
Pisa 28
Pokhara 377
pomegranate motif 18, 158, 221, 234, 264
Prayer rugs 18–19, 32–33, 34, 42, 53, 57, 61, 65, 69, 70, 74, 343

Qain 314
qamra sgira motif 414
qamra uni tmânia motif 414
Qamsar 300
Qum 118, 300–1, 309–13

Rahaq 300
ram's horns motif 340, 360, 425
Ravand 300
'Rhodes, rug from' *see* Megri
Romania 22, 27, 422–5
Rome 37
rug-making 83
running-dog motif 18, 24, 84, 91, 323

saadi dasteh gole design 192
Salar Khan 315
salat 32
salor-gul motif 347
Saman 268
Samarkand 18
Samarkand rug *see* Khotan
Samsun 70
Sarakh 314
Sarbished 314
sarchian motif 328
sandugh motif 162
Saph 69
Sarab 158
sarghola motif 328
Sarouk 167, 172, 175, 176, 179

Sebastia *see* Sivas
se hoze motif 291
Seichur 83
Seistan 314
Seljuk 9, 54
sel-selei design 196
selvedge 21
Senneh-Kilim 24
Senneh-Sanandaj 237, 245, 246, 249, 250
Seraband 167, 180
serpent motif 78, 103
Seydan 275
Shah Abbas design 188
Shahar pareh pichi motif 291
Sharabiyan 145
Shanghai 386
shekeri motif 54, 180
Shiraz 13, 20, 24, 275–87, 288, 292–9, 335
Shirvan 83, 84, 87, 112, 315
shou motif 404
Shurtepa 360
Siebenbürgers 32
Siirt 33
Sileh 24, 81, 107, 111
Silk 13
Sirjan 295
Sivas 33, 70
Songur 250
Soumak 9, 18, 24, 108, 208, 410
Spain 10
Spartan rugs *see* Macedonian
sshu-shih-pao motif 381
Star of David motif 328
sugar-loaf motif 99, 158
Suiyuan 404
swastika motif 18, 392, 404

Tabaristan 315
Tabriz 20, 27, 37, 112, 114, 117, 118, 121, 134, 154, 167, 314